GENDER IN HISTORY

Series editors:
Lynn Abrams, Cordelia Beattie, Pam Sharpe and Penny Summerfield

The expansion of research into the history of women and gender since the 1970s has changed the face of history. Using the insights of feminist theory and of historians of women, gender historians have explored the configuration in the past of gender identities and relations between the sexes. They have also investigated the history of sexuality and family relations, and analysed ideas and ideals of masculinity and femininity. Yet gender history has not abandoned the original, inspirational project of women's history: to recover and reveal the lived experience of women in the past and the present.

The series Gender in History provides a forum for these developments. Its historical coverage extends from the medieval to the modern periods, and its geographical scope encompasses not only Europe and North America but all corners of the globe. The series aims to investigate the social and cultural constructions of gender in historical sources, as well as the gendering of historical discourse itself. It embraces both detailed case studies of specific regions or periods, and broader treatments of major themes. Gender in History titles are designed to meet the needs of both scholars and students working in this dynamic area of historical research.

Imagining Caribbean womanhood

I0025673

MANCHESTER
1824

Manchester University Press

Myth and materiality in a woman's world: Shetland 1800–2000
Lynn Abrams

*Destined for a life of service: defining African-Jamaican womanhood,
1865–1938*
Henrice Altink

Love, intimacy and power: Marital relationships in Scotland, 1650–1850
Katie Barclay

*Artisans of the body in early modern Italy: identities,
families and masculinities*
Sandra Cavallo

Modern motherhood: women and family in England, c. 1945–2000
Angela Davis

Jewish women in Europe in the Middle Ages: a quiet revolution
Simha Goldin

The military leadership of Matilda of Canossa, 1046–1115
David J. Hay

The shadow of marriage: singleness in England, 1914–60
Katherine Holden

*Infidel feminism: secularism, religion and women's emancipation,
England 1830–1914*
Laura Schwartz

*The feminine public sphere: middle-class women and civic life
in Scotland, c. 1870–1914*
Megan Smitley

Being boys: working-class masculinities and leisure
Melanie Tebbutt

IMAGINING CARIBBEAN WOMANHOOD
RACE, NATION AND BEAUTY CONTESTS, 1929–70

⤛ Rochelle Rowe ⤜

Manchester University Press

Published by Manchester University Press
Altrincham Street, Manchester M1 7JA, UK
www.manchesteruniversitypress.co.uk

British Library Cataloguing-in-Publication Data is available

ISBN 978 0 7190 8867 4 hardback
ISBN 978 1 5261 5033 2 paperback

First published by Manchester University Press in hardback 2013

This edition published 2020

Typeset by Graphicraft Kimited, Hong Kong

For Rosa, Raphael and Mum

Contents

List of figures

Acknowledgements

I have many people to thank for their part in helping me to research and write this book. Thank you to the publishers Manchester University Press, and to the anonymous readers who commented on drafts. Thanks to the Arts and Humanities Research Council of the UK and the University of Essex for funding original research into this neglected and taboo subject area, including extensive travel to overseas archives and conferences. Many thanks to the patient archivists of the Caribbean; to the entire staff at the National Library of Jamaica; the National Archives of Trinidad and Tobago; the Barbados Department of Archives; the libraries and archives of the University of the West Indies, West India Collections at Mona and Cave Hill, and the West Indiana and Special Collections Division at St Augustine. Thanks especially to Jessica Lewis and Genevieve Jones-Edman. Thanks are also due to the staff of the Schomberg Centre of Black Research, Harlem. Of the British archives thanks especially to the staff at the British Library, the National Archives, the Institute for Commonwealth Studies, Lambeth Libraries and the Black Cultural Archives. I am also grateful to the Society for Caribbean Studies for being a forum for Caribbeanist researchers in Britain, whose conferences and seminars have been of great value to me. Thanks also to the network of Dress and the African Diaspora scholars who supported and critiqued earlier formulations of my arguments. Thanks also to the Women's History research seminar and Graduate Student research seminars at the University of London for their supportive critique and feedback of earlier drafts of these chapters.

Thank you to the Blake family for providing permission to use the fantastic images in their ownership. Thank you to all those who contributed their thoughts and experiences to this project by agreeing to be interviewed: Anna Adimira, Ngozi Aleme, Irico Aleme, Trevor Carter, Betty Hill, Jennifer Hosten, Frank Hunte, Sylvia John, Marcus Jordan, Olga Lope-Seale, Marvo Manning, Claudette Pickering and especially Donald Hinds, who also shared photographs from his collection.

For their generous critique and guidance thanks to Mary Ellen Curtin, Peter Gurney, Jeremy Krikler, Diana Paton, Alison Rowlands and Owen Robinson and the anonymous readers and editors of the *Radical History Review*, which published a somewhat different version of Chapter 4, reworked and extended here. For their encouragement and insights along the way thanks also to Henrice Altink, Emily Zobel Marshall, Monica Morena Figueroa, Mark Figueroa, James Robertson, Gordon Rohlehr, Claudia Hucke, Anyaa Adim-Addo, Phillipa Lane, Cathryn Wilson, Aisha Khan, Ambra Sedlmayr, Deborah Thomas, Leah Rosenberg, Sandra Courtman, Rivke Jaffre, Ian Robertson, Carolyn Cooper, Kate Quinn, Natasha Barnes, Carole Boyce Davies, Rose Matthews, Carole Tulloch, and David Dodman. Thanks especially to loved ones, Raphael, Reggie, Coreen, Rosa, Annette, Wendy, Nancy and Vita for inspiring and sustaining my journey.

The author and publisher gratefully acknowledge the permission granted to reproduce the copyright material in this book. Every effort has been made to trace copyright holders and to obtain their permission for the use of copyright material. The publisher apologises for any errors or omissions in the above list and would be grateful if notified of any corrections that should be incorporated in future reprints or editions of this book.

List of abbreviations

BWIA   British West Indies Airways
CBU   Carnival Bands Union (Trinidad)
CDC   Carnival Development Committee (Trinidad, state-run)
CIC   Carnival Improvement Committee (Trinidad, private)
JFW   Jamaica Federation of Women
JLP   Jamaica Labour Party
JWTU   Jamaica Workers and Tradesmen Union
PNM   People's National Movement (Trinidad)
PNP   People's National Party (Jamaica)
SCC   Savannah Carnival Committee (Trinidad, private)
UNIA   United Negro Improvement Association

Introduction – Caribbean beauty competitions in context

In 1949, the *Caribbean Post*, the brainchild of Jamaican feminist publisher Aimee Webster, announced the arrival of a new type of West Indian woman through its coverage of the pre-eminent beauty contest of British Honduras 'Queen of the Bay':

> This year's 'Queen of the Bay' is the true type of evolving West Indian womanhood. Young, she is just eighteen, attractive with a tanned olive complexion, dark wavy hair, and bright black eyes; she has a flashing smile. And her queenly bearing is so characteristic of Maya Indian and African ancestry.[1]

Webster's publication was proud to sponsor this new hybrid ideal of British West Indian femininity. A place was reserved for the 'Queen of the Bay' in the *Post*'s own regional 'Miss British Caribbean' beauty competition. Webster used the competition to assert the modernity of the British Caribbean, and to support plans for self-government through the proposed federation of British Caribbean colonies. Alongside beauty competitions, the *Post* championed modern Caribbean femininity. In articles such as 'Daughters of the Caribbean', it increasingly portrayed light-skinned 'mixed-raced' or brown women of the middle-classes as cosmopolitan, well-travelled, 'adventuresome' and 'eclectic'.[2]

The *Post*'s treatment of West Indian femininity reflected the growing significance of the beauty contest in the British Caribbean. The most prominent early beauty contest in the West Indies was the 'Miss Jamaica' contest, which began in 1929 and was sponsored by the national daily newspaper, the *Gleaner*. Though modelled in part on the new beauty competitions of North America – which aroused excitement and controversy in equal measure, for their parades of scantily clad women – 'Miss Jamaica' began modestly, as a debutante parade for white-creole women in ballgowns.[3] However, at this moment of cultural revolution in the West Indies, beauty contests were not to remain as private parties, restricted only to white elites and the wealthier coloureds who skirted the margins of elite social life. Gradually, as beauty contests grew in popularity, especially after the Second World War, they became a space to contest the nation itself through competing representations of ideal Caribbean womanhood.

As the predominantly brown middle-classes became ever more confident in asserting their leadership and stewardship of the mass of African and Asian-descended labourers and peasants, so they fought to influence the icons of nationhood and citizenship. They began to challenge the supposed cultural supremacy of the British and through that, the racial system itself. Particularly fascinating and under-examined are the gendered and racialised aspects of this competition for culture, and the struggle to enact non-white subjectivities and carve them into the national image. This book provides a cultural history of Caribbean beauty competitions in the Anglophone Caribbean and in London, examining the significance of the performances on the beauty contest stage, to reveal that the work of the beauty competition was to help to bring subjectivity, the body and citizen into being as these countries emerged from colonialism.

Caribbean cultural and literary criticism hosts a discussion on the politics of beauty in the Caribbean, reflecting on the obsessive debates that thrive in today's press over who ought to represent the nation, but with little or no examination of the history of these somewhat tabooed, public debates. This rich discussion reveals that beauty contests in the Caribbean are, in the words of literary and cultural critic Carolyn Cooper, 'far more serious than mere entertainment'.[4] Literary and cultural critic Belinda Edmondson, author of *Caribbean Middle-brow: Leisure, Culture and the Middle Class* has remarked on the lively 'regional obsession' over beauty contests in the Caribbean as a 'state-approved form of female spectacle . . . particularly useful in any discussion of the politics of femininity and public performance in the Caribbean'.[5] Edmondson offers incisive analysis of the success of images of eroticised yet sanitised and approved light-skinned femininity in beauty competitions, and other public spectacles including dancehall and carnival, that reveal the ongoing stratification in the middle-class press between decorous brown middle-class and 'vulgar' black working-class femininity. Edmondson also remarks that since the late 1990s, the interplay between paradigms of brown and black femininity has begun to change due to the effects of globalisation; 'in the age of black supermodels and the ubiquitous Oprah Winfrey', black beauty queens, she explains (those who can demonstrate middle-class values), are no longer unseen and unheard of.[6] Similarly Cooper, herself dedicated to reappraising the subaltern dancehall and black working-class culture in Jamaica as countercultural and defiant, dedicated a series of newspaper articles in the *Jamaican Observer* and *Gleaner* in the 1990s to critiquing the controversy surrounding the 'Miss Jamaica' competition and the ongoing marginalisation of blackness in constructions of Jamaican society.[7] More recently Cooper has also compared Jamaican beauty competitions with the rise since 2001 of professional modelling in Jamaica and argued that modelling makes more room for phenotypically African women, radically and sumptuously adorned, and in the process destabilises old beauty aesthetics valorised in the beauty competition.[8]

Most illustrative to date is the work of cultural critic Natasha Barnes, whose important essay 'Face of a Nation', originally published in 1994, was the first scholarly work to suggest that beauty competitions in the Caribbean had a history worth exploring, and shed light on the infamy of racialised politics surrounding the 'Miss Jamaica' pageant. Here I build upon Barnes's study, and the crucial commentary of Edmondson, Cooper and other cultural critics to elaborate a thorough historical discussion of the cultural history of beauty in the Caribbean as the process of decolonisation took hold.[9]

However, these works that have emerged from literary and cultural studies are written by scholars of literature and culture, and speak to other works of postcolonial literary criticism. Therefore whilst they provide essential observations, insights and a basis for new research into beauty, they lack detailed examination of the process of the development of racialised paradigms of beauty over time, and their political and cultural applications, in short their historical formation and contexts. The history and politics of constructions of racialised femininity and desirability in the Caribbean are not self-evident and need to be further explored and their origins accounted for.[10] Clearly beauty contests are not only significant, but have a history steeped in power, marginalisation and contestation. For the first time this study contributes a book-length work to the discussion of the politics of beauty in the Caribbean, a detailed historical study that centres on the theme of beauty. It is based on thoroughgoing analysis of the origins and development of the beauty competition over time in the Anglophone Caribbean in this crucial period of the twentieth century.[11] It draws upon valuable archival sources of African Diaspora history spread between the UK, the Caribbean and New York, including newspapers, magazines, pamphlets, periodicals, and government records, as well literature and oral testimony gathered by the author. As a result of this wide research, it seeks to contribute to studies of beauty, gender, 'race' and postcolonialism.[12] In the process this book addresses a number of gaps in the existing literature on beauty in the Caribbean. It clarifies the mystery overhanging beauty competitions before the 1960s, the dawn of independence in the British Caribbean; it analyses the steady rise of competitions invested in brown femininity in the postwar period; at the same time, it challenges the notion that black women had little or no role to play in the spectacle before the 1990s by bringing contrary evidence to the surface that demonstrates the ongoing construction of ideals of (dark-skinned) black femininity in the Caribbean. It aims to reveal that through the performance of cultured, modern femininity in the beauty competition that developed over time, brown and black women helped to enable creole-nationalist projects that sought to bring the subjectivities, embodiment and citizenship of people of colour into being. Although the construction of idealised femininity and not masculinity is under the lens in this book, it becomes clear that men had an investment in the beauty competition delivering these vital ends, and in many cases the organisation of the beauty competition was evidently 'too important' to be left to women.

This book is distinct in that it aims to highlight the significance of beauty to the wider social and political context of the transformation of the Caribbean within the twentieth century. By demonstrating that the performativity surrounding the beauty contest was used as a mode for realising racialised subjectivities, it aims to reveal that beauty was important for the possibility of nationhood and modernity amongst Caribbean people, both within the Caribbean and in the UK. As such, it is a work of feminist cultural history, adding to a growing, yet still tiny, body of critical feminist studies on beauty that look beyond the United States. This work in particular aims to help to fill the lacuna of such studies that specifically address the Caribbean and the black experience in Britain, in historical perspective.[13]

The beauty contest emerged in tandem with the cultural revolution, forced by labour unrest in the 1930s. It is, therefore, a primary site to examine racialised femininity under construction and reconstruction, in connection with the growth of interlinked public discourses on identity, national identity and decolonisation. By engaging the Caribbean middle brow culture, to use Edmondson's phrase, this book aims to build upon Caribbean cultural criticism on the rise of the Caribbean nation. However, this cultural history of Caribbean beauty competitions may also supplement political histories, which as literary critic Veronica Gregg has observed, have produced a 'nationalist creation story', focused in particular on the political life of a 'handful of remarkable men', and which has unsurprisingly, 'created many absences'.[14] Furthermore, as historian Howard Johnson has pointed out, Caribbean scholarship of the past has at times tended to focus upon the black 'sufferer' in isolation from the rest of the society.[15] In contrast, of particular interest to this study are the middle-class and the aspiring middle-class, as they were drawn into the saga of the beauty competition, either as nationalist activists subtly critiquing or openly protesting the idealised parade, or as self-conscious audiences examining themselves and the candidates in a circuitous flow of surveillance, or as consumers enticed by the alluring and glamorous spectacle of the beauty competition, its display of luxurious lifestyle and thrilling prizes.

Performativity and the beauty contest

As sociologist Shirley Tate has shown, 'feminist ideas on beauty are "raced", classed and the site of othering others'.[16] Therefore, this book emerges out of the need for more feminist historiography that engages race, beauty and politics, in the vein of Maxine Craig's landmark study of African American beauty competitions. I take up Tate's elucidation of race performativity to examine the work of the Caribbean beauty competition and the significance of brown and black women's involvement therein. Tate has theorised black beauty as performative, that is, 'designed activity', and:

> [A]n ongoing negotiation of aesthetics, stylization and politics produced through the mobility and mobilization of beauty knowledge, stylization technologies, feminist and anti-racist/Black Nationalist ideology in the Black Atlantic diaspora.[17]

Taking up a Butlerian grounding in performativity Tate argues that 'racialized subjects bring into being what they name, within the reiterative power of discourse on "race"'.[18] By extension the participants in Caribbean beauty competitions, be they audience members, organisers, judges or contestants, continue to shape and identify race as they participate in creating and affecting the performance of cultured, modern femininity in and around the beauty competition. This book will explore how the competition itself becomes a mode of articulating particular performances to deliver certain ends. The performance of cultured modern beauty, the idealised femininity of women of colour in the beauty contest, became the mode for projecting the wholeness and citizenship of Caribbean subjects.

However, in the process contradictions and occlusions occurred that reveal the limitations of the beauty competitions for this mode. Crucially Cooper's work on dancehall has addressed the 'pejoration of vulgar', which marks binaries of high and low culture in Jamaica, and has become 'encoded in the Jamaican body politic'.[19] Racialised notions of vulgarity are embedded in discussion of the performance of idealised femininity and are teased out here through the journey of the beauty contest from elite leisure to national product. And yet, the history of Caribbean beauty also bears the influence of counter-cultural anti-racist discourses, focused on locating blackness in so-called 'natural' stylisation processes and politics. This cultural history of Caribbean beauty competitions provides some much-needed examination of the surprising and little-known interventions of radical anti-racist voices into the beauty contest fray and considers the impact they had on the development of competitions in the Caribbean.

Hybridity and creolisation

As Edmondson writes, concepts of hybridity and creolisation have been used to theorise 'the development of a society that is the blend of ethnicities and influences'.[20] However, these concepts continue to be the subject of great debate among Caribbean and postcolonial scholars and still need to be further unpacked and their multiple historical and current usages examined. Here I take up Edmondson's observation that hybridity has somehow been posed as democracy-at-work and mysteriously become a romantic paradigm of Caribbeanness in popular culture.[21] Similar work has been done by anthropologist Donna Goldstein, who suggests that scholars wishing to understand the survival of discourses of racial democracy in Brazil ought to examine the much neglected question of the role of gender in the construction of a national mythology.[22] Here, I engage hybridity, as Edmondson suggests, not merely as a theoretical postcolonial trope, but for the way it was imagined on the beauty contest stage, specifically the use of the beauty contest to make literal representations of harmonious racial and cultural blending in the Caribbean through performances of cultured, modern beauty, created by contest organisers, beauty candidates and observers.[23] Through the examination of the beauty contest this book explores the serviceability of the concept of hybridity within the different nationalist projects of the mid-twentieth century in Jamaica, Trinidad and Barbados, and how these projects were challenged, in the Caribbean and in London. Beauty competitions provided the opportunity to orchestrate a national romance underpinned by idealised hybrid feminine beauty, a pageant of national self-realisation that attempted to harmonise racial, social and ideological conflicts and set forth a model for nationhood, according to the vision of its middle-class authors. However, as I have argued elsewhere, Caribbean gender constructions have, since the colonial encounter itself, used female bodies as the markers of racial difference and Euro-American travellers in the Caribbean continued to draw typologies of racialised femininity through the nineteenth century.[24] This cultural history of beauty competitions will therefore engage a history of essentialising and standardising types, a mode to which the beauty contest is inordinately suited, and will therefore uncover the limitations of such a project to bring Caribbean subjectivities into being.

The legal and social structuration of slavery and colonialism objectified brown and black women as sexual objects and tireless labourers, and thereby put them outside of the boundaries of proper femininity. Nevertheless, as historians Diana Paton and Pamela Scully have shown, the process of emancipation was also gendered and imagined, wrongly, that the liberal paradigm of male-headed households and female dependents would emerge in the postemancipation Caribbean.[25] The setting for this book, therefore, is the presence of lingering and unresolved ideological contradictions over race, gender, subjectivity, the body and citizenship which were formed in colonialism, slavery and emancipation, and were foundational to nationalist movements in the British Caribbean. Over 100 years after abolition in 1838, as the islands emerged from the paradox of 'colonial freedom', the beauty contest became a central arena in which idealised visions of femininity, articulated through performances of cultured, modern beauty, could be imagined and designed, in the attempt to bring full personhood into being.

Beauty contests, therefore, contained the possibility for postcolonial critique. As Mimi Sheller has shown, the Caribbean has been put outside the scope of the West by othering discourses that have allowed it to be consumed at a distance. This consumption which defined the colonial relationship, Sheller defines as 'mobile flows' of:

> [E]dible plants (sugar cane, bananas, tropical fruits); stimulants (coffee, tobacco, rum, cannabis); human bodies (slaves, indentured labourers, contemporary 'service workers'); cultural products (texts, images, music,); knowledge collections (studies of botany, ethnology, linguistics); and entire 'natures' and landscapes consumed as tropical paradise.[26]

Thus, postcolonial scholarship, from its architects including Caribbean intellectuals such as poet and writer Eduoard Glissant and psychoanalyst Frantz Fanon, has ever since striven to reconnect the history of the 'other' to the history of the West.[27] The influence of postcolonial theory on the practice of history is the ongoing project to transform studies of the past by demonstrating that Caribbean subjects were central to the formation of modernity. As historian Antoinette Burton has shown in *Gender, Sexuality and Colonial Modernities*, concepts of modernity were negotiated between the representative of colonial authority and the colonial subject. Analysis of the processes of making colonial modernities demonstrates that colonial 'regimes that were, [never] self-evidently hegemonic but . . . always subject to disruption and contest, and therefore never fully or finally accomplished, to such an extent that they must be conceived as unfinished business.'[28] This book takes up such theories to show that beauty contests were used to help to contest colonialism and othering, and that through the demise of colonialism, the beauty contest allowed its participants to use performance of cultured, modern beauty to bring Caribbean subjects and citizens into being.

The racial system in the British West Indies

The distinctiveness of the historical experience of the Caribbean is, in the words of sociologist O Nigel Bolland, the persistence and pervasiveness of colonialism and slavery.[29] Postcolonial scholars have demonstrated that the Caribbean was not merely pre-industrial in its economic and labour systems, but in fact intrinsic to the development of industrial capitalism.[30] In support of this process, race in the Caribbean was maintained and perpetuated through societal structuration, class, gender and culture. Historians Brian Moore and Michele Johnson show that one aspect of this structuration and projection of race was the British civilising mission, which ordinary Jamaicans engaged with only selectively, whilst they pursued their own cultural imperatives alongside it; they practised Christianity and Afro-Jamaican religions, Myal and Pokumina, simultaneously and did not regard these practices to be in conflict.[31] By contrast the British civilising mission particularly targeted elites, who as the 'standard-bearers of civilization' threatened to undermine the British imperial project if they could not convince as morally and culturally superior beings.[32] Church, schooling and the press were some of the main instigators and regulators of the programme to institutionalise good and bad behaviour, with the most sustained resistance to this programme residing in the subcultures of the urban slums.[33] Not only did the aspiring middle-classes determinedly pursue improvements in their lives through the outward signs of the acquisition of respectability and 'refined' culture, but they readily challenged biological racism that threatened to altogether block their path to equality.[34]

Social theorist Daniel Segal's analysis of race and colour in pre-independence Trinidad shows that race could be mitigated by conduct, such that for the aspiring coloured and black middle-classes 'achieved lightness' was possible, to a degree, through respectable living standards, marked in particular by education, legal marriage and church-attendance, as well as by bodily signs, or performance.[35] However, these could never entirely outweigh the significance of skin colour, facial features and hair texture as outward 'racial' markers that helped to position the individual within the social hierarchy. Race finds multiple assignations in appearance and behaviour, outward signs of physiognomy and culture and throughout this book I refer to a racial continuum that historically attempted to define people as black, 'coloured' or white, black having the most associations with African, white with European and coloured or 'brown' with mixed. This continuum selectively included and excluded former indentured persons. For example, Portuguese-Creoles in Trinidad were historically regarded as less than white by the hegemonic regime, because of their former dependent-labourer status and intermingling with other racial groups, and Jewish-Creoles in Jamaica became socially white only upon entering the plantocracy from the end of the nineteenth century. This continuum was and is, ever a matter of negotiation and the beauty contest provided a platform for altering one's racial designation and even acquiring a new one.

The acquisition of dominant culture by people of colour was thus an important outward sign of ascription, and it bred a pragmatic response among the aspiring middle-classes, described by Segal succinctly as 'upward identification and downward distancing'.[36] Segal has observed that notions of cultural preservation were deeply ingrained in the racial system, such that blackness was signified by a lack, an absence that represented the erasure of even the idea of African culture within the imperial project, while Asians (so-called 'East Indians' and Chinese descended people) represented the 'unassimilated', 'non-creole' element whose supposed backwardness was signified by clinging to ancestral culture. This socially constructed notion of cultural preservation was present in the nationalists' programme for unity in the mid-twentieth century. Hence the Mayor of Port of Spain, Tito Achong, an advocate of unified cultural nationalism, wrote in 1942, that Chinese and Indian Trinidadians ought to join the national project by 'forsak[ing] the past glory of their ancestral homelands', whilst Afro-Creoles should learn about 'all culture', and 'synthesise' these into an 'organic whole, harmonising the end product with their social history'.[37] Thus culture, whether British or creole, was a category overshadowed by imperial systems of racialisation, and burdened by a history of the pursuit of racialised respectability. This book explores the ways in which the acquisition of 'refined' culture, an imperative transformed by the anticolonial awakening of the 1930s, was heavily dependent on the performance of femininity.

This story of Caribbean beauty competitions unfolds largely in chronological order, taking the case of Jamaica, Trinidad and Barbados in turn, before returning to Jamaica and then journeying to Britain. Jamaica, by virtue of its size and importance to this story, earns two chapters. This structure allows the examination of the ways in which the problems of competitive beauty were differently apprehended in Jamaica, Trinidad and Barbados, and finally London. It begins with perhaps the earliest Caribbean beauty competition, 'Miss Jamaica', launched in 1929 on the cusp of Jamaican cultural blossoming. This chapter considers the 'Miss Jamaica' contest as a vehicle for elitist white-creole nationalism in resistance to the unfolding drama of labour rebellion and cultural awakening of brown and black people, one that placed upper-class Jamaicanness on a par with Britishness. It also provides the opportunity to explore the radical feminist voices that emerged amidst the cultural revolution of the 1930s. Fittingly this first chapter examines feminist-nationalist Aimee Webster's orchestration of the pan-Caribbean competition, 'Miss British Caribbean' that began to mould a brown feminine ideal that all of the English-speaking Caribbean, she proposed, could invest in.

We then journey to Trinidad, where the postwar beauty competition developed on a different basis, in spite of Webster's appeals. In Trinidad the battle for culture centred on Carnival, the 'national fete'. Here Afro-Creole nationalists competed with whites to assert their proprietorship over the transition to self-rule through the moral upgrade of Carnival, focusing particularly on conduct at Carnival, reorganising Carnival and the pageantry and performance of the 'Carnival Queen' competition. This chapter explores the 'Carnival Queen' beauty competition as part of this programme of moral and cultural 'cleaning' that shaped and projected racialised femininities onto the beauty competition stage. In the process it demonstrates that the Carnival-refinement process engaged only selectively with ideals of hybridity to deliver modern beauty, and through it subjectivity and citizenship.

Chapter 3 moves to Barbados where, historically, racial discourse has been so submerged as to become an almost infamously taboo subject. Yet, after a slow start, beauty competitions in Barbados thrived. Their development reveals the active process of shaping and reshaping complex identities on the beauty contest stage, identities that were bound to the modern nation and attempted to bring the citizen and the racialised subject into being. This chapter examines the signs and symbols of the performance of cultured modern beauty in this process, drawing upon oral testimony. It discusses the different processes that constructed brown and black femininities as the beauty competition began to take hold as legitimate national entertainment in Barbados.

Chapter 4 returns to Jamaica, not merely because it is the largest of the Anglophone islands and had a throng of beauty competitions, but because from this sustained activity Jamaica produced a 'remedy' to the saga of beauty competitions that by now gripped the Caribbean. This remedy, the 'Ten Types-One People' competition, it was suggested, set an example not just to the rest of the Caribbean, but to the wider watching world. The 'Ten Types' multi-competition of 1955 imagined ten racial-colour categories of Jamaicanness and became highly influential as a model of fair play and harmonious racial coexistence. It attracted regional and international attention, and formed a symbolic template for outward shows of equality and fairness in the cultural nation-building of Jamaica thereafter. However, I argue that the 'Ten Types' model aimed to conceal racial and social conflicts, and this chapter examines the institutionalisation of the 'Ten Types' model and provides examples of copycat competitions elsewhere in the Caribbean.

Having closely examined the development of beauty competitions in the Caribbean, the final chapter visits Britain, the destination for thousands of West Indian migrants after the Second World War. It highlights the radical vantage point of exiled Trinidadian-born communist-feminist Claudia Jones who launched a Caribbean beauty competition in London and persuaded the BBC to televise it. This chapter reveals that Jones modified Caribbean cultural nationalism and the performativity of the beauty competition in response to new challenges in Britain, at the metropolis of empire. Jones's innovative use of anti-racist campaigning and cultural affirmation revealed the circuitous travel of African Diaspora ideas of politicised 'black beauty' and challenged the effects of racism both in the UK and the Caribbean.

Notes

1 'Carib, Spanish and Negro', *Caribbean Post*, Sugar No. (1949), p. 10. The surviving records of the *Caribbean Post* at the National Library of Jamaica are incomplete. The publication was short-lived and during its demise, from around 1949 onwards, issues appeared less frequently and were not dated but named by theme, i.e. 'Sugar No.', 'Money No.' and 'Building No.'

2 'Daughters of the Caribbean', *Caribbean Post*, 1 (1946), pp. 24–25. I make reference to 'white', 'coloured' or 'brown' and 'black' people throughout this book. These were just some of the contemporary racialised identifiers used in British Caribbean societies. Although 'coloured' appeared to be a polite referent, especially used for and by people of mixed-race during the period, 'brown', and variations on brown,

'red', 'yellow', were also used in practice. The boundaries of each group were porous, subject to change according to temporal and social contexts, as will be explored, not least through the work of the beauty contests. Whiteness, brownness and blackness, however, carried both class and colour connotations; whiteness was associated with the power of colonial rule, blackness with the lower rungs of society, and brown or 'racially-mixed' identities became increasingly associated with the upwardly mobile middle-class in the mid-twentieth century. However, the middle-classes also featured people classed as black, and people ranging in skin tone were also present among the poor.

3   The term 'creole' in the British Caribbean usage signifies 'local', or originated in the locality. White-creole identity describes that of a local-born, white-identified person.

4   Carolyn Cooper, 'Caribbean Fashion Week: Remodelling Beauty in "Out of Many One" Jamaica', *Fashion Theory* 14(3) (2010), pp. 387–404; p. 388.

5   Belinda Edmondson, 'Public Spectacles: Caribbean Women and the Politics of Public Performance', *Small Axe* 13 (2005), p. 8. See also Edmondson, *Caribbean Middlebrow: Leisure, Culture and the Middle-Class* (Ithaca, New York: Cornell University Press, 2009) and Edmondson, 'Trinidad Romance: The Invention of Jamaican Carnival' in Edmondson (ed.), *Caribbean Romances: The Politics of Regional Representation* (Charlottesville: University Press of Virginia, 1999).

6   Edmondson, *Caribbean Middlebrow*, p. 120.

7   Cooper has written extensively on dancehall and in particular the 'erotic disguise' of black women's dancehall performance, *Noises in the Blood: Orality, Gender and the 'Vulgar' Body of Jamaican Popular Culture* (Warwick: Macmillan Caribbean, 1993).

8   Cooper, 'Caribbean Fashion Week', pp. 387–404.

9   Natasha Barnes, 'Face of the Nation: Race, Nationalisms, and Identities in Jamaican Beauty Pageants' in Conseulo Lopez-Springfield (ed.), *Daughters of Caliban: Caribbean Women in the Twentieth Century* (Bloomington: Indiana University Press, 1997) pp. 285–305 (an earlier version of this essay appeared in the *Massachusetts Review*, 1994) see also Barnes, *Cultural Conundrums: Gender, Race, Nation, and the Making of Caribbean Cultural Politics* (Ann Arbor: University of Michigan Press, 2006). Belinda Edmondson's informed discussion of beauty competitions relies for its reflections on the past on Barnes's analysis in 'Face of a Nation'.

10 Patricia Mohammed has indicated the need for greater historicisation of this racialised typology of desirability: Patricia Mohammed, ' "But Most of All Mi Love Mi Browning": The Emergence in Eighteenth and Nineteenth Century Jamaica of the Mullatto Woman as Desired', *Feminist Review* 65 (2000), pp. 22–48.

11 In this book the term 'black beauty' connotes a post-1960s counter-cultural statement of pride in the African Diaspora. However, it also embraces a history of engagement by African-descended people with the politicisation of feminine beauty in the New World, hence it is applicable in this instance to describe a study that explores African-descended subjectivities in the Caribbean.

12 I refer to 'race' here in inverted commas to acknowledge its place in this study as a social construct under examination. Hereafter I will refer to it in the same sense, without inverted commas.

13 For the growing body of works on race and beauty in the African Diaspora that look beyond the United States see: M.G. Moreno Figueroa, 'Displaced Looks: On

Being Beautiful, Ordinary, Ugly or Insignificant: The Lived Experience of Beauty and Racism in Mexico,' Feminist Theory (forthcoming in 2013), 14(2). Patricia Pinha, 'Afro-Aesthetics in Brazil,' in Sarah Nuttall (ed.), Beautiful/Ugly: African and Diaspora Aesthetics (Durham, NC: Duke University Press, 2006), pp. 266–289; Rita Barnard, 'Contesting Beauty,' and Zimitri Erasmus, 'Hair Politics,' in Sarah Nuttall and Cheryl-Ann Michael (eds), Senses of Culture: South African Culture Studies (Oxford: Oxford University Press, 2000) pp. 380–392; 343–62; for a discussion of 'Miss France d'Outre-Mer' competition in 1937 see Elizabeth Ezra, The Colonial Unconscious: Race and Culture in Interwar France (Ithaca, New York: Cornell University Press, 2000) pp. 36–38. And for fascinating examinations of the globalisation of femininity and consumer culture see Alys Eve Weinbaum et al. (eds), The Modern Girl Around the World: Consumption, Modernity and Globalisation (Durham: Duke University Press, 2008).

14 Veronica Marie Gregg, 'How with this Rage shall Beauty Hold a Plea: The Writings of Miss Amy Beckford Bailey as Moral Education in the Era of Jamaican Nation Building'. Small Axe 23 (2007), p. 18.

15 Howard Johnson, 'Introduction', in Howard Johnson and Karl Watson (eds), The White Minority in the Caribbean (Kingston: Ian Randle, 1998), p. ix.

16 Shirley Ann Tate, Black Beauty: Aesthetics, Stylization, Politics (Farnham: Ashgate, 2009), p. 1.

17 Ibid., p. 6.

18 Ibid., p. 8.

19 Cooper, Noises in the Blood, p. 8.

20 Edmondson, Caribbean Middlebrow, p. 49.

21 Belinda Edmondson, 'Introduction to Caribbean Romance: The Politics of Regional Representation', in Edmondson (ed.), Caribbean romances (Charlottesville: University Press of Virginia, 1999), p. 2.

22 Donna Goldstein, ' "Interracial" Sex and Racial Democracy in Brazil: Twin Concepts?' American Anthropologist 101 (1999), pp. 563–578.

23 Edmondson, Caribbean Middlebrow, p. 125.

24 Rochelle Rowe, 'Glorifying the Jamaican Girl: The "Ten Types – One People" Beauty Contest, Racialised Femininities, and Jamaican Nationalism', Radical History Review 103 (2009), 36–58.

25 Diana Paton and Pamela Scully, 'Introduction', in Paton and Scully (eds), Gender and Slave Emancipation in the Atlantic World (Durham: Duke University Press, 2005), p. 16.

26 Mimi Sheller, Consuming the Caribbean: From Arawaks to Zombies (New York and London: Routledge, 2003), p. 4.

27 Ibid., p. 2.

28 Antoinette Burton, 'Introduction', in Burton (ed.), Gender, Sexuality and Colonial Modernities (London: Routledge, 1999), p. 1.

29 O Nigel Bolland, The Politics of Labour in the British Caribbean (Kingston: Ian Randle, 2001), p. 2.

30 Ibid., pp. 1–8.

31 Brian Moore and Michele Johnson, Neither Led Nor Driven: Contesting British Cultural Imperialism in Jamaica, 1865–1920 (Mona, Jamaica: The University of the West Indies, 2004), p. 203.

32 Ibid., p. 147.

33 Ibid., p. 46.

34 For instance, a well-known debate unfolded in the pages of radical Trinidadian literary journal the *Beacon* in which CLR James challenged English geneticist Sydney Harland's racist theories of a white 'natural mental advantage' over blacks; Harvey Neptune, *Caliban and the Yankees: Trinidad and the United States Occupation* (Chapel Hill: University of North Carolina Press), p. 30.

35 Daniel Segal, 'Race and Colour in Pre-independence Trinidad' in Kevin Yelvington (ed.), *Trinidad Ethnicity* (Knoxville, University of Tennessee Press, 1993), pp. 91–93.

36 Ibid., p. 91.

37 Ibid., p. 96.

1

The early 'Miss Jamaica' competition: cultural revolution and feminist voices, 1929–50

Introduction

THE FIRST 'Miss Jamaica' beauty competition took place in 1929 and was sponsored by the national newspaper the *Daily Gleaner*, then closely aligned with planter-merchant interests. The *Gleaner's* editor was Herbert G. de Lisser, the most dominant figure in Jamaican literature and publishing, whose reign at the paper extended from 1904 to 1944. 'Miss Jamaica' represented an attempt to mark the cultural and racial supremacy of the white-creole planter-merchant class over the rest of Jamaica. This campaign was shaped by de Lisser and sustained through his literary and journalistic publications.

The 'Miss Jamaica' beauty contest developed in the 1930s, a decade that witnessed a surge in anticolonial activity: popular uprisings, feminist development, the formation of political parties, and an artistic and literary cultural awakening. However, the 'Miss Jamaica' beauty competition did not emerge as *part* of this cultural revolution, but in *resistance* to it. The competition became the pre-eminent social gathering among the elite, even as the tumultuous 1930s unfolded around them. However, it also aroused the contempt of middle-class nationalists, including taboo-breaking feminist, poet and playwright Una Marson. Marson attacked the beauty competition and, as her anticolonial position developed, began to interrogate the politics of feminine beauty brought to light by the mood of resistance to British colonialism and the advance of American consumerism in the island. Through an analysis of de Lisser's dedicated construction of idealised white femininity and Marson's and her contemporary Amy Bailey's feminist-nationalist critique of Jamaican national identity, this chapter establishes the context for the origins of a Caribbean beauty competition before the Second World War. Finally it considers the new beauty competitions which emerged immediately after the war and only for a short time: 'Miss British Caribbean', and 'Miss Kingston'. These new competitions projected modified formulations of femininity, through the performance of cultured, modern beauty by women of colour that would signal the islands' emergence from colonialism.

The Jamaican labour uprisings and political formation

The British civilising mission that sought to mollify the lower classes in post-emancipation Jamaica was only partially successful and the lower classes continued to organise and resist the colonial regime as the twentieth century dawned. However, attempts to organise labour were most successful in the decades between the wars. This period saw the return of ex-servicemen to the island, disillusioned with the black experience at home and abroad, the onset of global economic depression that forced the return of thousands of migrant labourers, and still other migrants leaving rural areas for Kingston in search of work. The unemployed and underemployed converged on the capital's slums and shanty towns. The city rapidly doubled in size, growing from 117,000 to 237,000 between 1921 and 1943.[1]

Radical black leader Marcus Garvey, having formed the United Negro Improvement Association (UNIA) in Kingston in 1914, and seen it grow throughout the region and in the United States, returned to Kingston from the US in 1927 as a deportee. The UNIA spread rapidly amongst working people, and became a catalyst for their politicisation and organisation. Garvey won a seat on the Kingston and St Andrew Council, a public representative body, and formed the People's Political Party, but was unable to breach the Legislative Council in the elections of the following year.[2] In addition to Garveyism, other forms of race-conscious nationalism were growing among middle and lower-class blacks. Ethiopianism was an international anticolonial movement, also present in the US and South Africa, which saw free-governed Ethiopia as an affirmative vision of black Africa. Ethiopianism in Jamaica emerged from the anticolonialism of the black churches in the nineteenth century, formerly the basis for missionaries' model societies.[3] Also present in interwar Jamaica was Rastafarianism, formed after the coronation of Ras Tafari as Emperor Haile Selassie of Ethiopia in 1930. The Italian invasion of Ethiopia in 1935 became an important element in anticolonial protest in both Jamaica and Trinidad.[4]

Jamaican labour protests began on the north coast in 1935 with striking banana workers in St Mary and dockers at the port of Falmouth, protesting against low wages. In the following year the Jamaica Workers and Tradesmen Union (JWTU) was formed among rural peasants and catalysed protests in the countryside. Its leaders were Allan Coombs and Hugh Buchanan, both the sons of rural peasants. Coombs was a former policeman and had served in the West Indian Regiment during the First World War. Buchanan had likely been radicalised in the UNIA.[5] By 1937 workers were in open and spontaneous rebellion, with major riots and strikes in Kingston and 'rolling' strikes throughout the country.[6] This rebellion, reported in the British press, was a major embarrassment to the colonial government, who were increasingly in competition in the region with American imperial interests and sought to appear as benevolent rulers.[7] The rebellion provoked a Royal Commission, headed by Lord Moyne, into the causes of poverty and underdevelopment in Jamaica and the wider British West Indies. However, with the outbreak of war, the publication of the report of the Moyne Commission was postponed to 1945.

Coloured middle-class men sought a role in the labour rebellion and by 1937 had emerged as labour leaders, although they were some-times mistrusted by the lower-classes who had succeeded in organising themselves in much of the action. Alexander Bustamante, for instance, began his involvement as a money-lender to the JWTU, and went on to become a charismatic leader and founded his own eponymous union, the Bustamante Industrial Trade Union. This became the largest trade union and the basis for the Jamaica Labour Party (JLP), which Bustamante also led. His cousin Norman Manley, an Oxford educated lawyer, enjoyed a favourable reputation among the nationalist activists of the Jamaica Progressive League, formed in New York City in 1936, and was committed to British Fabianism, that is to say he favoured a programme for evolutionary rather than revolutionary change, in Jamaica. Manley became leader of the People's National Party (PNP) when it was formed in 1938. The JLP pursued a populist agenda, and was less disconcerting to the elite, because unlike the PNP it did not pursue the socialist reorganisation of society, only better wages and living conditions for the poor. In contrast, the PNP wanted to stimulate nationalism and socialism in the island and initially appeared the more intellectual party. It attracted middle-class activists in greater numbers than the JLP, which lacked an internal structure for many years, but struggled to persuade its labour following of the need for a unified national identity.[8]

As both parties grew they lacked meaningful participation from the mass of working people who, though they had provided the initial mandate for the parties' existence, were denied leadership roles. Instead middle-class proprietorship of the transition to self-government on behalf of a supposedly immature majority black population emerged. This order ignored the rise of race-conscious politics amongst blacks and preferred instead to engender a harmonious national unity. However, though it would be erased in the march towards nationhood, black nationalism had nonetheless provided the impetus for much of the social and cultural activism that thrived during this period.[9]

Herbert de Lisser, *Planters' Punch* and the origins of 'Miss Jamaica'

Drawing a veil over the social upheaval and cultural awakening that rocked Jamaica during the interwar years, Herbert de Lisser's 'Miss Jamaica' competition instead espoused a narrow nationalism that affirmed the white-identified creole elites. De Lisser's ideological projection posed white-creole Jamaicans as the natural leaders of Jamaica, worthy inheritors of the British regime. The new beauty contest attempted to distinguish the femininity and distinctive beauty of the white-creole Jamaican woman by placing these Jamaican qualities on a par with those possessed by English and American women. De Lisser produced a voluminous body of fiction during the course of his career, controlled the *Daily Gleaner* for forty years, and produced another journal, *Planters' Punch*, at Christmastime each year, between 1920 and 1944. Thus de Lisser enjoyed a near monopoly over the written word in Jamaica at this time, an influence which literary critic Veronica Gregg has described as the ability to produce 'memory, history, value, wealth and desire'.[10]

Literary critic and historian Leah Rosenberg has produced an incisive and detailed account of Herbert de Lisser's career and writing, which betrays his long-standing preoccupation with drawing typographies of Jamaican womanhood, and is worth repeating here in brief, as it informs his development of the 'Miss Jamaica' competition. From his advantageous position de Lisser augmented his wealth and social standing, and as he grew in stature, he affected both a change in political alignment and in racial designation. De Lisser had identified himself as brown in the 1890s but had become a member of the white elite by the 1920s.[11] His ascent went in hand with a new 'corporate oligarchy' of Jewish-Jamaican families, who along with the United Fruit Company and other foreign capitalists entered the plantocracy as fruit and sugar growers, and came to dominate the Jamaican economy by the 1920s.[12] Early in his career de Lisser preached a liberal progressivism and had enjoyed a brief flirtation with Fabian politics. In 1913 he produced a novel, *Jane* (which would later be published as *Jane's Career*), and a body of essays entitled *Twentieth Century Jamaica*. In both publications de Lisser set forth his ideas concerning Jamaican advancement through a mixed-raced class, neither very light-skinned, nor 'unmixed' African, a 'type' he referred to as 'sambo', who would progress the nation toward modernity. The eponymous Jane, imagined as this dark mixed-raced 'type', charts this transformation as she leaves the rural backwater and achieves domestic respectability in the capital. However, later in de Lisser's career, as his interests became steadily more identified with the oligarchical elite, he used his influence to oppose universal suffrage and labour organisation. De Lisser became prolific in what Rosenberg calls anti-black, anti-labour fiction, which belittled moments of popular uprising in Jamaica, including the Baptist War of 1831 to 1832, the largest slave rebellion in Jamaica's history.[13] From this context of social ascent and resistance to popular political mobilisation, de Lisser invented and sustained the 'Miss Jamaica' beauty competition in the pages of the *Gleaner* and *Planters' Punch*.

The *Punch* was adorned by white ladies, from North America and Britain, especially tourists who wintered in the island. These provided instructive images of ideal femininity, including photographic portraits and an accompanying commentary written by de Lisser. For instance, 'Here Are Ladies Delightful', provided an array of 'greatly admired' visiting wives, including Mrs Bishop, whom de Lisser praised as a 'great fisherwoman and intrepid traveller . . . albeit perfectly feminine and charming'.[14] The *Punch* pictured a white-creole Jamaican society on genial terms with pre-eminent Euro-American company. In one feature, two English-educated upper-class white Jamaican women, Lucille Parks and Rita Gunter, favourably compared Jamaican young ladies to their English counterparts.[15] 'Types of English Beauty' harped upon the unchanging quality of Anglo-Saxon beauty through the ages.[16] Other features included 'Jamaican Entertains Royalty', 'A Woman as Empire Builder' and 'Ladies in the Working World', all of which attested to the Jamaican elite as the natural inheritors of the prevailing colonial order, yet on terms with modernity.[17]

Once English superiority had been rhetorically affirmed, and visually and discursively related to local feminine standards, de Lisser defended the particular attributes of the (white, upper-class) Jamaican woman. 'The Jamaica girl . . . possesses her full share of beauty; and perhaps climate and associations have added to her something that the girls of some other countries do not possess'.[18]

1.1 Types of English beauty, *Planters' Punch*

The task of affirming white femininity in Jamaica was particularly well served by the 'Miss Jamaica' beauty competition. In *Punch* it featured alongside similar material, including 'Some Beauties of Jamaica', all of which underscored upper-class Jamaican women as the true 'Daughters of Jamaica'.[19] Whereas women of colour were previously foremost in de Lisser's vision of the Jamaican future, they were now erased from his construction of Jamaican modernity and appeared only in anachronistic spaces in the journal, identified with the rustic past.[20] However, in the process de Lisser modified the racial boundaries of whiteness, as he included the daughters of prosperous Jewish and Syrian families in this clique, who would have been barred from white society before their rise to wealth. Miss Barbara Samuel, a woman of Syrian descent, and educated in London, was affirmed as a society belle through her appearance in

Punch; and, crucially, it was suggested that an *English* lady had remarked 'are all your Jamaica girls as nice and as good-looking as this one?'[21] 'Miss Jamaica' of 1930 was Helene Myers, an upper-class Jamaican of Jewish descent. As Rosenberg writes, the effects of de Lisser's widening of the boundaries to upper-class whiteness was that by implication whiteness could at this moment include light-skinned Jamaicans like himself.[22] The imagined racial boundaries to whiteness in Jamaica had always been porous in reality. However, de Lisser became the architect of a project to visually and discursively consolidate the new upper-class which had ascended after the decline of sugar, through his idealised formulation of white-creole Jamaican femininity and invention of 'Miss Jamaica' to cement this process.

Though it was well-publicised in both the *Gleaner* and *Punch*, 'Miss Jamaica' remained an exclusive and essentially private occasion, associated with the close-knit social world of wealthy white-identified families. Lucille Iremonger, a member of the elite descended from a French-Creole family with its roots in Saint Domingue, recalled the sense of entitlement that marked the early competition in her memoirs: 'The prizes were reserved for the daughters of the white planting plutocracy and the other old island families of the dominant caste. My family had come to regard themselves as having almost a prescriptive right to a place on the short list of finalists.'[23] The 'Miss Jamaica' competition thus recorded changes in social mobility, as it was a prize enjoyed by the old-elite and a litmus test of who else may be admitted to the 'dominant caste'. Whilst *Punch* had signalled that the wealthier Chinese could be potentially assimilated into the Jamaican elite, with a feature entitled 'Our Jamaica Chinese Ladies – An Influence', there was reportedly a private outcry among the white audience, as well as from middle-class nationalists, when a Chinese-Jamaican woman, Daphne Chen, was chosen as 'Miss Jamaica' in 1938.[24]

Responses from middle-class observers of the 'Miss Jamaica' competition were varied. Some women of colour attempted to breach the acknowledged racial boundaries of the competition by putting themselves forward as candidates, but they seldom featured on the short list of finalists Iremonger refers to. Una Marson, a young writer, had recently arrived in the capital and established the *Cosmopolitan* journal, the organ of the Jamaican Stenographers Association, and in so doing became the first woman publisher-editor in Jamaica. The organisation was essentially the trade union of aspiring professional women of colour, who along with the Jamaica United Clerk's Association, organised to gain greater access to civil service and business sector work.[25] Marson would later emerge as one of the artistic narrators of the cultural revolution. She described the labour uprisings of the 1930s in Jamaica as the 'birth of a[national] soul'.[26] Marson revealed the infamy with which the all-white 'Miss Jamaica' contest was regarded among the brown and black middle-classes, saying: 'Some amount of expense and disappointment could be saved numbers of dusky ladies who year after year enter the beauty competition if the promoters of the contest would announce in the daily press that very dark or black beauties would not be considered.'[27] Furthermore Marson aligned anticolonial nationalism to race and to the notion of the representativeness of the bodies of beauty queens, '[T]here is a growing feeling in many quarters that 'Miss Jamaica' should be a type of girl who is more truly representative of the majority of Jamaicans.'[28]

This race-conscious commentary was taboo and disrupted the colonial government's efforts to submerge racial discourse and discourage race-conscious politics. With her remarks Marson questioned the mythology of colour-blind liberal meritocracy that underpinned the British Empire. Marson belonged to a radical community of black nationalists and feminists who were increasingly challenging the colonial establishment and the prevailing social order in the interwar years.

Jamaican feminism: speaking up, speaking out

Black nationalism and feminism had emerged together in the late nineteenth century in Jamaica. Bahamian-born Robert Love, founder of the People's Convention, a pan-Africanist organisation, argued for the social elevation of black women through education and cultural refinement, as part of a programme for racial equality. A prominent feminist within the Convention was Catherine McKenzie. McKenzie campaigned for women's rights, birth control and better living conditions and typically framed these demands within a discourse of respectable Victorian house-wifery and good citizenship.[29] McKenzie trained as a teacher, and through her activism, became an essayist and public spokeswoman. During the interwar years the UNIA took up Pan-Africanism and produced another cohort of Caribbean feminists. However, although black nationalism stimulated the growth of feminism, its male leadership was often in conflict with the demands of assertive, educated women.

Like McKenzie, middle-class Jamaican feminists in the interwar period attempted to agitate within the constraints of the cult of domesticity. Respectable feminist activity in Jamaica was conflated with English notions of upstanding womanhood, and a woman's duty towards social work. This ideology rendered invisible the grass-roots activism of lower-class women in the trade unions.[30] A handful of elite female philanthropists concerned themselves with Jamaican poverty, led by Lady Denham, of the Jamaica Women's League, and were driven by English feminism and the moral imperative towards charity and 'uplift' as part of Empire-building. However, coloured middle-class feminist Eulalie Domingo charged that the majority of upper-class women's clubs were frivolous and indifferent to suffering, concerned only with 'the latest bridge or card game, the latest dance, and above all the latest gossip'.[31] There were also the English feminists who worked as teachers in Jamaican secondary schools, imparting robust Christian principles of hard work and public service to the coloured and black women they educated.[32] In turn educated brown and black feminists developed a feminist position around widening female political participation, alleviating poverty and improving women's job prospects in the civil service.[33]

However, as this picture indicates, feminism was fragmented by class-colour hierarchy and the separate identifications it encouraged and preserved. Middle-class brown and black women were ostracised from the charitable works of the elite, and, among middle-class feminists themselves, there was a tendency to seek to preserve class distinctions between their cohort and the lower-class poor. As historian Henrice Altink points out, although suffrage had been extended to 3000 educated and propertied women in 1919, feminists did not seek universal suffrage. Instead they directed their efforts at mobilising educated women into public life.[34] What these upper and middle-class feminists had in common was that they broadly strived for the alleviation of poverty amongst the lower-classes, but it was only the radical middle-class core, who publicly directed this effort at racial equality and national unity. Furthermore, women of colour in the feminist movement battled against what would later be called white liberal feminism's 'universalising of the category of woman' as middle-class and white which obscured the racial and class-based oppression they also suffered.[35]

Eulalie Domingo laughed at class snobbery, and appealed to other educated women to join the political effort, by crossing class and colour boundaries, and abandoning their pursuit of upward social mobility:

> Mrs. Mary Jane Brown is *afraid* to be seen with plain Mary Jane though they could arrange things for their mutual betterment, but Mrs. Mary Jane Brown is quite *flattered* to be seen in company with Lady Mary Jane deBrown who tells her she is much too good to fraternise with such a vulgar person as plain Mary Jane.[36]

In this sketch Domingo makes clear the powerful sway of all-too-important colour-class boundaries between unmarried lower-class (black)

Mary-Jane, respectable, middle-class, married (brown) Mrs. Mary Jane Brown, and distinguished upper-class (white) Lady Mary Jane deBrown, who though she may well patron a charity, discourages solidarity between women. Mary Jane is plain and worse still 'vulgar', and as such Mrs. Mary Jane really cannot afford the association. In a similar vein, Una Marson also attempted to rally better-off, educated women of the middling sort, 'Where are the hundreds of girls who leave secondary schools annually?' she asked, in an appeal that they enter social work and use that as their apprenticeship to politics.[37]

Class-colour hierarchy also affected the ways in which feminists responded to the moral panic surrounding the single lower-class women who migrated in large numbers to Kingston annually during this period, and were often accused disdainfully of promiscuity and prostitution.[38] Amongst the most progressive voices were Marson and feminist activist Amy Bailey. Marson called for a Secretary of Labour to be appointed who would directly address female as well as male unemployment.[39] Radically, she also proposed a tax on bachelors to provide a fund for neglected children.[40] Bailey rebuked Jamaican elites for their meagre sympathy with local poverty whilst they donated willingly to charitable fundraising drives abroad.[41] With their feminist collaborators Domingo, Mary Morris-Knibb (who after the Second World War would be elected to the Legislative Council), and Bailey founded the Women's Liberal Club in 1936, to stimulate feminist activism, particularly around poverty. Bailey also attempted to raise the status of the domestic work that most black women were forced to take by founding a training school that aimed to professionalise standards and raise salaries.[42]

As Marson's attack on 'Miss Jamaica' revealed, middle-class feminists did not restrict their commentary to socioeconomic issues alone, they were inevitably drawn into discussing the conditions affecting black women, which ultimately reflected the racialisation of power in everyday life. They particularly addressed the marginalisation of black femininity and the supposed debasement of black women. In defending black working women of Kingston, Amy Bailey detailed the meagre wages women received and the weight of social expectation that determined that they should spend their earnings on the trappings of respectable femininity, not least the cultivation of beauty:

> Let us take the case of a girl who gets nine shillings a week. Out of that she may have to pay car fares, but granted that she walks to and from her work, we will allow her one shilling for the days when she is too tired to walk home. She must pay between two shillings and three shillings a week for her lunch ... Out of the remainder she must provide

clothes good enough to look *respectable*, shoes and toilet articles. In these days of beauty culture, she must straighten her hair so as to be attractive, perhaps feed herself entirely and pay rent. Well, good readers, it can't be done, however masterly that girl may be at mathematics and high finance [italics my emphasis].[43]

Here Bailey began to question the emerging racial politics of consumption: the expectation, if not the responsibility, placed upon single black women of the working class to meet certain standards of outward respectability and attractiveness as they lived and worked in the city. Not only was the performance of respectability achieved through appearance and conduct, but also performing beauty was increasingly tied to the new modern ritual of hair straightening. These factors were regarded as crucial to achieving successful outcomes for such women, a living wage in the first instance, and ultimately, at least in the eyes of the bourgeois observer or charitable do-gooder, marriage and social acceptance into respectability.[44] Readers of *Public Opinion*, a nationalist journal founded in 1937, to which a number of feminists contributed, appealed to Bailey directly, after she had written an article exposing men's preference for light-skinned female partners in marriage, which she argued was another means by which dark-skinned women especially, were excluded from entering into respectability. In response to readers' calls for further comment, Bailey extended her critique of colour prejudice to consider women's behaviour in the matter of light-skinned preference. Bailey identified two groups of ambitious dark-skinned women. First, the cheerless black woman who had struggled so hard to achieve meagre recognition in clerical work that she was constantly on her guard in her effort for social acceptance and economic security:

[A] minority group, is to be found holding good positions in offices, schools, post offices, etc. They obtained these, often through much tribulation and heart ache, despite merit, and having got there *somehow* they can never allow themselves to forget it. In their effort to be dignified and modest a very commendable effort they go to the other extreme and become painfully stiff . . . They do not wish to be cheap and so wrap themselves with an air of unapproachability that goes far beyond their best intentions. The men seldom appreciate this [italics my emphasis].[45]

The woman Bailey describes here faces an impossible bind. Her hard-won position offers a modicum of respectable status that is nonetheless always precarious and requires constant self-policing, and by implication, the sublimation of sexuality, not least because married women were expected to relinquish clerical work. This black woman in the 'civilised' professional surroundings of the office must guard against *reverting* to what Bailey calls 'cheap' behaviour, or in other words, the racialised slur of vulgarity. It is particularly critical that Bailey, herself an educated, dark-skinned unmarried black woman, was sympathetic to the infamous character she had drawn, and created the image so as to draw attention to the workings of the colonial system in gendering black bodies.

The second group Bailey identified, also struggling to keep their place in the respectable clerical office, were accused of seeking socially advantageous company amongst their 'fairer sisters':

> They pride in telling you that they have few, if any dark friends; that at their parties the black girls are few and far between; that they prefer to have business transactions with those of lighter pigment, and other such ridiculous arguments which do little credit to their intelligence and less to their self-respect.[46]

Bailey continued by addressing the crux of the matter, that light-skinned preference was now being articulated not only among coloured men and women, not only by black men, but also by *salaried* black women, as well:

> [T]here is a growing tendency amongst some of our black girls today that is as alarming as it is absurd, that they also do not want to marry black men. They give as their reason the all-important one of 'raising the colour of their children'. If it is true that imitation is the sincerest form of flattery, then the men should be flattered that the girls have taken a leaf out of their book.[47]

Bailey continued by reassuring the reader that she was an advocate of greater social mingling, and a breakdown of class-colour hierarchy, but that this should be the 'natural sequence of love'.[48] This pattern of 'raising one's colour', she warned, would lead to the 'ironical justice' of lighter children resenting their darker parents.[49] Finally, Bailey revealed how class, race, shade and gender worked together to affect the individual's place on the social register: 'Imagine the consternation that the coloured son would give to his family were he to announce to them that he was going to marry a black girl *of his class*. He would be ostracised as having no mind, as having stepped down, as having disgraced the family'[50] [italics my emphasis]. Bailey thus revealed that acquiring education and clerical work was no guarantee of social acceptance or upward social mobility, and that the classes also preserved social distinctions through cloistered feminine sexuality and respectable marriage that hinged on greater pheno-typical distinctions. Though she had been asked to condemn women's behaviour, Bailey instead provoked her readers to consider the state of the nation's collective psyche, thereby situating the discussion of colour prejudice and marriage within the broader themes of the anticolonial struggle: '[T]here must be something diabolically wrong with the psychology of this country. It affects the highest to the lowest . . . I have seen too many occasions on which the market value of an individual rises or falls according to shade.'[51]

Similarly Marson used her journalism, especially in her own publication the *Cosmopolitan*, to stimulate feminism and rebut the denigration of women in the press. In 1929 Marson responded with wry humour to a public outcry against 'flapper' fashions of the 1920s; the trend for shorter skirts, make-up and bobbed hair. 'The poor modern woman!' she wrote, '[H]as the modern Jamaica girl given just cause to those of the opposite sex whose pastime is to criticise women?'[52] Marson was aiming to be doubly effective here, she attacked the scrutiny women were subjected to and asserted their freedom of expression, and ultimately used the opportunity to once more call for greater feminist participation.[53]

Marson continued to develop an anticolonial stance that criticised the racial politics of femininity, beauty and consumption, through her poetry. In 1937 she published her third collection, *The Moth and the Star*. This publication followed a stay of three years in Britain, between 1932 and 1935. Marson's British experience heightened her radicalisation, which was followed by her return to Jamaica where she witnessed the unfolding labour rebellion. Whilst in Britain Marson was ostracised from society through alarming experiences of aggressive racism in London. She was subject to verbal assaults in the street, and found herself barred from even basic secretarial work. These were more direct and startling experiences of the racial system than she had felt at home in Jamaica, where from her position of relative privilege – educated, middle-class and 'brown' – she had formulated a radical position and become a spokeswoman for brown and black women. In Britain by contrast Marson was part of a highly visible and victimised minority, subject, in the words of Fanon, to 'being dissected by white eyes'.[54] In *Little Brown Girl* Marson wrote about herself as a lonely curiosity:

Little brown girl
Why do you wander alone
About the streets
Of the great city
Of London . . .
Why do you start and wince
When white folk stare at you?[55]

In London Marson found refuge with the League of Coloured Peoples, an organisation formed primarily to challenge the 'colour bar' in employment. She was employed as the League's secretary, edited its literary publication *The Keys* and lodged with its founder, Jamaican-born doctor, Harold Moody. Towards the end of her time in London Marson also worked as secretary to Haile Selassie, when in 1935 he attended the League of Nations to assert Ethiopia's sovereignty against the imperial machinations of Italy.[56] Marson's deep sense of alienation from the 'Mother Country' was therefore mitigated by finding herself amongst the cosmopolitan environment sustained by 'coloured' colonials from all over the Empire who convened within the organisation.[57] It was through the League that Marson was exposed to circuitous flows of African Diaspora culture. Marson now experimented in her verse with the blues voice used by Harlem artists and with the Jamaican creole vernacular. In 'Brown Girl Blues', 'Canefield Blues', and 'The Banjo Boy', Marson recreated scenes from Jamaican popular culture, documented hardships and affirmed the sentiments of ordinary Jamaican people. She thus blazed a trail in the cultural revolution while some of her artistic peers remained highly Anglophile in their perspective and failed to be inspired by local scenes.[58] In 'Quashie Comes to London', Marson adopted the persona of a wide-eyed Jamaican visitor who tours London and records his impressions in Jamaican-Creole.[59] Quashie is mostly disillusioned but exclaims at joyous experiences of transatlantic black culture; jazz orchestras and a performance by famous African American singer, performer and activist Paul Robeson:

> I see some ob me own folks democratic
> In dese here music hall,
> An' if hear Paul Robseon sing
> You feel you wan' fe bawl.[60]

In this collection Marson employed pronounced aesthetic in blackness itself, which betrayed the influence of the Harlem Renaissance on her writing. She described skin as 'copper', 'black, bronze and brown', 'chocolate and high-brown', 'black ivory' and 'blackest ebony'.[61] Marson thus imagined a black identity affirmatively and inclusively as a range of brown hues, effectively reversing the Caribbean racial system characterised by 'upward identification and downward distancing', which prized how much white and not black identification one could claim.[62]

Marson also turned her attention to uncovering taboos of racial and sexual politics from the vantage point of brown and black women in Jamaica. In 'Brown Baby Blues', a mother despairs of her loneliness and poverty after abandonment by a white seaman, but is glad, in Bailey's words, to have 'raised the colour' of her child.

> My sweet brown baby
> Don't you cry.
> My sweet brown baby
> Don't you cry.
> Your mamma does love you
> And your colour is high.[63]

From this broad questioning standpoint, Marson confronted the invisibility of black people, women and men, as attractive figures in the mass culture industry, American cinema and magazines, and criticised these harmful forms of erasure. In 'Cinema Eyes' the subject is a brown woman who says, 'I grew up with a Cinema Mind', who asserts her light-skinned appearance as an agent for upward social mobility in colour-obsessed Jamaica:

> My ideal man would be a Cinema type
> No kinky-haired man for me
> No black face, no black children for me.
> I would take care
> Not to get sun burnt
> To care my half Indian hair
> To look like my cinema stars.[64]

Marson here accuses Hollywood films of exacerbating the already endemic racialised social hierarchy of Jamaican society.[65] The subject, schooled in protecting her skin and hair, begins to style herself to look like Hollywood stars. She rejects her black lover as she rejects blacks in general, 'they were black, and therefore had no virtue', identifying 'upwards' for self-preservation.[66]

Feminist scholar Honor Ford-Smith has extended Fanonian analysis to Jamaican life stories as a means of revealing the importance of gender to the construction of the self under colonialism.[67] Ford-Smith's study of two mixed-raced families revealed how racialised shame and humiliation within the colonial order could pass from parent to child. This chimes with Bailey's and Marson's commentary on the insidious role colour played in society. In the moral fable of 'Cinema Eyes' the female subject seeks out a light-skinned partner, who in fact becomes cruel, and she eventually bears a dark-skinned child, 'dark like your grandmother'.[68] The poem ends with a call for black cinema stars to grace the silver screen, and warns against black folk who 'fed on movie lore, lose pride of race'.[69]

Though Marson's poetry can be critiqued for its oversimplification of good black folk and misguided colour-struck subjects, it is worth remembering that her outspoken position as a coloured woman of letters was radical and bold for its time. Furthermore her rejection of Caribbean racial structuration was formulated from lived experience, and in response to her own complex position within the racial system. Marson's own background echoes Smith's observations of the influence of racialised shame on the construction of the colonial self. Marson was born in 1905 to a respectable middle-class family in the rural parish of St Elizabeth, the daughter of a black Baptist parson and a 'devout' coloured housewife.[70] As a family of the respectable middle-class, the Marsons occupied a typical position of relative privilege and social precariousness. They were a degree removed from the peasantry, and were able to uphold a respectable lifestyle in that they employed a servant, accessed secondary education and Marson's mother was able to refuse paid work outside the home. Yet within the relative privilege of her upbringing, Marson acquired an uneasy place in the system that judged status according to skin colour and the acquisition of 'refined' English culture. Marson's biographer, Delia Jarrett Macauley, reveals that Marson was differentiated from her siblings, as the darkest of three girls, and was apparently lacking in the feminine accomplishments of her sisters, preferring the outdoors to piano and needlecraft.[71]

Education reinscribed Marson's social lessons. Secondary education of a minority of children from the middle-class produced a reserve of civil servants, aimed to instil consent for colonial government and to deter middle and lower-class collaboration.[72] Marson received the Jamaican equivalent of an English public school education, as one of only ten (of 200 pupils) darker-skinned scholarship girls at Hampton High School. Hampton's teachers were white women educated in Britain and were employed to breed loyalty to the British Empire and an investment in an English identity, a process Smith has called 'making white ladies'.[73] Hampton on the one hand instilled English feminist values of the day, and prepared girls to be either educated, cultured wives or 'career' women, and on the other, exposed Marson to the racist bullying of fellow students and teachers alike. This process underpinned Marson's alienation from the privileged category of Englishness.[74] In 'Kinky Hair Blues' Marson cemented her commentary on the ravages of colonial and consumer culture on the black psyche. This poem explored the arrival of new beauty treatments which encouraged black women to consume white-dominated beauty standards. In 'Kinky Hair Blues' the subject is dark-skinned, lower-class and speaks in creole. The poem begins with the subject asserting a bold love of her African features. However, under social pressure the subject eventually capitulates and begins using the new American products, targeted at black women in particular, to bleach dark skin and straighten curly hair:[75]

> I hate that ironed hair
> And that bleaching skin
> Hate that ironed hair
> And that bleaching skin
> But I'll be all alone
> If I don't fall in.[76]

Here the subject must compromise her self-esteem, to attract lovers. Though the subject's would-be lovers are also black, Marson, like Bailey, shows men expressing an aspirational desire for light-skinned partners. Marson's warning to readers here was that if the black lower-class had barely survived British colonialism with their cultural originality and pride intact, then this identity was now being eroded by a new wave of American imperialism in form of films and beauty treatments. It is also worth considering that Marson assumed a purely negative relationship to beauty culture for lower-class black women, forced only by pressure to confirm and attract a mate, rather than an attraction to glamour and enjoyment of beauty culture, whilst at the same time she defended the choice of her middle-class sisters to style themselves as 'modern flappers'. However, in spite of the faintly patronising tone towards black working women, the poem is nonetheless bold and taboo-breaking in its attempt to affirm blackness and raise questions about creeping consumerism in the island.

In 'Black is Fancy' Marson depicts the cultural awakening of Jamaica through the eyes of a black female domestic labourer who is given a mirror, from her Aunt Liza, and begins to see herself anew. The subject takes down an image from her wall, an image she had previously admired of an attractive white model, an aspirational figure of beauty, and replaces it with the mirror in which she admires herself as she ties her bandanna or headscarf here, a culturally affirmative symbol of creole dress.[77] Furthermore, the subject identifies the white woman in the social order, and rejects her own position as labourer in a white woman's household, 'Besides she is not my friend, She is my mistress.'[78] In taking down the picture, which 'used to make me ashamed', the subject is enacting a social process of self-discovery, which Marson as a cultural nationalist, advocates for the future success of the nation.

Soon after the publication of the *Moth and the Star* war broke out, and most beauty competitions were suspended. However, *Spotlight*, a news magazine launched in 1940 by Afro-Jamaican Evon Blake, experimented briefly with a beauty competition which seemed almost to protest the genre. In June 1941, apparently in response to a request from its female readers for a return of the competition, *Spotlight* crowned white-creole Una Goldbourne, 'Miss Spotlight'. Goldbourne presented a very demure image, with simple dress, folksy hairstyle and little make-up. For the cover, she was photographed in profile in slightly sombre pose. The message seemed to be anti-glamour:

> One girl stood out as the morning star among all the other stars in the firmament. She wore a dancing frock as remarkable in its simplicity as her make-up. Life, youth, and vitality radiated from her oval face. The spotlight caught her raven-black hair, dimpled cheeks when she smiled shyly, provocative lips, large, dark, wistful eyes.[79]

The image of 'Miss Spotlight' perhaps represented a conservative response to consumerist glamour, a sober morality aided by wartime conditions, that stood in contrast to the 'modern' woman, who wore make-up, coiffed hair and shorter skirts, that Marson had attempted to defend some years before. However, following the war the beauty contest would be vividly revived with no less a political object than Herbert de Lisser first conceived for it.

'Miss British Caribbean': patriotism and nation-building in the wake of war

The war had catalysed the growing imperial crisis for Britain, and after 1945 the British West Indies moved towards democratisation and self-government.[80] Universal suffrage came to Jamaica in 1944, and most other British Caribbean colonies by 1951. Some form of economic and political association between British Caribbean colonies had been proposed for three centuries. After the war plans for British West Indian Federation were seriously revived as a means for sustainable self-rule that would especially protect the smaller territories.[81] Britain was also increasingly overshadowed in the region by the US, most significantly by the Bases-for-Destroyers Deal which during wartime had allowed the US Armed Forces to build military bases in British Caribbean territories. In exchange the US gave Britain fifty old American warships and agreed to defend the Caribbean zone from German attack. In the first half of the century the US had extended its presence in the Caribbean, through occupation or annexation (Haiti, Cuba, Puerto Rico); the building of the Panama Canal; corporate expansion into plantation production (Cuba, Dominican Republic, Jamaica); and extraction of minerals (Guyana and Trinidad). After the war, during which US service personnel had been present in many Caribbean countries, the US continued this economic expansion in the region through Caribbean markets.[82]

The Moyne Commission at last published its findings after the end of the war in 1945. Gender historian Joan French has shown that, though generally under-examined, the labour rebellion and the ensuing Moyne Commission determined colonial policy towards women in the postwar era. The report of the commission broadly recommended the domestication of lower-class women. Black families were living in poverty, it determined, because of the lack of a male breadwinner and dependent wife in the typical lower-class family structure. It preached female domestication and failed to acknowledge the impact of the decline in women's incomes or the present high rate of unemployment on the poverty and hardship felt in the islands. Following emancipation the majority of women remained land labourers and were therefore especially affected by the decline in sugar prices, global economic depression and the resulting urbanisation of the working poor. The female work force shrank from 125,000 in 1921 to 45,600 in 1943.[83] However, female promiscuity and the lack of a nuclear family structure were blamed for, in French's words, 'the entire suffering of the masses, for poverty, for infant mortality, for venereal disease, and for "the lot of their unfortunate children".'[84]

The report reaffirmed the notion that social work ought to be the vocation of the modern middle-class woman. Educated women were to encourage lower-class women to accept domestication. Historically, and to the exasperation of the respectable classes, many poor black women rejected marriage, in proverbial terms, as 'too much work', preferring instead to retain their economic autonomy.[85] Middle-class women were advised to seek work as nurses and teachers, and to volunteer as unpaid social workers, advising fellow women in everything from hygiene to child welfare. In return middle-class women would gain greater access to public bodies, in an advisory and executive capacity, where so-called feminine expertise was required, in welfare and education. As a direct result of the report the Jamaican Federation of Women (JFW) was founded in 1944, headed by Lady Molly Huggins, wife of the Colonial Governor. French writes that the JFW was modelled after the British Women's Institute, or WI, and strengthened the image of the domesticated housewife who pursued public good works. The JFW was expressly apolitical in its constitution. The avowedly feminist Women's Liberal Club disbanded and some of its leading members joined the Executive Committee of the JFW. Colonial policy therefore not only bolstered the image of housewifery in Jamaica, but was also responsible for depoliticising the feminist agenda, by fragmenting one of its most important activist groupings.[86]

After the war, patriotic feminist publisher Aimee Webster took over the running of the 'Miss Jamaica' competition and incorporated it into a regional competition of her own making, 'Miss British Caribbean'. This beauty contest was intended to increase the circulation of Webster's new publication, *Caribbean Post*, and to boost the postwar Caribbean economies through tourism. Webster and her staff canvassed support for the beauty contest in 1945 among each country's Chamber of Commerce and travel bureaux, and launched the competition two years later. The queen would be selected annually, as before, but would now enjoy a prize trip to the United States or Canada, and thereby encourage North Americans to visit the British Caribbean.[87]

However, for Webster, boosting West Indian economies was merely complementary to the deeper purpose of her new publication and the new beauty competition: unifying the British Caribbean for Federation and eventual self-government. Webster, a committed nationalist and federalist, believed that the disparate countries of the British West Indies had to be spiritually connected. A common identification was needed to replace the rivalries and prejudices harboured between the territories. Webster referred in an editorial, 'Beauty and Federation', to the Montego Bay Conference on Federation of September 1947, at which Norman Manley, representing Jamaica, and Grantley Adams of the Barbados Labour Party, had called for the necessity of 'federating the *people* as opposed to the *territories*' of the British Caribbean.[88] The beauty competition would be an agent for this, Webster wrote. It would encourage a common West Indianness as people followed the progress of the candidates, and travelled between the countries to attend the parades and fêtes of the competition.

Webster was an unusual figure among the Jamaican upper-middle-class. Her background was privileged and white-identified, and she was the daughter of planters.[89] Webster had trained as a journalist on the *Daily Gleaner* and therefore enjoyed a rare opportunity among professional Jamaican women, for a cerebral career. Webster had also collaborated on the relaunched *New Cosmopolitan* with feminist maverick Una Marson. By working alongside Marson, and by publishing in dissident journal *Public Opinion*, Webster was exposed to, and mixed with, radical race-conscious nationalists and feminists who challenged her own background. However, Webster was never converted to black nationalism though she became an avowed feminist, albeit within the confines of her own class snobbery.

Webster wrote in the *Post* of the need for the 'emancipated' West Indian woman to become more politically effective: 'The West Indian has opportunities to be [as] educated, polished, and accomplished as her vis-a-vis anywhere in the civilised world. Measured by existing standards of mass effectiveness, she is a failure.'[90] Webster charged West Indian women with failing in their 'personal and public responsibilities'.[91] They were indifferent to their right to vote, Webster argued, and, like feminists before her, she advocated they join the national effort through social work.[92] However, Webster's diatribe showed the particular influence of the report of the Moyne Commission, and betrayed her class position as one who could afford to berate her social 'inferiors' with licence. Provocatively, she accused Caribbean women of failing to make the home either a haven or a place of intellectual stimulation, of maintaining poor standards of cleanliness in the household, of being responsible for high infant mortality rates, and finally, she charged that 'in every West Indian capital prostitution is a flourishing industry'.[93] Besides ignoring the endemic and structural causes for Caribbean poverty, Webster's comments revealed her raced, classed composition of the category 'woman'. Although Webster repeated many of the charges levelled at lower-class women by the Moyne report, her desire for 'educated, polished . . . accomplished' and 'civilised' women to take centre stage ironically exposed her concern with middle-class respectability. She revealed that the racial boundaries to proper femininity were increasingly under question. Webster's intervention in feminine ideology was reflected in the beauty competitions she oversaw, and in the *Post*'s regular features on exemplar Caribbean women. The best of Caribbean women were cosmopolitan, stylish, erudite and attractive, boasted 'Daughters of the Caribbean', a typical *Post* picture-article featuring Caribbean housewives with their children. They were also typically light-skinned, sometimes white and more often of mixed heritage, 'as eclectic as . . . the many races that forge the destiny of the Caribbean'.[94] Such features marked the journal's agenda to feature sophisticated brown middle-class women prominently.

The beauty competition, under Webster's management, was intended to be properly public to reflect the shift towards impending self-rule and democratisation. 'Miss Jamaica', would now be decided by regional finals, with each parish sending a candidate. Sponsors included a group of large fruit growers who formed the 'Buy Jamaican' campaign. Each parish in Jamaica sent a candidate to highlight their local produce. Of the 'country' candidates *Spotlight* commented smugly that 'Kingston has seen possibly more beautiful girls', but agreed that they were 'cultured-looking and decidedly charming'.[95] Culture and charm were the bearers of class position, and were therefore crucial to the judging criteria, which also included, 'general knowledge and deportment', 'intellectual gifts', 'gay conversation' and being of 'good birth'.[96] To this end, winners were required to produce a self-penned journal of their prize trip for publication in the *Post*. Furthermore, judges were now publicly announced and appointed from the Chamber of Commerce, the US services, newspapers and tourist boards throughout the Caribbean, with some effort towards ethnic diversity.[97]

In keeping with Webster's commitment to national and regional unity, and under pressure from an increasingly expectant public, efforts were made to enlarge the scope of the beauty competition and to show that brown women could win. The first 'Miss Jamaica' and 'Miss British Caribbean' winner of 1947 was brown-skinned Leonie Samuels. Thereafter finalists and winners of 'Miss Jamaica', as well as the regional representatives entered in 'Miss British Caribbean', tended to be light-skinned brown women, the daughters of coloured lawyers and businessmen, with only a few white candidates remaining.

1.2 'Miss St Kitts', cover girl and candidate in the 'Miss British Caribbean' competition of 1947

These brown women represented the emerging potency of 'brownness' as a new political force in the Caribbean. Phyllis Wong, a contestant of coloured and Chinese heritage, was chosen as 'Miss Trinidad' for 1947 and was described in the *Post* as 'a true cross-section of Trinidad's cosmopolitan population,' and the authentic choice of a multiracial audience who 'instinctively recognized [Wong] as typifying the exotic West Indian of tomorrow.'[98] Similar glowing terms were heaped upon 'olive-skinned, raven-haired', Phyllis Woolford, 'Miss British Caribbean' of 1948. Woolford was from British Guiana, and was the daughter of a Queen's Council barrister, Sir Eustace Woolford. Woolford was pictured on the cover of the *Post*, epitomising modern Caribbean womanhood, as she stood before a modern aircraft, waving to an unseen crowd of well-wishers. Sheila Cunliffe, 'Miss British Guiana' in 1949 typified, 'the blending of racial characteristics that has resulted today in a very definite West Indian type'.[99] The *Post* responded with ambiguity towards darker women of colour. Features including the regular column 'West Indian Nebulae', which honoured a different young woman in each issue, occasionally remarked on the 'grace, charm and subtle attractiveness' of mid-brown and dark-brown women who, though not beauty queens, were successful, according to the *Post*, in displaying demure femininity.[100] In such descriptions 'subtlety' signalled their upward trajectory from the pitfalls of lower-class vulgarity. This sort of positive depiction was distinct from other descriptions of black women as 'native', in the journal. The 'native' label, as Rosenberg has shown in relation to de Lisser's writing, confined black women to anachronistic spaces of the past, and separated them from the modernity project.

Although it is evident that Webster intended to broaden the racial representation of both competitions during her brief tenure from 1947 to 1950, contests were still open to charges of being too aloof from their expanding audience. *Spotlight* wrote of the 1948 competition, that a noisy audience readily voiced their objections. The winner in that year was Hampton-educated, Joy Mott-Trille, a white Jamaican from the parish of Manchester. Whilst the crowd broadly approved of the candidates, which is perhaps an indication that the audience were also largely coloured and middle-class, they objected to the judges, who were by implication, mostly, white and wealthy, or, as the journal reported it, 'too much of one type and class'.[101] According to a retrospective piece which appeared later in another of Evon Blake's publications, *Newday*, Webster's beauty competitions stimulated a flurry of questions that would continue to surround the competition in years to come. Audiences asked especially, *who* could be defined as typical, and *who* had the authority to choose a national representative.[102] However, Webster's *Post* and the 'Miss British Caribbean' contest revealed the beginnings of the marriage of cultural nationalism to the ideal of mixed-raced female beauty. The progressive West Indian identity Webster espoused would come into being through the female mixed-raced body. Assured performances of cultured modern beauty by Caribbean women would deliver the modern Caribbean citizen of tomorrow. For this reason, brown femininity now carried a special purchase over West Indianness itself.

At the same time the PNP demonstrated that it too was alert to the possibilities of elaborating the party's project of economic and cultural nationalism through a beauty contest. In 1950, it sponsored a contest that divided the city of Kingston by district. Titles included 'Miss West Kingston' and 'Miss East Kingston,' and winners were featured in the *Caribbean Post* as 'Dark Beauties' alongside a column of beauty advice tailored to women of dark complexions, from 'chocolate to Ebony'.[103] These competitions, which were local and directly addressed Kingston's black populations, at least in their preliminary rounds, were thought to be a good vehicle for aiding the PNP's project of cultural nationalism among the aspiring middle classes and poor.

Webster's expansive Caribbean-wide competition was short-lived and she relinquished control of it after 1950, when the *Caribbean Post* also ran into decline. Nonetheless it was a broadly successful venture, drawing large audiences, sponsorship and media attention. Webster put forward her idea of proper West Indian womanhood forthrightly and her bold display of assured performances of cultured, modern beauty in the figure of the brown woman marked the sign of things to come. In the process of launching 'Miss British Caribbean' she had laid the way for new competitions to spring up throughout the region. Furthermore her programme for 'federation and beauty' tested the political service-ability of the ideal hybrid beauty that would usher in a new Caribbean future.

Notes

1 Bolland, *Politics of Labour*, p. 301.
2 Ibid., p. 302. These were the first elections to the Legislative Council after the franchise was expanded in 1919 but with property and education qualifications remaining.
3 Anthony Bogues, 'Nationalism and Jamaican Political Thought', in Kathleen Monteith and Glen Richard (eds), *Jamaica in Slavery and Freedom* (Mona: University of the West Indies Press, 2002), pp. 363–387, 381.
4 Bolland, *Politics of Labour*, p. 302.
5 Ibid., pp. 305–307.

6 Ibid., p. 313

7 Ibid., pp. 381–388.

8 Trevor Munroe, *The Politics of Constitutional Decolonisation: Jamaica 1944–1962* (Institute for Social and Economic Research, University of West Indies Press, 1983), pp. 37–41.

9 For more on the theme of the marginalisation of black-nationalism in the official memory of nation-building and state formation see Bogues, 'Nationalism and Jamaican Political Thought'.

10 Gregg, 'Beauty Hold a Plea', p. 21.

11 Leah Rosenberg, *Nationalism and the Formation of Caribbean Literature* (Basingstoke: Palgrave Macmillan, 2007), p. 67.

12 Ibid., p. 68.

13 Ibid., pp. 83–90.

14 'Here Are Ladies Delightful', *Planters' Punch* 2 (1929–1930), p. 2.

15 Lucille Parks and Rita Gunter, 'English and Jamaican Society – Two Views', *Planters' Punch* 4 (1938–1939), p. 57.

16 'Types of English Beauty', *Planters' Punch* 3 (1933–34) p. 3.

17 Gregg, 'Beauty Hold a Plea', p. 2.

18 'Some Beauties of Jamaica', *Planters' Punch* 3 (1932–1933) p. 1.

19 Ibid.

20 Rosenberg, *Nationalism and Caribbean Literature*, pp. 79, 89.

21 'Miss Barbara Samuel', *Planters' Punch* 3 (1934–1935) p. 6.

22 Rosenberg, *Nationalism and Caribbean Literature*, p. 81.

23 Lucille Iremonger, *Yes My Darling Daughter* (London: Secker and Warburg, 1964), p. 65.

24 'Our Jamaica Chinese Ladies – An Influence', *Planters' Punch* 2 (1929) pp. 8–9; 'Beauty Contests Are Bad Business', *Newday* 2 (1958) p. 43. *Spotlight* magazine also hinted that even the 'social revolutionists', i.e. the nationalists, were angry about a Chinese 'Miss Jamaica': *Spotlight* 16 (1955), p. 27.

25 Honor Ford-Smith, 'Una Marson: Black Nationalist and Feminist Writer', *Caribbean Quarterly* 34 (1988), p. 26.

26 Quoted in Rosenberg, *Nationalism and Caribbean Literature*, p. 1.

27 Una Marson, 'Kurrent Komments', *New Cosmopolitan*, April 1931, p. 20. (*Cosmopolitan* and its successor *New Cosmopolitan* appeared intermittently and surviving volumes are numbered erratically, hence date and year of publication are given here.)

28 Ibid.

29 Linette Vassell (ed.), *Voices of Women in Jamaica, 1898–1939* (Mona: University of the West Indies, 1993), pp. 5–6, 16–19.

30 For a more detailed discussion of working-class female organising see Linette Vassell, 'Women of the Masses: Daphne Campbell and "Left" Politics in Jamaica in the 1950s', in Verene Shepherd, Bridget Brereton and Barbara Bailey (eds), *Engendering History: Caribbean Women in Historical Perspective* (Kingston: Ian Randle, 1995), pp. 318–336.

31 Vassell, *Voices of Women*, p. 35.

32 For instance, the Principal of Shortwood College, Anna Marvin, instructed women of the Onward and Upward Society; Vassell, *Voices of Women in Jamaica*, pp. 6–8. Una Marson's English teachers at Hampton School delivered similar instruction; Delia Jarrett-Macauley, *The Life of Una Marson* (Manchester: Manchester University Press, 1998), pp. 16–22.

33 Joan French, 'Colonial Policy Towards Women after the 1938 Uprising: The Case of Jamaica', *Caribbean Quarterly* 34 (1988), p. 39.

34 Henrice Altink, 'The Misfortune of Being Black and Female: Black Feminist Thought in Interwar Jamaica', *Thirdspace* 5 (2006), pp. 4, 13.

35 This issue has been foundational to theorising black feminism. For further discussion of black feminist theory see: Bell Hooks, *Ain't I a Woman: Black Women and Feminism* (Boston: South End Press, 1981); Heidi Safia Mirza (ed.), *Black British Feminism: A Reader*, (London: Routledge, 1997); Lola Young, 'What is Black British Feminism?', *Women: A Cultural Review* 11 (2000), pp. 45–60; and for the implications of black feminist theory on writing history see Evelyn Brooks Higginbotham, 'African-American Women's History and the Metalanguage of Race', in Ruth-Ellen B. Joeres and Barbara Laslett (eds), *The Second Signs Reader* (Chicago: University of Chicago Press, 1996), pp. 3–26.

36 Vassell, *Voices of Women in Jamaica*, p. 44.

37 Ibid., p 30.

38 Altink, 'Black and Female', pp. 1–6.

39 Jarrett-Macauley, *Una Marson* (Manchester: Manchester University Press, 1998), p. 111.

40 Ford-Smith, 'Una Marson', p. 27

41 Gregg, 'Beauty Hold a Plea', p. 30.

42 Altink, 'Black and Female', p. 6.

43 Quoted in Gregg, 'Beauty Hold a Plea', p. 24.

44 Ford-Smith, 'Una Marson', p. 34.

45 Vassell, *Voices of Women*, p. 37.

46 Ibid.

47 Ibid., p. 38.

48 Ibid.

49 Ibid.

50 Ibid.

51 Ibid, pp. 38–39.

52 Vassell, *Voices of Women*, p. 12.

53 Ibid., p. 13.

54 Fanon (*Black Skin, White Masks*, p. 116), cited in: Delia Jarrett-Macauley, *The Life of Una Marson. 1905–65* (Manchester: Manchester University Press), p. 50.

55 Una Marson, *The Moth and the Star* (Kingston: published by the author, 1937), p. 11.

56 Ibid., p. 26; Jarrett-Macauley, *Una Marson*, pp. 98–105.

57 In Britain the term 'coloured' took on a different meaning, referring to people of African and Asian descent from imperial possessions.

58 Jarrett-Macauley, *Una Marson*, p. 33.

59 Marson's use of the name 'Quashie' was most likely a play on the derogatory Quashie/Quasheba caricatures elites used to mock the lower-classes.

60 Marson, *Moth and the Star*, p. 18.

61 Ibid., pp. 11, 12, 76, 77.

62 Segal, 'Race and Colour', p. 91.

63 Marson, *Moth and the Star*, p. 97.

64 Marson, *Moth and the Star*, p. 87. 'Indian' in this context may have had an ambiguous meaning, like 'Spanish' in Trinidad with its ambiguous and multiple assignations of mixed-raced identity. For further reading see, Aisha Khan, 'What is "a Spanish"?: Ambiguity and "mixed" ethnicity in Trinidad', *Trinidad Ethnicity*, pp. 180–207.

65 Harvey Neptune has shown that many cultural nationalists were suspicious of the encroachments of American mass culture, and the American presence, through wartime occupation, on the Trinidadian populace; Neptune, *Caliban and the Yankees*, p. 50.

66 Marson, *Moth and the Star*, p. 87.

67 Honor Ford-Smith, 'Making White Ladies: Race, Gender and the Production of Identities in Late Colonial Jamaica', *Resources for Feminist Research* 23 (2005), p. 55.

68 Marson, *Moth and the Star*, p. 88.

69 Ibid.

70 Jarrett-Macauley, *Una Marson*. p. 8.

71 Ibid., pp. 1–9.

72 Ford-Smith 'White Ladies', p. 57.

73 Ibid., p. 55.

74 Frantz Fanon, *Black Skin, White Masks*, (London: Pluto Press, 1986), Stuart Hall, 'The After-Life of Frantz Fanon: Why Fanon? Why Now? Why Black Skin, White Masks?', in Alan Read (ed.), *Fact of Blackness* (London: Institute of Contemporary Arts, Institute of International Visual Arts, 1996).

75 Marson's own short-lived journal *Cosmopolitan* had accepted advertising revenue, perhaps faced with little choice, from a company offering a whitening face cream, hair-straightener, and face powder which came in 'White, Pink, Hi-Brown and Extra-Hi Brown' shades. The US mass cosmetics industry, which featured both white and black manufacturers, is discussed at greater length in Chapter 5.

76 Marson, *Moth and the Star*. p. 91.

77 For further discussion of the headscarf see Carol Tulloch, ' "That Little Magic Touch": The Headtie and Issues Around Black British Women's Identity', in Kwesis Owusu (ed.), *Black British Culture and Society, A Text Reader* (London: Routledge, 2000), pp. 207–219.

78 Marson, *Moth and the Star*, p. 75.

79 'Women', *Spotlight* 2 (1941), p. 17.

80 Bolland, *Politics of Labour*, p. 449.

81 Elisabeth Wallace, *The British Caribbean: From the Decline of Colonialism to the End of Federation* (Toronto: University of Toronto Press, 1977), pp. 85–91.

82 Bolland, *Politics of Labour*, pp. 120–126.

83 French, 'Colonial Policy', p. 39.

84 Ibid., p. 40.

85 Ibid., p. 42.

86 Ibid., pp. 50–51.

87 'Editorial', *Caribbean Post* 2 (1947), p. 4.

88 Ibid.

89 Jarrett-Macauley, *Una Marson*, p. 38.

90 'Editorial', *Caribbean Post*, titled the 'June-July Number' (date and volume unknown due to incomplete records), p. 1.

91 Ibid.
92 Ibid.
93 Ibid.
94 'Daughters of the Caribbean', *Caribbean Post* 1 (1946), p. 24.
95 'Carload of Queens', *Spotlight* 9 (1948), p. 35.
96 Aimee Webster, 'My View of It', *Vanity* 1 (1959), p. 4; 'My View of It', *Vanity* 2 (1960), p. 13.
97 'Beauty – What a Business', *Caribbean Post* 3 (1948), p. 10.
98 'West Indian Nebulae: Phyllis Wong of Trinidad', *Caribbean Post* February 1948, p. 20.
99 Betty Bachus, 'A Good Queen', *Caribbean Post* July 1948, p. 19; 'Carib, Spanish and Negro,' *Caribbean Post* (The Sugar No) (1949), p. 10.
100 'West Indian Nebulae: Thelma Niles of British Guiana', 3 (1948) p. 42; 'Native Artistes', *Caribbean Post* (1947) (Industrial Number), p. 16.
101 'Carload of Queens', *Spotlight*, p. 36. Certainly some of the crowd were affluent as there were reports of men taking bets of £5 and £10 on their favourite candidates to win.
102 'Beauty Contests Are a Bad Business', *Newday* 2 (1958), p. 43.
103 'One Hundred Percent for Dark Girls', *Caribbean Post*, (Building Review) (1950), pp. 12–13.

2

Cleaning up Carnival: race, culture and power in the Trinidad 'Carnival Queen' beauty competition, 1946–59

There is no reason why Carnival should not gain in attractiveness what it loses in vulgarity. A first step towards better things may be to give it more coherence by establishing a central feature of wide public appeal and this purpose is served . . . by the 'Carnival Queen' contest.[1]

Trinidad Guardian, 1949

THE 'Miss Trinidad' beauty competition doubled as the search for an annual 'Carnival Queen'. It began in Port of Spain in 1946, the first year in which Carnival was again allowed after a four-year wartime ban. From the outset the competition played host to the battle for culture between white-creole elites and middle-class nationalists that steered Trinidad's passage through the 'crisis of decolonisation'. As in Jamaica before the war, the beauty competition began in Trinidad in 1946 as a projection of the primacy of white-creole identity, intended to show the mastery of the creole elite, rather than the British, over leadership and power in the emergent Trinidadian nation. However, middle-class nationalists of the People's National Movement (PNM) challenged the 'reign' of white beauty queens and produced their own rival candidates. The drive to create an alternative Afro-Creole feminine icon produced the world's first black airline stewardess. At the climactic moment of the confrontation, the new PNM government banned the 'white' beauty competition and revealed its desire for pre-eminent influence over Carnival as a potent symbol of Trinidadianness.

On the face of it, as Barnes has suggested, the 'Carnival Queen' competition represented the power of the moneyed white elite against an emergent black political force.[2] This chapter builds upon this framework of the waxing and waning of new and old establishments. However, it delves into the culturally embattled origins of 'Carnival Queen' and complicates the assumption of a polarised confrontation between black and white. Instead it approaches 'Carnival Queen' from the perspective of contending bourgeois programmes, whose aims for carnival-refinement often ran on parallel lines, with whites asserting a white-creole leadership akin to Herbert de Lisser's project in Jamaica, and a brown-identified middle-class championing Afro-Creole nationalism. Both parties saw 'Carnival Queen' as a crucially important symbol of power and influence. It therefore considers the competing investments of the white-creole elite, and the brown middle-class, in the beauty contest as a cultural agent. In the process it considers the role of the competition's brown middle-class audiences who watched 'Carnival Queen' keenly and invested a great deal in the success or failure of brown candidates.

As a postwar development at a time when self-government seemed imminent, the white-dominated 'Carnival Queen' was immediately contentious to the growing Afro-Creole national project. Progressively, through Carnival, the patriotic brown middle-class sought proprietorship over authentic 'creole' identity, especially through their attempts to steward and temper subaltern creative life and public behaviour.

However, in the Trinidadian context, the term 'creole' takes on particular nuances, referring formally, pre-independence, to the white–brown–black social matrix to the exclusion, again formally, of Indian, Chinese, Venezuelan ('Spanish'), Syrian, Jewish and Portuguese groups. Ideologically the national project was invested in the paradigm of nurturing an Afro-Creole root for culture. Indeed many patriotic middle-class artists and emerging leaders in Trinidad, though diverse in heritage, favoured this model at the time as the most fitting and unifying for Trinidad.[3] Within this political setting therefore, the battle for beauty and visibility in the pre-eminent Port-of-Spain beauty competition, evolved into a dispute over the dominance of white winners, at the expense of brown. Whilst Indo-Trinidadians sometimes made the San Fernando competition in the south of the island their focus within this period, in general their exclusion from the pre-eminent 'Carnival Queen' extravaganza in the capital, both as winners or hopefuls, signalled their exclusion from the paradigm of creole nationalism. I argue here that this context of bitter rivalry over Carnival between whites and browns, restrained the development of the model of hybrid Caribbean beauty that Aimee Webster's 'Miss British Caribbean' competition had decreed as the way forward.

Very little has been written about the 'Carnival Queen' beauty competition. Led by historian Gordon Rohlehr, a handful of scholars have referred to what I will call a bourgeois Carnival-refinement movement that intervened in subaltern creative expression. Carnival-refinement attempted to 'improve' and 'sanitise' the festival, thus echoing in Carnival, the broader middle-class investment in shaping lower-class culture that emerged in the British Caribbean during the revolutionary 1930s.[4] This chapter begins by drawing together the threads of a diffuse discussion of Carnival-refinement, a process which began in the last two decades of the nineteenth century. It identifies Carnival-refinement as the cultural work of contending white and brown nationalisms. Carnival-refinement was replete with its own language of 'cleaning', used by the press and by the civic watchmen overseeing improvement strategies. Both arms of this movement preferred to remove, control and replace the 'coarser' elements of Carnival with that which was thought to be more desirable. However, brown nationalism placed more value on what it regarded as the critical African basis from which Trinidadian culture would grow. The process of Carnival-improvement implicated differentially gendered bodies; from the active male citizen of the improvement-committees, to the feminine ideal of the 'Carnival Queen' pageant, to the unruly woman of the *jamette* lower class. Each played a role in shaping the development of the 'Carnival Queen'.

Creolisation, class and Carnival

John Cowley suggests Shrovetide festivities in Trinidad were introduced by early Spanish settlers who formed a sparse population in the island, but the transformation of Carnival into an annual pre-Lenten festival on a grand scale was made by the influx of mainly French-speaking white and brown planters and their slaves after 1783.[5] Enslaved Africans and Afro-Creoles were officially excluded from festivities, particularly the public rites of Carnival, but in the period of elite licence that prevailed, they also observed the festive season where opportunities arose.[6]

As Milla Riggio has argued, part of the complexity of Trinidad Carnival lies in its history, which 'emerges as much from the mythology . . . as from the history of Trinidad'.[7] The making of Carnival history itself is in part the story of the movement for national sovereignty that has 'weaved an evolutionary narrative' of change and development in Carnival.[8] Though there has been a resurgence of interest in writing about Carnival, significant gaps and questions remain in accounting for the history of Carnival in Trinidad. For instance, more research is needed into the changes wrought on Carnival by the emergence of an educated brown and black middle-class after emancipation.[9] This lack is particularly salient to the following discussion, which identifies an important role for the middle-classes in the twentieth century, when the movement to improve Carnival took hold. Middling sorts of people provided both rapt audiences of the 'Carnival Queen' pageantry and the source of its main detractions.

Cultural theorist Richard Schechner has shown that the complexity of Trinidad Carnival confounds the Bakhtinian model of the carnivalesque as popular inversion of official culture. Although these elements of transgression and comic inversion were of course important, in the case of Trinidad, Carnival practices bear the imprints of both the former slaveholders and the formerly enslaved, who, as Schechner points out, were satirising *and* revelling in each other's cultures in their masquerades.[10] Carnival is therefore the quintessential creolised cultural form, a symbol of complex and contested cultural integration forged where huge disparities of power exist. While Bakhtinian theory may illuminate radical imperatives from below, it is less useful to this discussion of how competing elites used Carnival to constitute themselves as superior and autonomous amidst the crisis of decolonisation.

Instead literary critic Joseph Roach's analysis of New Orleans Mardi Gras is more instructive. Roach has examined New Orleans Carnival in the post-emancipation South as a stage for bourgeois reformulations of identity and history.[11] Whilst the contexts of Carnival in New Orleans and Trinidad are not identical, their common histories of African-European creolisation provide a basis for comparison. Common to both was the exclusion of slaves from the festivities during slavery, and the potentially revolutionary effects on Carnival after emancipation when former slaves participated as free persons. Roach has shown that 'bourgeois Carnival cleanses as it dignifies'.[12] In the power vacuum left by the Civil War a group of New Orleans businessmen recast themselves as an aristocratic elite and used Mardi Gras to sustain the new brotherly clans and societies they invented. The brethren used Carnival to assert their challenge to the liberal reforms of Reconstruction, creating spectacles of 'violent ridicule' of African Americans.[13] In Roach's words, Carnival was thus, 'not an occasion for seeking release from a way of life . . . but an institution dedicated to its perpetuation'.[14] This context of elites attempting to direct Carnival after emancipation provides the basis for understanding the bourgeois competitions for supremacy through control of Carnival in Trinidad. To grasp the racialised context for twentieth-century Carnival-refinement it is necessary to discuss here its origins in postemancipation Trinidad.

Canboulay Carnival and the Canboulay riots

After slave emancipation in Trinidad, freed people, claiming their entitlement, made public Carnival celebrations in the streets. A period of Afro-Creole domination of Carnival, though contested and uneven, spanning roughly from the 1850s to the 1880s, has been historicised as 'Canboulay Carnival'.[15] Competing accounts of the origins of the term Canboulay circulate. Derived from the French for burning cane, *cannes brulees*, it is thought to refer to the routine of slaves being driven to quell plantation fires, either caused by accident, by act of slave resistance, vandalism or as a controlled part of the agricultural cycle.[16] The planter class created a Carnival masquerade, the *negre jardin* (meaning field slave in this context) to parody this plantation scene of slaves being driven to put out burning cane fires. After the end of slavery freed people creatively reinterpreted the burning cane ritual. Canboulay was broadened into a range of Carnival practices enjoyed by Afro-Creoles, and practised on the opening night of Carnival, *Dimanche Gras*. JD Elder has described the subversive elemental features of Canboulay. These include:

> [E]nacting the African pageant inside the white-dominated Carnival (trespassing); processing through the streets at dead of night; satirising the ruling-class in popular song; beating African drums – a symbol of savagery; performing African-type dancing condemned by white moralists as profane; carrying lighted torches in a wooden city; blowing cow horns and conch shells at dead of night; burlesquing the Europeans' lifestyle, as in Dame Lorraine (a transvestite masquerade mocking French-plantation wives);[17] [and] arming with bois for duelling (stickfighting) on the streets.[18]

Canboulay Carnival dramatically altered what had been a season domin- ated by the festive play of white French-creoles, and in general enjoyed by the better-off, including some free coloureds. Canboulay became the dominant element of Carnival, featuring the masquerades (or mas' in creole dialect) of the *jamette*, that is, the subculture of the urban, creole- speaking, black poor. The term *jamette* was derived from the French for lower-class, literally below the diameter. Other mas' that thrived under *jamette* Carnival were *pissin-lit, jab molassi* and *baby doll. Pissin-lit* (wet the bed) has been remembered as a transvestite masquerade performed by men dressed as women carrying or wearing soiled menstrual cloths, comically humiliating notions of upper-class gentility. However, as Pamela Franco has argued, women's performances of *pissin-lit* have been drastically understated. Drawing attention to the menstrual bleed through *pissin-lit* can be interpreted as a radical disavowal by women of their marginalisation and powerlessness relative to the colonial state.[19] *Jab molassi* was a devil character daubed in black to represent a slave who has fallen into the boiling molasses in the hazardous process of refining sugar.[20] The *baby doll* masquerade was a character in which women demanded money from 'accused fathers' in the crowd.[21] Subaltern *jamette* women predominated as the *chantuelle*, the singers of topical song, who led bands of people in Canboulay rituals, including *kalinda* (stick-fighting). The *chantuelle* were the forerunners of the predominantly male calypso artists who emerged as popular singers in the twentieth century.[22] Women's participation in *kalinda* as fighters has also been written out of Carnival history.[23]

Meanwhile the Carnival performance of the 'respectable' classes was largely transferred behind doors. The wealthy, conspicuous by their absence from street masking, at least by day, poured scorn on Carnival through the press, creating a gendered discourse of degeneration and disorder around the black *jamette* Carnival. They reserved particular ire and disapprobation for the behaviour of poor women at Carnival. Women's deliberately subversive behaviour became, according to the Catholic-oriented *Port of Spain Gazette*, the cavorts of prostitutes, the 'ostentatious promenade of those ladies whose existence is usually ignored or accepted as a necessary evil'.[24] Subaltern women at Carnival were readily labelled as the bearers of venereal disease. They were targeted for violence and incarceration under the Contagious Diseases Ordinance of 1869, which was a model of the English Contagious Diseases Act of 1864. As Franco writes, this sweeping campaign to clean the streets of prostitutes coincided with the peak of resistance through the female *pissin-lit* masquerade.[25] Eventually the term *jamette* became synonymous with promiscuity and explicitly gendered black, female and lower-class.[26]

In 1881 a series of violent confrontations occurred. Known as the Canboulay Riots, these were armed clashes between the *jamette* and the colonial police.[27] The government used law and order to control subaltern cultural expression at Carnival. A series of ordinances were passed which effectively banned large gatherings, drumming, *kalinda*, lighted torches and other key components of Canboulay.[28] This climactic confrontation between the subaltern and official authority provided pathways for the bourgeoisie to cast itself as the legitimate proprietors of Carnival. It marked the start of the gradual return of middle and upper-class revellers to the festivities. Canboulay Carnival was too much dominated, in the minds of the reforming bourgeois, by the vivacity of subaltern culture, its subversive humour, violence and frequent crossings of middle-class gender norms that marked respectability and modernity. Amidst the male-dominated campaign for improvement of Carnival, middle-class women's participation was circumscribed by the boundaries of respectable femininity, which meant chaperoned, supervised participation, under the watchful gaze of male relatives.[29]

In New Orleans the postemancipation ruptures of the Civil War left a power vacuum for the bourgeoisie to fill with creative formulations of a white supremacist future. In postemancipation Trinidad quelling Canboulay provided opportunities for the middle and upper-class to 'refine' Carnival and 'clean up' plebeian festivities in line with values of respectability and modernity. For people of colour particularly, this was an opportunity to constitute themselves fully as citizens and in the process, to foster a nascent nationalist movement.

Middle-class influence over Carnival

Carnival was subject to successive waves of elite influence after the government put down Canboulay. There were the efforts of the 'City Fathers', wealthy white and brown statesmen, to act as patrons of Carnival by instigating prize-giving competitions, which began to rationalise the apparent disorder of subaltern Carnival. There were also the middle-class entrepreneurs, such as respectable black calypsonian Chieftain Douglas, who sought to refine calypso music by making it suitable for middle-class practitioners and fee-paying audiences.[30] This process, removing male competitive violence and replacing it with verbal combat, saw the further marginalisation of women, as Smith writes; 'the former male fighters appropriated the feminine *cariso* [early Calypso] that emphasise[d] banter, gossip and abuse transferring the physical challenge of the *kalinda* to the [verbal] challenge of the song'.[31] Carnival-improvement therefore instigated a bourgeois gendering of prominent competitive participation at Carnival. It aimed to confine female performance to approved spaces and refine a manly competitiveness, as it rationalised and commercialised Carnival. This progressively effaced the cultural work of lower-class women. The gradual onslaught of this process in the twentieth century would provide the conditions for that arch spectacle of bourgeois femininity at Carnival, the 'Carnival Queen' beauty contest.

During the interwar period middle-class activism for Carnival-improvement became characterised by rival campaigns between the Afro-Creole journal, the *Argos* and the liberal middle-class newspaper the *Trinidad Guardian*, which had the larger white readership.[32] This was a bourgeois competition for manly citizenship that prized cultural authenticity, but also morality, respectability and modernity. The *Argos* led the campaign, successfully persuading the Governor to allow a Victory Carnival after the end of the First World War in 1919. In triumph it boasted the support of an ethnically diverse group of businessmen and professionals – 'Merchants ([of] provisions, cocoa, dry goods), doctors, lawyers, chemists, financiers, and others, have thrown in their lot with the people's cause and the petitioners rest assured that they have with them, men who represent the intelligence and wealth and the thinking body of the community.'[33] In Rosenberg's words the success of this campaign established its backers as the 'power brokers between the black working-class and the colonial government'.[34] It boosted the political and social aspirations of middle-class professionals, including Afro-Chinese trade unionist Alfred Richards and African-born lawyer Emmanuel Lazare. The *Argos* particularly emphasised the relationship between the middle-class reformer and the lower-class figure in need of guidance. 'A strong committee will be formed to assist and direct you', it advised.[35] Prizes were offered for good conduct and decent European-derived costuming, such as the 'Lorraine Peasant'.[36]

The *Argos* led preparations for a Carnival in the city, whilst the *Trinidad Guardian* with its more affluent white-creole readership sought to deliver Carnival at the Queen's Park Savannah, the racetrack adjoining the wealthy St Clair neighbourhood. This rivalry overstated the distinction between competing bourgeois visions for Carnival. As Garth Green has pointed out, this was actually a competition to decide 'which middle-class reincarnation of the Carnival would emerge victorious'.[37] Whilst the *Argos* positioned itself as the more attuned to the 'true Carnival of the people', and attacked the *Guardian* for being too aloof, in fact both papers aligned themselves with the middle-class merchants of the city, offering opportunities for advertising and sponsorship. Indeed both papers made proposals for Carnival that aimed to 'de-Africanize' the festival, replacing *jamette* costumes with European ones. Both called for censorship of calypso, and both advocated the removal of 'tamboo-bamboo' and 'bottle and spoon' bands of the *jamette*.[38]

The *Argos* instigated the first committee of 'prominent citizens' who delivered public lectures to direct people in how to practise a 'cleaner' Carnival. Meanwhile the *Guardian* created its own committee, to organise a Carnival at the Savannah, imagined in the 'continental', i.e. European, style.[39] Though they were rivals, the competing efforts of the journals actually represented a consensus of the respectable around the moral upgrade of Carnival. However, while whites sought to affirm their leadership role in society, for middle-class Afro-Creole nationalists this was an opportunity to establish themselves as the 'moral arbiters' of Carnival, in other words to prove their leadership ability by guiding and controlling the lower class.[40]

However, as in Jamaica, the labour uprisings of the 1930s brought middle and lower-class collaboration and established middle-class nationalist leadership more properly, albeit over a far older and more fragmentary Trinidadian labour movement than existed in Jamaica.[41] By 1939 the foremost committee of nominated civic watchmen attempting to bring respectability to Carnival, was the Carnival Improvement Committee (CIC), which was affiliated with the new Tourist and Exhibition Board. The Committee was formed of the Mayor of Port of Spain and labour leader Captain AA Cipriani; it also included a representative of the Catholic Church, and another from the police, as well as Wilson Minshall, a Carnival patron who would later be heavily involved in the 'Carnival Queen' competition.[42] High on the CIC's agenda was public order, censorship of calypsos, and stimulating a tourist audience. Carnival-improvement complemented the zeal of special proprietorship of the enlarged brown and black middle-classes. For the middle-class, as Rohlehr writes, the lines were blurred between self-improvement and Carnival-improvement:

> [The] brown/black bourgeoisie, larger than in 1919, and seeking at times most successfully, to re-enter and reshape the folk culture for their own ends, often by taming or toning down the *loa* of energy. The fruit of much effort towards self-improvement during the twenties and thirties, this section of the Creole middle-class had created and sustained many of the institutions by which self-improvement was achieved; cultural clubs, friendly societies, literary groups, drama and dance groups.[43]

Before the war, the CIC began publishing a set of rules of conduct. In 1946, the first year of 'Carnival Queen', the rules extended to the following:

> Don't dress in an immodest or scanty costume; don't dress in a vulgar way; don't sing any immoral or suggestive tunes; don't lose your temper or behave in a violent manner, but give and take; don't indulge in obscene language; don't over-indulge in intoxicating liquor: don't forget that others are seeing you and hearing you; don't forget that your children and your neighbour's little ones are looking at you; don't carry about your person any weapon of offence; don't leave any room for regret.[44]

In the same year the leadership of the Carnival Bands Union (CBU), the association that represented bands of working and middle-class steel pan players, allied with the CIC and made its own appeal to revellers for a 'clean' Carnival.[45] Union leader and politician Aubrey James adopted a parochial role in offering a guiding moral hand to its members:

> [P]lay your Carnival as formerly, in a clean and orderly way, worthy of the name of Trinidad. We appeal to you to avoid indecent gestures and immoral songs in your streets and squares, in your downtown Carnival and further appeal to the sense of good citizenship to keep cool and calm during the two days of your own Trinidad Carnival.[46]

Thus even before the first appearance of the 'Carnival Queen' beauty competition, Carnival-improvement was a project of competing racialised nationalisms, which made new leaders in the middle-classes. However, this programme would be made flesh by the appearance of a white beauty queen, with special competencies in casting a civilising, sanitising and modernising influence over Carnival.

Making 'Carnival Queen'

After the end of the Second World War, Crown Colony rule was gradually dismembered as Trinidad prepared for democratic self-governance. The first elections under universal suffrage were held in 1946, but the new constitution was deliberated for a further decade in the Legislative Council. Trinidad still had no clearly defined leading political parties; its relatively mature workers' movement lost momentum as the labour vote was fragmented between multiple parties.[47] In the intervening years an unpopular semi-responsible regime was imposed and led by former radical trade unionist Portuguese-Trinidadian Albert Gomes, who was now less concerned with the labour movement and more with attracting capital investment to Trinidad.[48]

In 1946 a new multiethnic Savannah Carnival Committee, headed by secretary James Smith, invited women to enter the first 'Carnival Queen' beauty competition by attending any of eight cinemas in the environs of Port of Spain at their evening showings. From each preliminary round, two finalists would be chosen for the grand competition at the Queen's Park Savannah, before His Excellency the (British) Governor Sir Clifford Bede. Prospective entrants were advised that the competition was 'Open to all ladies, irrespective of class, colour and nationality.'[49] However, if ladies need not be Trinidadian-born, they certainly ought to be resident in Trinidad, and willing to perform as 'Miss Trinidad' at the national festival and at other regional competitions. They would be doing 'national' work as a new Carnival figurehead in the capital city.[50] Smith underlined that the Savannah programme was part of the nation-building effort. He encouraged all to 'team together and uplift our beautiful island home'.[51] Significantly, the female contestants would not be asked to parade on stage at the cinemas, but instead would be discreetly judged as they purchased their admission tickets.[52] However, in the final competition they would parade twice, once in masquerade costume, and then in ballgown.

A glittering list of public dignitaries, carefully selected for their ethnic diversity, in the year of Trinidad's first fully democratic elections, was convened to judge the competitions. The judges were arranged into two panels, male and female. The men included Jewish-Trinidadian Alfonso Behrens De Lima of the well-known Y De Lima jewellers of Frederick Street; Wilson Minshall, already involved with the tourist-oriented CIC; and Charles Espinet, a Carnival enthusiast and folklorist.[53] Among the female judges were Mrs B Perez (wife of prominent lawyer JM Perez); Mrs Jones; Mrs Foo-Wong Sue, and Mrs Hadeed. The lady judges were mostly married women, emblems of respectability and representatives of their prominent husbands.[54] For instance, Mrs Wooding was wife to black lawyer Hugh Wooding, who would later receive a knighthood and, following independence, serve as Trinidad's first Chief Justice. Here was a panel cherry-picked from respectable middle-class society, each seeming to present the best 'face' of their respective ethnic enclaves.

The cinema auditions, multiracial judges, and the egalitarian banner made a show of the putative openness of the first competition, albeit a competition restricted to young, slim, unmarried, women. The organisers were unusually candid in suggesting there would be no bars of class or colour. However, organisers clearly had an idea of the sort of upper-class young woman they were seeking, as they had also approached private social clubs to nominate female candidates, but this attempt was a partial failure, as was reported in the *Caribbean Post*:

> In spite of the lack of full-cooperation from some of the island's high society clubs which tabooed the contest as too public and embarrassing the committee gathered together a real eyeful of beauties with many entries from country districts. The original plan to select finalists from a number of social clubs which would hold their own eliminations fell flat but the public was certainly satisfied with the result.[55]

As sociologist Lloyd Braithwaite's taboo-breaking study of 1953, 'Social Stratification in Trinidad' revealed, Trinidadian club life, which could range from sporting clubs, to cultural societies, to fee-paying leisure clubs, revealed the workings of a colonial social system. Putatively they symbolised the myth of liberal meritocracy that underpinned British rule, while in fact they were patently rigid in enforcing codes of class and colour.[56] At each rung of the ladder, a small minority of successful social climbers were to be found. These 'privileged exceptions' perpetuated the system.[57] A social directory from 1950 *Trinidad Who, What Where and Why* provided the description of leisure clubs below:

> [The Country Club] ... claims a certain amount of exclusivity but there is a certain line of demarcation between the top local and the middle-class whites. It lays no claim to exclusive white membership as there is quite a fair share of fair-skinned and coloured members ... [The Perseverance] is less exclusive in nationality, race or other rank or class. Its membership and entertainment cards are pretty well varied. Perseverance caters for the very mixed of Trinidad society ... Still less exclusive is the Palm Beach club. It is mainly a club for middle, lower middle and non-descripts of the island's social strata. There are no barriers whatsoever as to colour, rank or class, the main object being to cater for respectability in the social ranks of the colony ... [The Palms Club] is the result of South Trinidad's Indian coloured society. Here again there are no pretensions to exclusivity though a stern effort is occasionally made to be selective rather than allow promiscuity in its membership roll.[58]

Though the directory was intended to present an attractive picture of Trinidadian social life by illustrating a liberal social scene, it offers rather dubious proof of tolerance and intermingling. Ironically the references to colour, ethnicity, exclusivity and respectability actually confirm the presence of extensive stratification, varying only in degrees of severity from club to club and of racial prejudice that is slow to dissolve.

Yet perhaps it was *because* the invitation to the little-known 'Carnival Queen' competition seemed to flout, even if superficially, tightly regulated social stratification, that it was initially snubbed by the 'best' clubs. The elitist clubs at the top of the hierarchy had the most to lose from a competition that seemed to celebrate horizontal participation in nationhood. In the event, the organisers assembled a troop of white-identified finalists from the upper and upper-middle-classes, and these included a smattering of brown participants. The competition was putatively open, but in real terms, closed to all but the few. For all its efforts at transparency and democratic structure, darker-toned women, especially Indian and black-identified were absent from the final selection. Thus in common with the Jamaican competition, 'Carnival Queen' emerged as a competition that affirmed white-creole identity in the tropics.

The new programme of events was more akin to a gala evening than the 'world turned upside-down'. Organisers promised a ticket-buying public, 'A colourful display of disguised performers in a variety programme of folk lore, music, songs, dancing and community singing'.[59] This was the maturation of the competing visions for bourgeois Carnival proposed by the *Argos* and the *Trinidad Guardian* in the interwar years. Calypso and steel band music, now increasingly legitimate as Trinidadian national products, not least because of their wartime popularity with US servicemen, were fixed on the programme. But these were carefully managed performances by favoured artists performing approved songs and music. There was no place in the programme for the unchoreographed exuberance of Canboulay. Instead the programme included the parade of themed bands, competing under the following headings: 'Historical', 'Original', 'Indian' (a mas' based on the trope of the Hollywood 'Red Indian'), 'Dragon and Devil', and 'Advertising'. The advertising bands ranged in sponsorship from local businesses such as 'Coehlo's Bread' and 'Trinidad Dairies' to foreign brand names including 'Coca-Cola', 'Shell products', and 'Andrews' Liver Salts'.[60] On the opening night of Carnival, *Dimanche Gras* (Fat Sunday), the beauty competition was interspersed with events 'previewing' Carnival proper, with the tourist audience in mind.[61] This pageantry not only rehearsed Carnival for tourists, but also reflected a refined image of Carnival at its upper-middle and middle-class ticket-buying audience. Here was a sanitised, modern view of Carnival, with more order and less 'chaos'.

In the first beauty competition in 1946 the committee showed that they had not yet learnt to fully exploit the commercial potential of the beauty candidate's glamorous allure. The portraits of the twelve women received almost equal billing with the faces of seven multiracial men of the grand Savannah committee who had organised events. This marketing blip unwittingly affirmed that such men were as important to Savannah Carnival, as symbols of modernity and nationhood, as were the beauty competitors themselves.[62] In 1946, winner Joy Burke led a courtly procession from a fairytale coach and was accompanied by a Guard of Honour through the commercial streets of Port of Spain, and back up to the Savannah.[63] Savannah Carnival continued in this manner for the following two years. The pattern of Savannah Carnival was emerging. Decorative white-creole femininity, prominent male citizenship and corporate sponsorship, mingled as symbols of the new, improved Carnival.

In 1949, the *Trinidad Guardian*, who had been proposing Carnival at the Savannah since 1919, assumed a public role in leading the organisation of the beauty competition and its accompanying programme of sanitised Savannah Carnival.[64] The *Guardian* campaign had succeeded in lifting Carnival celebrations above the confines of the waterfront city to the Savannah and its leafy suburban surrounds. Ralph De Boissiere's social documentary novel, *Crown Jewel*, set in the labour uprising of the 1930s, captures the stark distinction between two worlds in the long walk of seamstress Aurelia Luna, who travels uptown, from her ramshackle dockyard home to a grand house in St Clair, to take orders from wealthy British expatriates.[65] This pre-eminent location, marked uptown Carnival and the beauty competition as important and worthy of national attention.

The *Guardian*'s new visibility as sponsor and patron of the Savannah Carnival had immediate implications for the beauty competition; 'Carnival Queen' became a more serious business venture overnight. Gone were the auditions by surveillance at public cinemas, now each candidate would be nominated by a business sponsor, or some other organisation with the necessary funds, typically a private social club. Commercial sponsorship was better organised. Linda Misjewski has described twentieth-century glamour, essentialised through the bodies of women, as the 'business of female spectacle'.[66] The *Guardian* conjured an aura of feminine glamour around the beauty contest by pairing female beauty candidates with prominent firms and luxury commodities. It boasted, 'Firms Rush to Send Candidates for "Carnival Queen" Contest'.[67] The *Guardian* posed the contest as a ' "battle" of the blondes and brunettes'; in Barnes's words, 'fetishising phenotypes associated with whiteness'.[68] The newly revitalised Savannah committee, it seemed, could attract the brightest stars of Trinidad's upper set to the competition. In 1949 it announced a new beauty candidate, Yvette Piddack, who was not only an air hostess with British West Indies Airways (BWIA), but also the fiancée of West Indies cricketer Gerry Gomez.[69]

The advent of *Guardian* sponsorship in 1949 also signalled the start of expensive prizes for the winner and finalists, donated by business sponsors. As prizes grew the *Guardian* foregrounded its charitable fundraising associated with the Savannah Carnival. It donated over $100,000[70] to its charity, the Guardian Neediest Cases Fund between 1949 and 1958.[71] In 1949 the first prize cache included an all-expenses paid return trip to Barbados, honorary Perseverance Club Membership, free beauty treatments at 'three leading parlours', lingerie, a solid-gold wristwatch and other jewellery.[72] Such prizes were racially coded. Barbadian social life, particularly hotels and private clubs, were infamous for their racism and segregation. The chosen winner would have to be acceptable to the proprietors and patrons encountered on her trip. Similarly, she would have to be agreeable to the clientèle of the Perseverance Club and its social mores. These prizes affirmed proper femininity as white-identified and underlined the association between leisure, luxury and consumption and the ascriptive values of whiteness.

The *Guardian* stridently promoted its new competition, now awash with money and graced by glamorous, elegant young women. The committee refocused the rules and judging criteria and published these for clarity:

1. Candidates must be sponsored by a club, business firm or similar organisation, have been born in Trinidad & Tobago or resident here for two years,
2. have left school,
3. be unmarried,
4. and be not over 25 years of age.

Candidates will be judged for Beauty, Poise and Charm.[73]

The paper endorsed 'Carnival Queen' as *the* defining element of Carnival-improvement.[74] The beauty competition should substitute for the vulgarity, excess and the backwardness of subaltern Carnival. Through 'Carnival Queen', Carnival could 'gain in attractiveness what it loses in vulgarity'. This was in the national interest.[75] Thus 'Carnival Queen' seemed to satisfy the remit that bourgeois Carnival-improvement had striven for, for half a century.

'Carnival Queen' as middle-class market-place

The *Guardian*'s Savannah Carnival programme, with 'Carnival Queen' as its centrepiece, facilitated the advance of American consumer-culture, into the lives of middle-class Trinidadians. Patrons paid between $3 and $12 for a ticket in 1954, but it was reported that a black market had emerged with tickets selling for up to $50.[76] Paying audiences for the beauty show were 5000 strong, but the *Guardian* estimated in 1956 that there was demand for 20,000 seats.[77] Beyond the paying audience, the queenly parade, as it circuited town, exposed the spectacle to still thousands more revellers. As Braithwaite argued, respectable middle-class status in Trinidad was acquired through the accumulation of modern com- modities, such as a refrigerator, motor car, overseas vacation and lavish entertainment.[78] Soon all of these consumables featured in the 'Carnival Queen' spectacular, either on stage or in the prize cache of finalists. This culture of consumption has been conceptualised by historians Richard Fox and TJ Jackson Lears as an 'ideology and a way of seeing'. Consumer culture encourages the individual to strive for the accumulation of things which accommodate a good life measured by 'personal fulfilment', and were otherwise imagined at this time as an 'American standard of living'.[79] The 'Carnival Queen' competition, as it grew into an ever-more attractive display, delivered consummate performances of idealised femininity, racialised as white and adorned by modern consumables.

The beauty contest as commodity showroom functioned on many levels. Firstly, the audience were encouraged to share in a fantasy of aristocratic heritage as represented by the courtly spectacle of the queen, in crown and sceptre, and her assembled maids of honour. Business sponsorship brought ever-grander ballgown costumes, replete with bodice and crinoline skirt. As Franco has noted, this exaggerated, full-skirted femininity, emphasised chasteness and offered a stark contrast to the defamed, trousered *jamette* woman.[80] Instead of a benighted slave past, still a source of shame for many, middle-class patrons could consume an ennobled, vaguely French-creole heritage.[81] This romanticised past gained currency among some of the respectable classes in the wake of the Canboulay Riots as a response to the disdain for the *jamette*.[82] Furthermore, staging white-creole heritage in this way, called to mind masquerade balls, elaborate costumes and finery, and eschewed memories of more debauched elite traditions at Carnival, of drunkenness, excess and racially transgressive play in the *negre jardin* or *mulatress* masquerades. If the cultural revolution stimulated nationalist interest in an Afro-Creole foundation for culture that was still to be developed, 'Carnival Queen' affirmed the sophistication of the resident elite and claimed space for them in the new national order.

Secondly the 'Carnival Queen' candidates themselves were made consummately feminine through press coverage and especially in the high-gloss pages of the new 'Carnival Souvenir Programme'. This brochure was instrumental in the racialisation of the beauty pageant as white, rather than brown. Sophisticated portraiture transformed candidates into starlets worthy of Hollywood. Late entrants, typically women of colour with less well-heeled sponsors, typically did not appear in the brochure. Instead the brochure revealed that the progressive whitening of the competition and its professionalisation were concurrent processes. Not only was the pre-eminent beauty contest in Trinidad a predominantly white-creole domain, it was becoming more so under the *Guardian*'s zealous campaign to build the Savannah Carnival enterprise. Profiles for each prospective 'queen' affirmed affluent status through detail of family background, convent or foreign schooling, prestigious work (if at all), foreign travel and leisure time for hobbies. 1954 candidate, Vicki Taurel, was described as:

> [A] most accomplished young lady . . . daughter of the late Mr Victor Taurel and Mrs Elmo Bearden. Vicki is 18, 5'4" and has green eyes and brown hair. She was educated at Codrington High School, Barbados, where she played tennis and netball, and went horseback riding and swimming. She also took up art and dress-making and is now taking lessons in flying.[83]

Vicki Taurel was related to a prominent sponsor of the competition, car dealer Taurel and Co Ltd. Her 'society' wedding to BWIA pilot Richard Hamilton later made the *Guardian*'s pages.[84]

Thirdly, the brochure functioned as a shoppers' guide to Carnival, a veritable directory for consumers, locals and tourists. All prizes and their donors were listed in the brochure and thus small and large businesses alike were attracted to this medium of advertising. Of the large brands were the Colonial Insurance Company, who bought advertising space on the front cover of the brochure in 1951 and 1952, only to be replaced thereafter by 'Coca-Cola'.[85] In 1954 Esso Standard Oil, and Shell, who drilled Trinidad's oilfields, both offered cash prizes of $250 each for each of seven of the finalists. Other typical business sponsorship came from pharmaceutical, cosmetic, cigarette and alcohol companies. Firms also escalated press advertising and, with ever-more stylish adverts, began to employ beauty candidates as models. By 1956 the list of prizes awarded to the winner alone extended to the following:

> Volkswagen [Car]. Presented by Taurel and Co Ltd
> English Electric Refrigerator. Donated by Stephens and Todd Ltd in association with SK Watson Ltd (agents)
> Phillips Console Radiogram presented by Investments and Agencies Ltd
> The Singer 306 Automatic Sewing Machine
> New World Gas Cooker
> 19 jewel Diamond Elgin Wristwatch
> A free return trip to New York, for 'Her Majesty' and a chaperone via BWIA and BOAC Viscount service. Arranged by Messrs Trinidad Guardian
> Five days complimentary stay at the Waldorf Astoria Hotel, New York, donated by Hilton Hotels Inc.
> A CYP dressing table and stool
> A dress length of witchcraft lace
> A flask of Weil perfume
> Max Factor presentation set
> One year's guest ticket at the cinema on all releases by United Artists
> A beautiful bathing suit
> A Bond Street gift case[86]

The staggering array of prizes approximated to a marriage dowry. The prize list was an ideal 'wedding trousseau' of large electrical appliances, decorative aids and even a dress length of lace, ideal for a wedding gown.[87]

Fourthly, in the construction of the beauty competition a shopping gallery was effected through prioritisation in the *Guardian* of the North American tourist gaze, in response to the racialised femininity of the

'Carnival Queen' pageant. The press often featured praise for 'Carnival Queen' from American visitors. Jean Minshall, a female columnist at the *Guardian* (and perhaps wife of competition-organiser and Tourist Board employee Wilson Minshall), enthused about compliments paid to Trinidadian women by tourists in a piece entitled, 'Visitors Think Trinidad Women Are Well-Dressed'. Minshall reported a fascination with beauty contestants and other elegant women, as part of her report on the Canadian Trade Fair delegation.[88] Praise for the white-creole femininity when linked in this way to tourism and foreign investment, projected (white) feminine beauty into the economic development of the decolonising nation, and symbolically affirmed the importance of white-creoles to the postcolonial future.

2.1 Coca-Cola sponsors Hollywood glamour in the 'Carnival Queen' contest. Rosemary Knaggs, 'Carnival Queen', 1953

The serious matter of 'Carnival Queen'

Under the *Guardian*'s management of the beauty competition the expansive ethnically balanced judging panels, where respectable ladies seemed to be as important as prominent male citizens, were curtailed. There were 21 judges in 1946, but after 1949 the judges were never more than ten in number and sometimes as few as five. In its first year the new *Guardian* committee appointed two judges from the US Services, the commanders of an air base and a naval base. The Services were again represented in 1950 by Lieutenant Commander Carlton Goddard. By 1951 the judging panel had acquired a corporate and diplomatic tone. Present were Trinidadian Rex Stollymeyer, British West Indian Trade Commissioner in Canada; Grant Major, Canadian Trade Minister in Trinidad; Captain WA Deam, Commanding Officer of the United States Naval Operating Base; the Honourable JM Perez, Attorney General (whose wife had served on the panel in previous years). They were joined by only three lady judges; Mrs Wooding, Mrs Pertuz Jimeniz and Mrs JD Ramkeeson MBE. By 1954 the judges were limited to six. They again included Perez, who was by now Chief Justice, and who was joined by the Honourable Colin Tenant; the Canadian Trade Commissioner; the Indian Commissioner; and even His Royal Highness Prince Alexander of Yugoslavia. In that year, of heavyweight public dignitaries and international attachés, the number of lady judges dwindled to two.[89]

The professionalisation and commercialisation of the beauty competition extended to an increasingly masculine array of judges with far-reaching economic influence over capital investment, good trade relations and the expansion of tourism. Carnival-improvement had always involved civic-minded men, distinguishing themselves through public service for the national good. Now 'Carnival Queen', the ultimate agent for Carnival-improvement, implicated still greater transactions of power by annually convening an international judging panel of powerful men.

The *Guardian* oversaw a trio of processes from 1949 onwards – commercialisation, professionalisation, and the progressive whitening of the beauty competition. These interrelated processes were intended to affirm the nationalist vision of white-identified creoles who sought to distinguish themselves not only from the working-class majority, but also from brown nationalism. Meanwhile, however, downtown Carnival had remained the fiefdom of the Carnival Improvement Committee, a space for reform-minded, ambitious middle-class men to grow their careers in leadership and public service, in anticipation of self-government. Bridging this gap in Carnival-improvement were the brown middle-class audiences to the fantastic Savannah spectacle. They were both engaged in nationalist debates over identity, and drawn to the prestige and respectability of the Savannah Carnival, which did its best to identify the better parts of Carnival with white-creole identity.

Contesting national beauty

Evidently the grand 'Carnival Queen' spectacle enjoyed an audience of thousands. In 1956 social commentator Barbara Powrie remarked on the gradual return of the middle-classes to Carnival and of the social stratification of the audience of the 'Carnival Queen' show.[90]

> [T]he Carnival Queen Contest has become a major event in the Carnival programme. It has a certain amount of novelty and over-all appeal for the middle-class. A glance at the audience packed into the Grand Stand reveals it to be almost one hundred per cent coloured. The lower-class is very poorly represented in the audience. The fact which gives it special respectability is that the expensive arena seats are occupied by whites and wealthy coloured people.[91]

Segal has demonstrated that part of racial designation in Trinidad was determined by cultural behaviour, and that it was, to a limited degree, possible to achieve lightness through 'comportment and lifeways', including speech, education and a formality of legal marriage in the church.[92] 'Carnival Queen' was an opportunity for social ascription, a chance to be in social proximity to the wealthy.

Powrie acknowledged that many people disregarded the beauty competition, and that others objected to it in principle as a representation of Carnival. Nonetheless thousands were fascinated by the annual parade and avidly consumed the 'Hollywood' type of desirable white femininity it projected, albeit with much dissatisfaction:

> It might be thought . . . by an outsider [that] . . . a contest of this type could assist the coloured person to develop a standard of appreciation for female beauty which bore some relation to local reality, in place of the standard based on European or Hollywood ideals. [However] there is no desire to feel lumped in with a group referred to as coloured. The selection of a girl to typify coloured beauty serves to draw attention to the social distinction between white and coloured and this touches a very sensitive area of the mind and emotions.[93]

Even as Powrie suggests that 'Carnival Queen' was becoming a brown competition by dint of the composition of its largely brown audience, she also suggests that this audience were unwilling to identify readily as 'coloured', such was the tendency for 'upward identification and downward distancing'.[94] Evidently, however, there was some eagerness for the politicised prize of visual representation that a brown success in the beauty competition promised. 'It is felt that the winner should be representative of Trinidad, and to the middle-class this means someone representative of the middle-class. Most of the entrants are coloured girls, and popular middle-class verdict requires that a coloured girl be the winner.'[95] Powrie's somewhat condescending account of middle-class attitudes nonetheless reveals competing agendas, between the *Guardian*'s progressive whitening of the competition, and the growing middle-class audience who vied for a brown winner, even as they passionately debated how exactly this winner should be composed:

> [S]atisfaction over the result is invariably marred by some 'defect' which the girls is said to possess. She is too dark, too fair, she is ill-educated or notoriously lacking in academic brilliance, she has no talents, her accent is too broadly Trinidadian, her family background is not of the best . . . The winning girl is given a trip abroad as one of her prizes, and she will be very much in the limelight on this trip. This, too, arouses basic coloured middle-class fears. They believe that her behaviour and manner on this trip should be faultless, and, that one false move, which might reveal lack of education or sophistication, could result in their being dammed and laughed at by the outside world.[96]

This anxiety reflects the sort of haunting of the colonial psyche brought to light by Frantz Fanon. The fear of being ridiculed and objectified by the 'outside world' is a nuanced reference to fear of racial humiliation which Fanon made a power transaction between the white and black male.[97] It underscores the sense of limited personhood experienced by these not-quite citizens of the middle-class, and characterises the post-emancipation struggle as a fight, not only for democratic citizenship, but also for full-personhood. Particularly it reflects how these dilemmas were magnified and projected onto ideal femininity. The audience negotiates their expectation of visual representation in the national iconography, whilst they struggle against knowledge that refined English femininity has already colonised the space claimed for ideal womanhood. 'Carnival Queen' symbolised middle-class claims to proprietorship over the symbols of nationhood and Carnival in particular. Here the battle for culture was hinged on the battle for representation through a woman whose sophistication was marked by her ability to perform modern, cultured beauty, consisting of the correct physical appearance, phenotype, refined speech, and erudite conversation.

Not only was the contest popular among the brown middle-class, but also among the brown women who were choosing to put themselves forward for it. However, while Powrie suggests a brown-dominated audience and a steady stream of brown contestants, she fails to distinguish between the presence of upper-middle-class 'near-white' elites, and the majority of brown middle-class patrons. Nor does Powrie actually suggest the competition was dominated by brown *winners*, only by brown contestants. Indeed, whatever the efforts of brown contestants, white winners prevailed with few exceptions, the subject of a discussion below. Instead, Powrie's comments are most useful in what they reveal of the tension between shunning and claiming colouredness and by implication blackness. They reveal the making of racial meanings through the contest, where light-skinned beauty candidates can be deemed white or claimed as brown, by a riveted audience who postulate over the attributes of the ideal brown winner. They point to the instability of unfixable 'racial' categories that exist on a continuum of local understandings of race or colour and rely upon who is reading the body in question. This account can be viewed within the conceptual framework of African American 'passing' narratives, in which racial 'tells' form their own currency of racial knowledge and understanding in a social world of people of colour in particular.[98] Trinidad had its own situational incidences of 'passing'. For instance, the many accounts that emerged during the American occupation of white servicemen being 'fooled' by coloured women passing as white.[99] The de Coudray family in De Bossiere's second novel *Rum and Coca Cola* live prosperously amongst whites but are known to have black antecedents and this shared knowledge sometimes leads to their marginalisation in St Clair social life and at other times does not.[100] Among coloured middle-class 'Carnival Queen' audiences, widely differentiated within their own social bracket, beauty candidates represented racial liminality. The beauty competition, in its routine production of very light-skinned winners, became a metaphor for coloured social ascent. Coloured audiences hungry for 'representation', and social mobility, and, by dint of their racial knowledge, could make 'coloured' winners from 'white'.

However, if the audience to the 'Carnival Queen' pageant was predominantly coloured middle-class, save for an elite tier of mostly white-identifying people, it is also clear that the *Guardian* particularly courted an ever-greater North American audience. This group would increasingly be made up of tourists but initially included US servicemen. The American 'occupation' lasted roughly from 1941 to 1947. However, the presence of Base Commanders on the 'Carnival Queen' judging panel in the 1950s is testament to their lingering presence, their literal and psychological impact, extending far beyond the peak of wartime activity, even if many of the servicemen had been repatriated. As historian Harvey Neptune writes, the American occupation variously challenged and disrupted the norms of colonial Trinidad that maintained distinctions of class, race and gender, and facilitated white-minority rule. Of particular significance here is that white American servicemen had open relationships with Trinidadian women of colour, and thereby subverted racial codes that deemed that such relationships, though common practice, should always be covert and pursued in private. Servicemen, however, free from the social restrictions of home, felt free to embark on open interracial relationships that disturbed the white elite, and brought approbation from their military superiors, who advised them not to breach the social mores they would observe in the US. [101]

White upper-class society responded by attempting to restore social conventions that affirmed white superiority. Upper-class ladies operated special programmes, the Home Hospitality Programme and the United Servicemen's Organisation that brought servicemen into the company of respectable young white women.[102] Thus the question arises as to how 'Carnival Queen' featured in the ongoing project to defend and reassert the prestige of whiteness in a colonial regime. Whilst senior American servicemen sat on the panel of judges for the 'Carnival Queen' competition, rank and file servicemen made up large and vocal members of the audience as late as 1948.[103] The presence of the uproarious servicemen at 'Carnival Queen' shows was noted in some sections of the press, but few made direct reference to which candidates, be they white or brown, the troops favoured and cheered for, or furthermore, whom they consorted with amongst the audience. As we have seen, though the competition was renowned for crowning only white women and thereby endorsed white primacy that chimed with the elite women's cause, it was also a large draw for brown contestants, and brown audiences. Therefore it by no means ensured the separateness which was the concern of the upper-class social schemes. If anything Carnival and 'Carnival Queen' brought greater opportunities for interracial meetings. Therefore, even during the professionalisation and whitening of the competition, the American presence probably served to complicate and occasionally subvert the work for racial preservation managed by upper-class white women.[104]

Imagining an Afro-Creole 'Carnival Queen'

Implicit social stratification was intrinsic to the Savannah Carnival. The Parade of the Bands involved parties of people, typically formed of neighbourhood associations, and these bands tended not to be socially mixed beyond conventional colour-class boundaries. Savannah Carnival instantly made a judgement on the relative worth of calypso artistry as against the civilising influence of the 'Carnival Queen'. Here the cultural war pitted creole music against the symbolic purchase of sophisticated, refined white womanhood. Typically the winner of the 'Calypso King' competition won prizes ranging from a cup worth $5, to $50 in prize money, in stark contrast to the valuable prizes awarded the beauty queen, which could amount to $6000 in value.[105] Savannah Carnival divided participants into performer and spectator. With the exception of the glorified beauty queen, spectatorship was the more respectable role to occupy. In 1949 the *Port of Spain Gazette* published a letter from a Carnival enthusiast who challenged the process of carnival-improvement on the basis that it had become indistinguishable from commercialisation, to the exclusion of the masses.

> Imagine, with all that was done [in Carnival of 1949] we had no black or dark Carnival Queen. And yet the majority of the bands and the various leggoes [amusements] sprung from the unfortunate, [who] were in some form or other contributing to their more fortunate brothers and sisters in the merriment.[106]

However, in 1950 two politicians, identified with middle-class nationalism and cultural creolisation, were invited onto the 'Carnival Queen' judging panel. They were the Hon. Albert Gomes, de facto leader of the interim regime, and Norman Tang, Mayor of Port of Spain. This was the second year of the *Guardian*'s professionalisation programme for the competition, and these nationalists were part of a reduced panel of only six others. Together Tang and Gomes used their votes and influence to usher Marion Halfhide and Pearl Marshall towards first and second places. Halfhide was light-skinned, and was referred to in the knowing language of racial economy, as 'not exactly European'.[107] Marshall was brown-skinned, 'dark' by comparison with other brown competitors; she attracted epithets ranging from 'spice-coloured' to 'Ebony venus'.[108] The *Guardian*'s account of the competition in that year deliberately suppressed the furore that surrounded the unprecedented success of Marshall as runner-up.

When the controversial annual 'Carnival Queen' contest was some years later debated in the Legislative Council, Gomes wryly disclosed the subversive role played by himself and Tang in this unprecedented episode in 1949, which in effect suspended the normal process of 'queen' selection.

Hon. A Gomes: We have had reference to beauty contests. I propose to say a word about beauty contests. I hope no one has any doubt as my ability to adjudicate in a matter of this sort, because I regard myself as a sort of pioneer in the field. . . . I see the Hon. Minister for health and Local Government [Tang] looking at me across the table and I recall that when he was Mayor of Port of Spain on a certain memorable occasion both of us were part of a panel of judges appointed by the particular newspaper [*Trinidad Guardian*] to which reference has been made by the Hon. Member for Port of Spain East [Aubrey James], and I do not think anyone can suggest that on that occasion we followed the [racially selective] line that the Hon. Member for Port of Spain East suggests that beauty contests are following at the present time.

Hon. M. G Sinanan: Were the judges fired as a result?

Hon. A Gomes: I should prefer to say that we were never again invited.[109]

Gomes thus revealed that he and Tang acted against white domination of the 'Carnival Queen' title. Instead they sought to move non-white candidates Halfhide and Marshall from the margins to the centre. The outlandishness of their actions is confirmed by the fact that the *Guardian* and its committee excluded nationalist politicians from the judging panel thereafter, and preferred instead to solicit businessmen and foreign dignitaries.

Marshall was sponsored by the Little Carib Theatre. This was the movement founded by the 'mother of Caribbean dance', cultural nationalist Beryl McBurnie. McBurnie, along with her contemporaries Boscoe Holder and Sylvia Chen, was dedicated, as Neptune writes, to mining Trinidad's cultural originality through dance.[110] The Little Carib Theatre revived 'folk' dance, including motifs of Canboulay, and annually produced celebrated performances for the Savannah Carnival. This was Carnival-refinement, but with the accent on cultural nationalism carried by Afro-Creole cultural originality. In sponsoring Marshall, Little Carib attempted to affect a crossover of the black presence at Carnival from that of charming 'native' culture to privileged feminine parade. Marshall's bid for the crown was intended as a comment on the marginalisation of most Trinidadians from the glamour, financial reward and symbolic value of Carnival performance, even while contributing the cultural work to the festivities. Marshall's relative success – she became the de facto winner for many – was a dramatic reversal of normal order.[111] Nationalist efforts here combined in a somewhat subversive challenge to the white-creole 'Carnival Queen', with Marshall performing a rival paradigm of Afro-Creole femininity, culturally authentic, and locally rooted. Marshall's 'win', helped along by progressive politicians, did not represent the investment in hybrid beauty preached by Aimee Webster's competition, rather Marshall, with her dark skin and association with Little Carib, visually signalled the parity of Afro-Creole culture with the aristocratic pageantry surrounding the white 'Carnival Queen'.

Though the CIC continued to direct its efforts downtown, middle-class stewardship of working-class energy was seen to lapse in 1953. Violence broke out between rival steel bands at a special one-off Carnival celebration to mark the coronation of Queen Elizabeth II on 6 June, resulting in one death. The *Port of Spain Gazette* figuratively wrung its hands over a 'totally irresponsible lot who do not know better and must be saved from themselves' and renewed appeals for a 'Clean Carnival' following the violence.[112] 'Carnival Queen', though apparently not the cause of the outbreak of band violence, emerged, through investigation, as a figure of resentment of steel band players.[113] CBU leader and politician, Aubrey James, proposed the bands launch their own pageant of musical performances to raise money for its members, who were disgruntled by the huge disparity in their rewards and the prizes awarded to the beauty queen. James also assured his members that the Union would attempt to secure better prizes from the Savannah Carnival organisers.[114] Furthermore, the issue was debated in the Legislative Council, and James, addressing the speaker, asked: 'We hope, Sir, that the Committee will be strong enough to eliminate *that* feature [racism] so that there will be no cause for us to feel that one or two sections [white and 'high-coloured'] are determined to keep out the other races from what is intended to be a national festival.'[115]

This pressure did not alter 'Carnival Queen' on a permanent basis. However, in the following year at least, the competition crowned its first brown-identified winner, sixteen-year-old 'cinnamon-skinned' Marcia Rooks. The *Guardian* appeared bemused by its new queen. 'She is by no means the classic beauty or the sophisticated glamour girl type', wrote Carl Yip Young, 'but her eyes have fun in them, her face glows and sparkles, and she suggests all exhilaration, gaiety and delight.'[116] This coded language carried the weight of racialising and sexualising narratives, that placed Rooks outside of 'classic' Hollywood glamour and within instead, the confines of the exotic and seductive 'mulatta' stereotype. However, if the *Guardian* did not see that mixed-raced identity could chime with its modernising agenda, it certainly agreed that exotic 'mulatta' sexuality was marketable. It told how Rooks was 'discovered' by marketing executive Ronald Williams when walking through the business district of Port of Spain. Williams was 'immediately impressed by her fresh, invigorating and different type of beauty'.[117] Williams' firm sponsored Rooks, using her image to advertise Cow and Gate malted drink TONO. Displaying that it was alert to the success of the Rhumba-dancing *mulatta* to Cuban tourism, the *Guardian* made much of Rooks's own skills in the Rhumba and her similar appeal as an exotic and charming national figure to lure tourists, 'her youthful exuberance, bright tropical colour, cosmopolitanism and the joyous spirit of Trinidad and its national festival'.[118]

Here indeed was the first faint suggestion that Rooks's racial blend somehow represented the cosmopolitanism of the island, but such commentary surrounding Rooks proved scarce. The *Guardian* were more occupied with maintaining the status quo in the beauty competition than testing the success of hybrid beauty as the brand for 'Carnival Queen'. Rooks's win may have temporarily appeased some of the 'Carnival Queen' following. However, it did not set a precedent of brown middle-class winners, such was the stranglehold of the business elite over the competition. Rooks's win represents a lone attempt by the competition organisers to invest in the idea of hybrid Caribbean beauty, in spite of Aimee Webster's encouragement for this idea in her 'Miss British Caribbean' competition.

The dissatisfied nationalist contingent became louder and more public in their complaints against 'Carnival Queen'. Raymond Quevedo, otherwise known as calypso artist Atilla the Hun, launched his own protest with an anti-'Carnival Queen' song in 1955. Quevedo was also a former Mayor of Port of Spain, a former member of the Carnival Improvement Committee, and a serving member of the Legislative Council for slum-district Laventille.[119] As both Calypso artist and politician, Quevedo thus represented the spirit of creole cultural nationalism. Quevedo called the song, the 'Guardian Beauty Contest', which he punned as 'white people's business', literally the private reserve of 'whites' and awash with 'white' money.

'Guardian Beauty Contest', 1955

I really have to tell you Evelyn
Girls it's only time you are wasting
Why did you enter that beauty contest
Why all this hair-do and pretty dress
Evelyn you really cannot tell me
That you don't know they picked the queen already

Chorus:

For this Guardian Competition
Is nothing but real discrimination
One thing in this world will never be seen
Is a dark skinned girl as Carnival Queen.[120]

Subsequent verses continued to puzzle over the unerring appeal of the contest to dark women, whom he advised to abandon all hope of winning, even as he praised their beauty. Atilla mused over judges who appeared sympathetic to brown women but considered them 'too dark' to win, and over the despairing, yet enthralled, brown crowd. Finally, Atilla, called for a boycott,

> So it is time that our forces we enlist
> And put an end to all this stupidness.
> With protest from all over the country
> That when a beauty contest they are judging
> There must be no question of colour or skin
> And if no regard for our views are shown
> Then let us leave the white people business alone.[121]

However, such a boycott did not immediately materialise. For the moment Atilla's was virtually a lone voice amongst calypso artists, who in spite of the satirical tradition of Calypso chose not to attack or lampoon the 'Carnival Queen', perhaps because they did not want to jeopardise their position as performers in Savannah Carnival, however meagrely it was remunerated.[122] Furthermore, although calypso was a satirical and activist form, it had also become a male-dominated creative space, which, in spite of censorship drives, largely working-class male artists used to embarrass the upper and middle-classes, to resist negative characterisation and to assert masculine identities. This was often done at the expense of women, and black working-class women in particular, who were sometimes scapegoated in notoriously misogynistic lyrics.[123] In fact from the 1930s calypso had spawned its own genre of songs around the lure of the upper-class, particularly 'foreign', woman and the sexual largesse of the black lower-class man who demonstrated his masculine prowess through his ability to live a life of leisure while wealthy white women in his thrall provided his income.[124] Though subversive in its own right, as an attack on respectability, this trend of revelling in the appeal of glamorous white-creole femininity also provides some explanation for the relative silence on 'Carnival Queen' from the working-class black male artist at this time. Just as the origins of the Carnival-refinement movement that had produced the beauty competition were middle-class, so too were its most vocal and articulate detractors. Imagining a brown or 'dark' beauty queen in place of a white queen was the particular concern of the brown middle-class, who sought to decorate an iconography of Afro-Creole cultural nationalism with a feminine figurehead.

In 1956 the People's National Movement (PNM) completed its rapid rise to power. The PNM won the general election of 1956 on the basis of uniting a core of brown and black middle-class voters with the black working-class electorate, but in general alienated the Indo-Creole vote, more than one-third of the populace. The new government delivered Oxford-educated Dr Eric Williams, radical historian and author of seminal postcolonial text *Capitalism and Slavery* (1944), as Chief Minister of the semi-responsible administration, with the inauguration of the British West Indian Federation imminent. Williams's government gave confidence to the brown and black middle-classes and to cultural nationalism as a political force. Following the rise of Williams, more outspoken critics of the 'Carnival Queen' appeared.

Councillor Tywang, of Port of Spain's City Council, attacked the 'Carnival Queen' enterprise at a public meeting, as a conglomerate of privileged interests that systematically excluded most Trinidadians and kept black women away from the winner's spot.[125] Tywang accused the *Guardian* of withholding complementary tickets for the CIC to the 'Carnival Queen Show', a seemingly un-brotherly act amongst fellow Carnival-improvers. Furthermore Tywang accused the *Guardian* of colluding to restrict sales of tickets to ordinary Trinidadians and of attempting to seat American tourists separately from the Trinidadian crowd. Finally, Tywang accused the organisers of excluding dark women from the competition, saying that they would 'not even accept a nice cultured Negro girl' as winner of the competition, a comment which perfectly spelled out the nationalists search for exemplar respectable femininity in women of colour.[126]

The *Guardian* responded with an editorial, demeaning Tywang and challenging him to sponsor his own candidate. Tywang fought back with an open letter to the editor, reasserting his claims:

> [W]hy [is it] that young girls of a certain racial group here [are] never selected as 'Beauty Queens' to represent this island, and were never even sponsored? Surely this gives food for thought, and you cannot blame anyone for saying openly and in public what so many people feel but keep within themselves.[127]

Tywang's candour provoked a more serious rebuttal from the *Guardian* which reiterated the rules of the competition: 'Every girl, properly sponsored, who offered herself for the competition was accepted by the Committee. Will Councillor Tywang sponsor a girl of any racial group he likes for the next competition?'[128] In fact community and cultural organisations had, in the wake of Pearl Marshall's success, begun sponsoring their own contestants for the competition. A contingent of middle-class small-businessmen had also attempted to launch the 'Miss Port of Spain' competition as a rival to 'Carnival Queen', crowning brown winners, but this was eventually subsumed into the preliminary rounds of the larger 'Carnival Queen' competition, and the chosen 'Miss Port of Spain' became merely another contestant in the finals.[129]

In this context Marshall's win took on all the more significance. Marshall continued to symbolise racial and cultural pride through the 1950s. In post as favourite symbol of Afro-Creole nationalist destiny, Marshall gained access to new symbols of elite femininity, otherwise barred to Trinidadian women of colour. Marshall was not celebrated as a hybrid beauty, harmoniously blending all of the races of Trinidad, but rather as a black woman infiltrating previously white-only domains, just as she had the beauty competition. In 1956 Marshall joined the staff of BWIA as an air hostess and was roundly celebrated as the first black woman *in the world* to achieve that feat.[130] Her identity was inscribed pointedly as 'black' by Jamaican publisher of *Spotlight* magazine, Evon Blake, the better to mark the moment as an international first. Blake, a liberal advocate of black 'uplift', invested heavily in Marshall's image. Marshall appeared on board a BWIA aircraft for the cover of the September 1956 cover of *Spotlight*, above the heading 'The world has a lot to learn from the West Indies'. Marshall was thus paraded as a testament to progressiveness; the acquisition of modernity in the British Caribbean. The feature was entitled 'A New Career for West Indians' and accompanied the news that BWIA, a subsidiary of imperial carrier British Overseas Airways Corporation, was expanding its operations.[131] Blake's excitement was warranted. Here was a profession steeped in glamour. As historian Kathleen Barry has shown, airline stewardess was ranked beside beauty queen and topped only by Hollywood actress in the popular imagination.[132] As if to emphasise the vaunted platform Marshall had now ascended, the *Spotlight* wrote, 'All airline hostesses are attractive – some are even beautiful. BWIA accents the point. Three have been local beauty queens; several have been runners-up in beauty contests.'[133] There followed a profile of another new recruit, Judy Verity, 'Miss Jamaica' of 1954. Verity was white and displayed all the usual hallmarks of accomplished womanhood, from elite schooling to professional yet decorative prestige work as bank clerk and model. With the stage of proper femininity set, *Spotlight* then followed with a gushing account of Pearl Marshall's accomplishments – 'She combines athletic talent, dancing grace, personality and far-above-average brains. She bubbles with pride and enthusiasm at being the first obviously dark-skinned girl to be recruited as an air hostess'.[134] And yet, the role of race itself was downplayed in liberal meritocratic terms: 'The fact that she is the first Negro airline hostess the world has known doesn't bother Pearl Marshall one way or the other. She is naturally thrilled, but the big thing is her determination to be "one of the best hostesses on any airline. Period" '.[135]

In keeping with Blake's liberal principles, equality was presented as the reward of the deserving, willing to work hard and assimilate to middle-class respectability. Marshall, the very icon of black womanhood Tywang had pleaded for, symbolised the acquisition of the principles of liberal democracy in her performance of sophisticated femininity on board a modern aircraft.

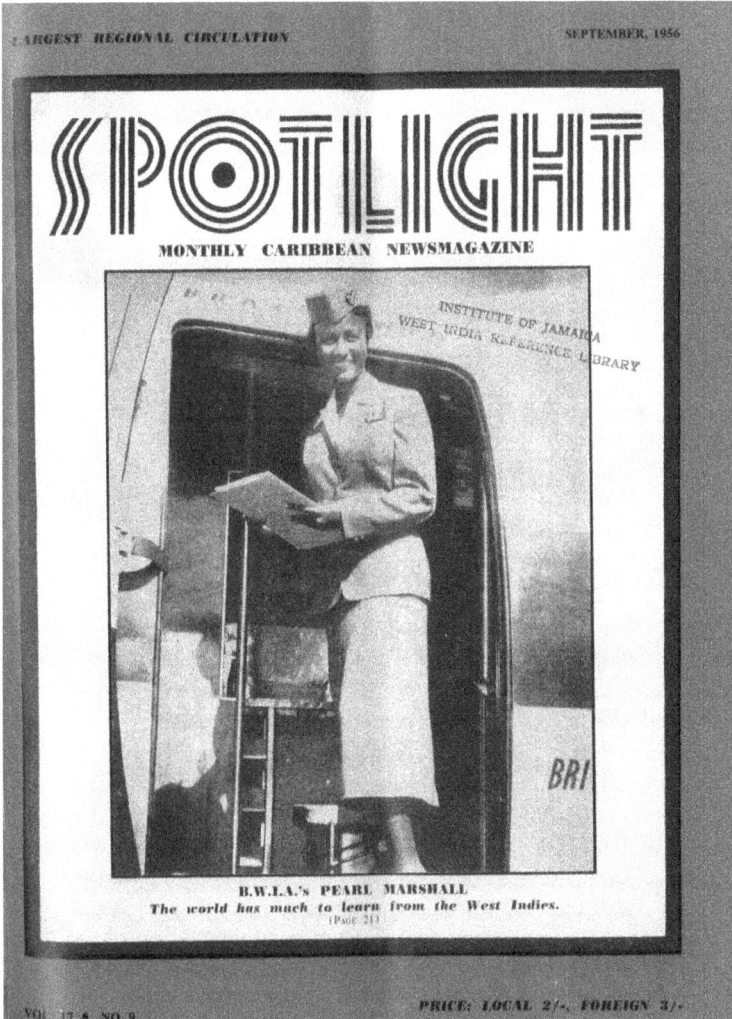

2.2 'The world has much to learn from the West Indies', 1956

In the United States the National Association for the Advancement of Coloured People and the Urban League had long been campaigning to integrate airline travel and particularly stewardess work. Activists tested New York's new anti-discrimination law, but faced great resistance from airline companies. Eventually in 1957 African American Ruth Taylor was employed by a small carrier, Mohawk Airlines.[136] When Marshall arrived in the United States on duty as a stewardess, she made front page news with African American paper, the *New York Age*. Marshall's welcoming committee included Sir Hugh Wooding, prominent black Trinidadian lawyer and BWIA board member, whose wife had served on previous 'Carnival Queen' judging panels.[137] I speculate here that Wooding, as a progressive Afro-Creole nationalist, who would later serve prominently in the postcolonial state apparatus, intervened to bring about Marshall's unprecedented appointment, at a time when blacks were still virtually invisible from prestigious jobs outside of the transitioning government. Though *Spotlight* boasted a multinational array of new West Indian beauties taking to the skies, the group were hardly multiracial in appearance, and Marshall was the only prominently African-descended woman among them.

'Carnival Queen' and the new nationalist government

In 1957 the task of the PNM leadership was to appease growing dissatisfaction, not least amongst its own ranks, over the seemingly unassailable Savannah Carnival enterprise. As the CBU threatened to boycott Carnival, Williams's government-in-waiting moved to 'nationalise' Carnival-refinement. It hastily created a state-run Carnival Development Committee (CDC), essentially appointing itself as the legal guardian of Carnival. Within a few years it would neutralise the other private committees and their claim to be legitimate or nationally representative bodies.[138] The *Guardian*, which did not want to meet the bands' demands for better prizes, handed over the running of glamorous Savannah Carnival to the government in 1957. The PNM offered the bands and calypso artists slightly better prizes and instigated appearance fees, thereby recognising them as cultural workers. However, these were not sufficient for the artists, who, emboldened by the atmosphere of political change, went ahead with a boycott.[139] Leading black calypso artist The Mighty Sparrow now provided a direct attack on the 'Carnival Queen', breaking the silence of black working-class artists at Savannah Carnival. However, he did not demand a darker queen like brown nationalist Atilla, but rather asserted his competitive rivalry with the white queen, who he cast as phoney icon beside the black male cultural worker.[140]

> I am going to play me mas' as usual
> Because I love Carnival
> I am going to play me mas' as usual
> Because I love Carnival
> But no competition for me
> In San Fernando or the City
> They could preach to Peter or Paul
> I won't even go to Savannah to see football
>
> I intend to keep all my costume on the shelf
> Let them keep the prizes in the Savannah for they own self
> Let the Queen run the show
> Without Steelband or calypso
> Who want to go can do up dey
> But me ain't going no way
>
> What really cause the upset
> Is the motor-car the Queen does get
> She does nothing for the Carnival
> She only pretty and that is all
> But men like me and you
> Saving money to play 'history' and Ju-Ju
> All we get is two case of beer
> And talk up as the band of the Year . . .[141]

The government was forced to intervene in the boycott, putting the new CDC into action to organise Carnival, in the words of Eric Williams, 'on a more national basis'.[142] It proposed to address the 'reorganisation of festivities, improvement in seating accommodation, the question of prize money and so on'.[143] These changes targeted the keynotes of rising nationalist complaints about Savannah Carnival, symbolised by the beauty queen; from the Little Carib Theatre's cultural activism, and the renegade judges of 1949, to Atilla's protest song of 1956, Councillor Tywang's outburst and the boycotting artists. The reorganisation, then, was intended to address the 'Queen' competition that, in the eyes of nationalists, humiliated the national image.

I speculate here that the pressure from the artist's boycott and the CDC's direct intervention led to the disintegration of the Savannah committee in an argument over the predominance of white beauty queens. The competition was suspended in 1958. Chief Minister Williams aired some clues to the dispute between committee members when he spoke in the Legislative Council:

> It was [the leader of the committee] who told me about his wife being a judge one year when a dark-skinned girl won the prize and was told by a foreign Consul who had given the first prize, that if *she* gets that prize I withdraw my trip for two to my country. I was told that, and we said, *no racial discrimination in this Carnival*. They will all get out and go. There is going to be no compromise on this issue, and where the Government is responsible, especially through the Ministry of Finance, for the proper control of public funds everybody is going to be controlled, or otherwise he goes out, and I am responsible to the Legislative Council of Trinidad and Tobago[144] [italics my emphasis].

Williams articulated the question of control over Savannah Carnival as the question of postcolonial power relations that it in effect had become:

> The issue to be decided is: who governs Trinidad? We say it is the Government of Trinidad and Tobago responsible to the Legislative Council and through the Legislative Council, to the people of Trinidad and Tobago. And those who do not like it could walk out and resign in a body. That is exactly what happened to the Carnival Committee. The Government is going to determine the policy. There is going to be no mistake about that.[145]

However, in spite of (or because of) this outburst, subsequent negotiations for the takeover of Savannah Carnival proved that an amicable relationship could in fact exist between government and the *Guardian* enterprise, and the broad similarity of their objectives for Carnival. The new PNM government quickly showed it was equally concerned to exploit the specular appeal and commercial potential of the Carnival and retained many facets of the Savannah variety show, only with more pronounced folk-creole elements incorporated into the programme. The CDC now appointed a full-time staff of civil servants to organise Carnival. By the end of the decade the CDC had the power to raise government funding of Carnival from \$15,000 to \$80,000.[146] The government proposed 25,000 extra seats for Carnival 'patrons' to watch the parade of the bands. The CDC commandeered the Savannah location and apparatus on *Dimanche Gras* night for a new nationalist-themed show in place of the 'Carnival Queen' competition. The new 'Dimanche Gras Show' would include a display of *kalinda*, masquerade competitions, steelband, and limbo contests.[147] The plans revealed the government's admiration for the refinement process with its emphasis on seated spectaculars and raising tourist audiences.

The new state-run show elevated the 'Calypso King' competition to the headline act and offered the winner more prize money than before.

It also created a new 'Queen of the Bands' competition as the King's female counterpart. The 'Queen of the Bands' was a prize awarded to the best-costumed female band leader. This role of female figurehead to each of the parading bands was, on the one hand, reminiscent of the leadership of the female *jamette chantuelle* of the previous century, and yet, on the other, a highly decorative role that prided in elaborate costume and feminine beauty. However, organisers were keen to stress it was not merely another beauty competition. The King won $1000 in prize money, and the Queen, $700.[148] This was a new domestic gendering of the King and Queen figures. Gone for the moment was the expansive glamour of the white beauty queen, and the disparity in prizes that dwarfed and humiliated black male calypso artists. In her place was a contest which rewarded its female winner mainly for her decorativeness and kept her in suitable second place behind 'her' man. This was bourgeois Carnival-improvement come full circle as a masculinist, nationalist process. The new King and Queen under-scored the marginalisation of women from prominent artistic cultural performance at Carnival, and towards allegorical and decorative roles, which began with Carnival-improvement at the turn of the twentieth century and was made flesh by mid-century by 'Carnival Queen'.

However, the original beauty competition was in fact revived in 1959 by the Junior Chamber of Commerce (Jaycees), a youth movement for business-minded young men that was sweeping the Caribbean. The new competition, like its predecessor, drew audiences of thousands, continued to raise large sums of money for charity, and to crown very light-skinned, white-identified winners for over a decade.[149] It now took place on the Saturday preceding Carnival, the night before the government's new 'Dimanche Gras' show, but both shows now shared the Savannah venue. The two rival spectaculars were symbolic of the competition between bourgeois nationalisms to steer Carnival towards modernity.

The ousted *Guardian* celebrated the revival of the 'Carnival Queen' contest and observed wryly that the government's 'Queen of the Bands' competition was merely another (and it was implied, lesser) beauty contest, by another name. 'Carnival Queen is a must', wrote David Wrenwick, '[enjoyed by] every man, woman and toddler in the land.' Wrenwick gloated over the *Guardian*'s ability to deliver assured, 'blonde' glamour that 'the people' enjoyed:

> [I]n 1956, the year people fondly recall as that of the most breathtaking queen competition ever, popular blonde 'monarch' Judy Edgehill, could count amongst her prizes a Volkswagen car, a trip to New York, a radio-gram, sewing machine, gas cooker, dressing table, refrigerator and expensive dresses too numerous to note on the fingers of both hands.[150]

In fact the eventual forced demise of the white 'Carnival Queen' competition took place over a decade later in 1971, in the aftermath of a surge
of African and Indian-Trinidadian race-conscious activism which began
in 1966, when Trinidad was rocked by local reverberations of the Black
Power movement.[151] In this atmosphere the competition finally crowned
only its second brown winner, Elicia Irish. Irish became celebrated as
the first 'Afro Queen' because of her 'afro' hairstyle. She was also the
last 'Carnival Queen' as the competition withdrew itself from the cultural
arena thereafter.[152]

After 1958 the government appeared to have retreated from its earlier
position on the 'Carnival Queen' beauty competition, which continued
to thrive from 1959 until 1971. However, though government accommodated the beauty competition, by allowing it to continue, it charged
the Jaycees a fee to host its events at the Savannah and was careful to cast
its own competitions as authentic, national and creole while it figuratively
marginalised the 'Carnival Queen' competition as the 'Commercial Queen',
or 'Jaycees' queen.[153] The lucrative white-dominated beauty competition
was permitted but denied its claim to the symbols of proper creole national
culture until its eventual demise in 1971.

The 'Carnival Queen' competition in Trinidad created and sustained
a spectacle of cultured, modern beauty invested defiantly in white-creole
femininity, in spite of loud protests from a diverse group of middle-class
nationalists, who believed by contrast in the Afro-Creole root for the
Trinidadian nation, and sought an Afro-Creole figurehead to infiltrate
the whites-only competition. Such actors sought brown beauty queens
who could, they believed, more properly embody the local and authentic
quality of carnival and nation. And in the spirit of radical defiance that
surrounded the battle to unseat the white 'Carnival Queen', black beauties
such as Pearl Marshall, and other 'nice Negro girls' were also encouraged
and took their chances. Marshall indeed became a crucial figure of
black parity challenging the stranglehold of white-creoles over all things
sophisticated and glamorous in the island. However, whilst brown audiences waited impatiently for the competition to deliver their icon, and
scrutinised each cohort very carefully, brown dominance of the competition, in the form of coloured beauty queens winning the title year on year,
failed to emerge. Marcia Rooks stood alone as an anomaly. Nationalists
focused on undermining the dominance of the white beauty queen, and
the 'Carnival Queen' competition failed properly to emerge as a space
for grooming brown beauties as it would do in other islands. Latterly
the effort for moulding a national ideal for Trinidadian beauty was taken
up by the 'Queen of the Bands' parade, where the spirit of the *jamette*

woman was tamed into a decorative symbol of Carnival. Winners of 'Queen of the Bands', who tended to be brown, and rarely black, were tasked with delivering femininity that combined elements of subaltern cultural authenticity, so prized by the middle-classes, harmonised with the aspirations of a modernising Carnival.

Notes

1   *Trinidad Guardian*, 27 February 1949, p. 6.
2   Barnes, *Cultural Conundrums*, p. 56.
3   Rosenberg, *Nationalism and Caribbean Literature*, p. 129; Neptune, *Caliban and the Yankees*, pp. 23, 47–48; Daniel, A. Segal, 'Race and Colour in Pre-Independence Trinidad and Tobago' in Kevin Yelvington (ed.), *Trinidad Ethnicity* (Knoxville: University of Tennessee Press, 1993), pp. 81–115. Rosenberg has reflected on the disproportionate influence of the tiny Portuguese-Trinidadian population in shaping politics and culture between the mid-1930s and the mid-1950s, especially writers Albert Gomes and Alfred Mendes, who helped shape the development of national literature in Trinidad from within the intellectual community surrounding the *Beacon* journal.
4   These scholars include dress historian Pamela Franco, musicologist Hope Munro Smith and literary-cultural critic Natasha Barnes: Gordon Rohlehr, *Calypso and Society in Pre-Independence Trinidad* (Port of Spain: Gordon Rohlehr, 1990); Pamela Franco, 'Dressing Up and Looking Good: African-Creole Female Maskers in Trinidad Carnival,' *African Arts* 31 (1998), pp. 62–95; Hope Munro Smith, 'Performing Gender in the Trinidad Calypso', *Latin American Music Review* 25 (2004), pp. 32–56; Barnes, *Cultural Conundrums*, pp. 56–61.
5   John Cowley, *Carnival, Canboulay and Calypso: Traditions in the Making* (Cambridge: University of Cambridge Press, 1996), p. 11.
6   Ibid., p. 12; Franco, 'Dressing Up', p. 64.
7   Milla Cozart Riggio, 'The Carnival Story – Then and Now: Introduction', in Milla Cozart Riggio (ed.), *Carnival: Culture in Action, the Trinidad Experience* (New York and London: Routledge, 2004), p. 41.
8   Ibid.
9   Ibid., p. 43.
10 Richard Schener, 'Carnival (Theory) After Bakhtin' in *Carnival: Culture in Action*, p. 8; Mikhail Bakhtin, *Rabelais and His World*, tran. Helene Iswolksy (Bloomington: Indiana University Press, 1984).
11 Joseph Roach, *Cities of the Dead: Circum-Atlantic performance* (New York: Columbia University Press, 1996), pp. 242–249.
12 Ibid., p. 256.
13 Ibid., p. 267.
14 Ibid., p. 246.
15 Bridget Brereton, 'The Trinidad Carnival in the Late Nineteenth Century', in *Carnival: Culture in Action*, p. 54. Brereton describes the 'distinct character' of Jamette Carnival as emerging in the 1860s, though adds that Jamette elements were disavowed by elites as 'disreputable' as early as the 1850s.
16 Carol Martin, 'Trinidad Carnival Glossary', in *Carnival: Culture in Action*, p. 285.

17 Ibid., p. 286.
18 JD Elder, 'Cannes Brulees', in *Carnival: Culture in Action*, p. 49.
19 Pamela Franco, 'The "Unruly Woman" in Nineteenth Century Trinidad Carnival', *Small Axe* 7 (2000), pp. 60–76.
20 Patricia De Freitas (Unpublished doctoral thesis), ' "Playing Mas"; The Construction and Deconstruction of National Identity in the Trinidad Carnival', June 1994, McMaster University, p. 82.
21 Martin, 'Trinidad Glossary', p. 283.
22 Munro Smith, 'Gender in the Trinidad Calypso', p. 34.
23 Pamela Franco and Susan Campbell in particular have countered this by restoring the infamous Boadicea, Alice Sugar and Piti' Belle Lily, renowned fighters, as well as a number of homosexual male stickfighters, to the historical record. Franco, 'Unruly Woman', pp. 70–76; Susan Campbell, 'Carnival, Calypso, and Class Struggle in Nineteenth Century Trinidad', *History Workshop* 26 (1988), p. 12.
24 Quoted in Andrew Pearse, 'Carnival in Nineteenth Century Trinidad', *Caribbean Quarterly* 4 (1956), p. 188.
25 Franco, 'Unruly Woman', pp. 62–70.
26 Franco, 'Dressing Up', p. 67.
27 Cowley, *Carnival*, pp. 84–90; Bolland, p. 71.
28 Dawn Batson and Milla Cozart Riggio, 'Trinidad Carnival Timelines', in *Carnival: Culture in Action*, p. 33. Ordinances included the Summary Convictions Ordinance of 1883 which fined the owner of yards where drum dances took place, the Musical Ordinance of 1883 that banned percussion instruments, and the Peace Preservation Ordinance which banned lighted torches, noisy dances and processions and sticks.
29 Barbara Powrie, 'The Changing Attitude of the Coloured Middle-class Towards Carnival', *Caribbean Quarterly* 4 (1956), p. 228; De Freitas, 'Playing Mas', p. 104.
30 Rohlehr, *Calypso*, pp. 90–92; Rosenberg, *Nationalism and Caribbean Literature*, p. 134.
31 Smith, 'Performing Gender', p. 35.
32 Rohlehr, *Calypso*, pp. 90–92; Garth Green, 'Marketing the Nation: Carnival and Tourism in Trinidad and Tobago', *Critique of Anthropology* 22 (2002), p. 294.
33 Rohlehr, *Calypso*, p. 90.
34 Rosenberg, *Nationalism and Caribbean Literature*, p. 131.
35 Ibid., p. 132.
36 Ibid.
37 Green, 'Marketing the Nation', p. 293.
38 Rohlehr, *Calypso*, p. 89.
39 Green, 'Marketing the Nation', p. 294.
40 Ibid.
41 Bolland, *Politics of Labour*, p. 250. See also Ralph de Boissiere's *Crown Jewel* (London: Picador, 1981) which describes the labour uprisings of the 1930s, and the attempts of middle-class leadership to become established.
42 Rohlehr, *Calypso*, p. 328.
43 Rohlehr, *Calypso*, p. 425; Green, p. 294.
44 *Port of Spain Gazette*, 3 March 1946, p. 6.
45 Rohlehr, *Calypso*, p. 328.
46 Quoted in Rohlehr, *Calypso*, p. 404.

47 Bridget Brereton, *A History of Modern Trinidad 1783–1962* (Exeter: New Hampshire, Heinmann, 1981), pp. 196–198.

48 Kirk Meighoo, *Politics in a Half-Made Society: Trinidad and Tobago 1946–1970* (Cave Hill: University of the West Indies, 1984), pp. 17–24.

49 *Trinidad Guardian*, 31 January 1946, p. 2.

50 The largest celebrations took place in Port of Spain but also in smaller towns, for example Arima and St Augustine, and especially in the 'capital' of the south, San Fernando, where another, increasingly grand, beauty competition thrived and became a preliminary competition of the Port of Spain 'Carnival Queen'. This competition grew so lucrative that gradually the prospect, however remote, of one winner claiming the prize for both the southern competition and the Port of Spain competition became a matter of concern.

51 *Trinidad Guardian*, 2 March 1946, p. 8.

52 *Trinidad Guardian*, 31 January 1946, p. 2.

53 Together with Harry Pits, another occasional judge and organiser of 'Carnival Queen', Espinet had authored *Land of Calypso: The Origin and Development of Trinidad's Folk Song* (Port of Spain: Guardian Commercial Printery, 1944).

54 *Trinidad Guardian*, 31 January 1946, p. 2.

55 'Trinidad's Carnival provides a "Queen" for Post's "Miss British Caribbean" 1948 Contest', *Caribbean Post* (2) 1948, p. 11.

56 Lloyd Braithwaite, 'Social Stratification in Trinidad: A Preliminary Analysis', *Social and Economic Studies* 2 (1953), p. 112.

57 Ibid.

58 Ibid., pp. 68–69.

59 *Trinidad Guardian*, 8 March 1946, p. 8.

60 Ibid.

61 Pamphlets were also produced for visitors, such as 'Trinidad's Sensational Calypso Dance', which advised tourists of the basic steps.

62 *Trinidad Guardian*, 8 March 1946, p. 8.

63 Ibid.

64 Rohlehr, *Calypso*, p. 414.

65 De Boissiere, *Crown Jewel*, pp. 11–12.

66 Quoted in Kathleen M Barry's *Femininity in Flight: A History of Flight Attendants* (Durham and London: Duke University Press, 2007), p. 6. See also Stephen Gundle's *Glamour: A History* (Oxford: Oxford University Press, 2008).

67 *Trinidad Guardian*, 26 February 1949, p. 1.

68 Barnes, 'Face of the Nation', p. 293.

69 *Trinidad Guardian*, 26 February 1949, p. 1.

70 The currency of the Eastern Antilles was undergoing successive waves of change during this period, but it is likely that the figure given was amassed in the Eastern Caribbean dollar.

71 'Carnival Queen Show' (Souvenir Programme), p. 19.

72 *Trinidad Guardian*, 1 March 1949, p. 7.

73 *Trinidad Guardian*, 28 January 1950, p. 13.

74 *Trinidad Guardian*, 27 February 1949, p. 6.

75 Ibid.

76 *Trinidad Guardian*, 4 February 1954, p. 1.

77 *Trinidad Guardian*, 15 February 1956, p. 8.

78 Braithwaite, 'Social Stratification', p. 115.

79 Richard Wrightman Fox and TJ Jackson Lears, 'Introduction' in Fox and Lears (eds), *The Culture of Consumption: Critical Essays in American History, 1880–1980* (New York: Pantheon, 1983), pp. vii–xvii.

80 Franco, 'Dressing up and Looking Good', p. 91.

81 See for instance Ivor Oxaal's mention of the powerful effect that PNM leader Eric Williams's oratory on African heritage had on middle-class audiences, in *Black Intellectuals Come to Power, the Rise of Creole Nationalism in Trinidad and Tobago* (Cambridge, Mass: Schenkmann, 1968), p. 100.

82 Carnival historian Errol Hill ruminated on the putative link between grand aristocratic masquerade balls of the nineteenth century and the 'Carnival Queen' competition some generations later. Errol Hill, *The Trinidad Carnival: Mandate for National Theatre* (London: New Beacon, 1997), p. 102.

83 'Carnival 1954 Souvenir Programme', p. 5.

84 *Trinidad Guardian*, 1 February 1959, p. 10.

85 Carnival Souvenir Programmes, from 1951 to 1955.

86 *Trinidad Guardian*, 3 February 1956, p. 2.

87 Victoria Pasley (Unpublished PhD thesis), 'Gender, Race and Class in Urban Trinidad: Representations in the Construction and Maintenance of the Gender Order 1960–1980', University of Houston, (1999), p. 80.

88 *Trinidad Guardian*, 25 February 1959, p. 11.

89 Carnival Souvenir Programmes, 1951 to 1955.

90 Though this contribution is widely cited and informative, it has been difficult to contextualise its provenance or the academic affiliation and discipline of the author.

91 Powrie, 'Coloured Middle-Class', p. 231.

92 Segal, 'Race and Colour', pp. 91–92.

93 Powrie, 'Coloured Middle-Class', p. 231.

94 Segal, 'Race and Colour', p. 91.

95 Powrie, 'Coloured Middle-Class', p. 231.

96 Ibid.

97 Lola Young, 'Missing Persons: Fantasising Black Women in Black Skin, White Masks', in Alan Read (ed.), *The Fact of Blackness* (London: Institute of International Visual Arts, 1996), pp. 87–97.

98 Nella Larsen's 1929 novel *Passing* (New York: The Modern Library, 2002) explored this notion of racial transgression, where previously black-identified individuals disappeared into white society.

99 Harvey Neptune, 'White Lies: Race and Sexuality in Occupied Trinidad', *Journal of Colonialism and Colonial History* 2 (2001) //E:\2.1neptune.html (accessed 24 June 2006).

100 Ralph de Boissiere, *Rum and Coca Cola* (Melbourne: Australasian Book Society, 1956).

101 Neptune, 'White Lies'.

102 Ibid.

103 'Trinidad's Carnival provides a "Queen" for Post's "Miss British Caribbean" 1948 Contest', *Caribbean Post* (2) 1948, p. 11.

104 Neptune, 'White Lies'.

105 Rohlehr, *Calypso*, pp. 450–451; *Trinidad Guardian*, 4 February 1954, p. 1.
106 *Port of Spain Gazette*, 8 March 1949, p. 10.
107 Hansard. Legislative Council Debates Fourth and Fifth Sessions of the Eighth Legislature of Trinidad and Tobago (1954), p. 1183.
108 Pearl Marshall was described as 'spice coloured' in the *Port of Spain Gazette*, as cited in Rohlehr, *Calypso*, p. 417, and as a 'stately, statuesque Ebony Venus' in the *Trinidad Guardian* (21 February 1950), p. 11.
109 Hansard. Legislative Council Debates Fourth and Fifth Sessions of the Eighth Legislature of Trinidad and Tobago, (1954), p. 1183.
110 Neptune, *Caliban*, p. 47.
111 Michael Anthony, *Parade of the Carnivals of Trinidad 1839–1989* (Port of Spain: Circle, 1989), p. 206.
112 *Port of Spain Gazette*, 28 February, 1954, p. 1.
113 The CIC was commissioned to investigate the disorder and proposed a number of restrictions only some of which were imposed.
114 *Port of Spain Gazette*, 23 January 1954, p. 1.
115 Hansard. Legislative Council Debates Fourth and Fifth Sessions of the Eighth Legislature of Trinidad and Tobago, p. 1172.
116 *Trinidad Guardian*, 2 March 1954, p. 1.
117 Ibid., p. 2.
118 Ibid., p. 1. See also Vera Kutzinski *Sugar's Secrets: Race and the Erotics of Cuban Nationalism* (Charlottesville: University of Virginia Press, 1994).
119 Donald Hill, *Calypso Callaloo: Early Carnival Music in Trinidad* (Gainsville: University of Florida Press, 1993), p. 104.
120 Raymond Quevedo, (Atilla the Hun) *Atilla's Kaiso: A Short Story of Trinidad Calypso* (St Augustine: University of the West Indies, 1983) pp. 126–127.
121 Ibid.
122 Calypsonian The Mighty Zebra is reputed to have also complained of 'Carnival Queen' along similar lines although no records could be found.
123 Smith, 'Gender in Calypso', pp. 36–39; on this subject see also Patricia Mohammed, 'A Blueprint for Gender in Creole Trinidad: Exploring Gender Mythology through Calypsos of the 1920s and 1930s', in Linden Lewis (ed.), *The Culture of Gender and Sexuality in the Caribbean* (Gainesville: University of Florida Press, 2003), pp. 129–168.
124 Rohlehr, *Calypso*, pp. 243–250.
125 *Port of Spain Gazette*, 8 February 1956, p. 1.
126 *Trinidad Guardian*, 15 February 1956, p. 8.
127 Ibid.
128 Ibid.
129 Rohlehr, *Calypso*, p. 431.
130 'New Career for West Indians', *Spotlight* 17 (1956), p. 21.
131 Ibid.
132 Barry, *Femininity*, p. 119.
133 'New Career', *Spotlight*, p. 22.
134 Ibid.
135 Ibid.
136 Barry, *Femininity*, pp. 115–116.

137 *New York Age*, 24 August 1957, p. 1.
138 Hansard. Legislative Council Debates First Session of the Ninth Legislature of Trinidad and Tobago. (1956–1957), pp. 911–913; De Freitas, 'Playing Mas', p. 118.
139 Rohlehr, *Calypso*, p. 449.
140 Barnes, 'Face of the Nation', p. 290.
141 Quoted in Rohlehr, *Calypso*, pp. 451–452.
142 Hansard. Legislative Council Debates First Session of the Ninth Legislature of Trinidad and Tobago. (1956–1957), p. 911.
143 Ibid.
144 Hansard. Legislative Council Debates Third Session of the Ninth Legislature of Trinidad and Tobago. (1958–1959), p. 512.
145 Ibid.
146 Hansard. Legislative Council Debates Fifth session of the Ninth Legislature Trinidad and Tobago. (1960–1961), pp. 2367–2368.
147 *Trinidad Guardian*, 3 February 1959.
148 Ibid.
149 'Carnival Queen Show' (Souvenir Magazine), 1964, p. 19.
150 *Trinidad Guardian*, 12 February 1961, p. 17.
151 Herman Bennet, 'The Challenge to the Post-Colonial State: A Case Study of the February Revolution in Trinidad', in Franklin W Knight and Colin A Palmer (eds), *The Modern Caribbean* (Chapel Hill: University of North Carolina Press, 1989), pp. 129–146.
152 *Trinidad Guardian*, 22 February 1971, p. 1.
153 'Trinidad Carnival and Calypso 1964 – What's On' (Souvenir Guide, published by the CDC 1964). In the protests of the late 1960s the beauty competition was referred to as the Jaycees queen.

3

Parading the 'crème de la crème': constructing the contest in Barbados, 1958–66

THE 'Carnival Queen' beauty competition began in Barbados in 1958 and was modelled after its lucrative Trinidadian equivalent. Anglican Barbados did not have an annual carnival celebration before 1958. The organisers of the 'Carnival Queen' competition, the newly formed Barbados chapter of the Junior Chamber of Commerce (Jaycees), invented a carnival, consisting primarily of the music, dance and glamour of the 'Carnival Queen Show'. The beauty competition formed the centrepiece of this show and featured the usual parades of young women contestants in glitzy, carnivalesque costume, and upper-middle-class judges awarding prizes and accolades.[1] The programme hosted performers from Barbados's fledgling entertainment industry, which came to be regarded, along with the glamour of the beauty contest, as a mark of Barbadian economic and cultural development, and a source of national pride. By 1958 the growth of beauty competitions in the wider Caribbean, into large-scale events with thousand-strong audiences, was well under way. Within this context, the Barbados 'Carnival Queen' competition was relatively late in coming, but quickly developed into the sort of grand event also enjoyed in Trinidad and Jamaica at this time, and could also boast audiences in the thousands.[2]

This chapter brings into focus the performativity of the beauty contest and considers particularly how modern, cultured beauty was imagined and constructed by its central agents, organisers and contestants. It examines the role of the Jaycees, a youth movement favoured by socially aspirant men, in organising the contests; crucially the Jaycees paired business sponsors to beauty candidates, and considers the experiences of candidates, tasked with delivering idealised femininity on the national stage. It also examines what happened when this process, of making displays of ideal femininity, was seen to lapse, as in the 1964 'Miss Ebony' competition, which was denounced as a failure and resulted in a booing fracas as the candidates were rejected by a racist audience. The chapter particularly draws upon the oral testimony of three former organisers, and four former beauty contestants who appeared in the main beauty show in its various incarnations as 'Carnival Queen', 'Festival Queen' and 'Miss Independence', and in the new 'Miss Ebony' show, between 1958 and 1966, the year of Barbadian independence from the British.

Background to Barbados

Barbados, not unlike the Bahamas and Bermuda, has been and continues to be discursively constructed as a distinctively English corner of the British Atlantic Empire. And yet, concurrently, Barbados (in common with the Bahamas and Bermuda) grew infamous among black West Indians and visitors for the extent of its racism and social stratification.[3] As political analyst Gordon Lewis observed in 1968, Barbados was simultaneously derided and admired for its supposedly English national character. 'Barbados', Lewis wrote, 'is an English market town, Cheltenham . . . with tropical overtones'.[4] Barbados was ruled by 'a white plantocracy proverbial for its reactionary conceit'.[5] Ironically, visiting Colonial Secretary Sir Cosmo Parkinson remarked in a report in 1942 that only revolution would resolve Barbados's extreme social stratification, which represented a huge bar to its economic progress.[6] Barbados's reputation among whites also meant that Barbados served as a beacon of white privilege to white minorities living elsewhere in the British Caribbean. It was, for example, the preferred place to educate elite children in the southern Caribbean, when schooling in Europe was no longer a viable option.[7] Social apartheid in Barbados was so legendary that it became the defining element of travel writer Wenzell Brown's description of the island in 1947. Brown toured the Caribbean basin pronouncing it a 'cauldron' of exoticism, malcontent and upheaval. Brown related a number of incidents of black anger directed towards him during visits to other islands, which he viewed, tantalisingly, as signs of a simmering racial pot that threatened to boil over on America's southern frontier. However, Brown's brief account of Barbados labelled it, somewhat blandly, as the 'Focus of racial discrimination' in the Caribbean. Completely absent were the tales of muscular black aggression that dotted accounts of other islands. So much was Barbados the seat of snobbishness and segregation, wrote Brown, that even he, a white American visitor, was barred from a certain social club, for not possessing the correct membership.[8] ' "Bimshire" is the mocking name which the Barbadians have given to their island. With a combination of irritation and pride, they point out that it is a "Little England" transplanted to the Caribbean.'[9]

Historian Mary Chamberlain has revealed some of the hysteria with which wealthy white Barbadians guarded their lifestyle and balked at the threat of democratisation as independence drew nearer, in this example of a letter by Mrs G. Skinner to the Rt. Hon. Oliver Stanley, Secretary for the Colonies in 1943:

> It is all very well for white people safe in their white country, with flowing words and a magnificent gesture of democracy, to sweep away the Colour bar and decided *for us* that the dear African shall be our brothers and associates. But how would these Democrats react if they lived in a small island populated by white and African people. Would they sit and rejoice to see their young white daughters dancing cheek to cheek with a woolly haired coloured boy? Would they rejoice to see their sons marry a chocolate-coloured African girl and bring that abomination, the little Half-cast into the world? [Original emphasis].[10]

To better understand the context for contesting racialised femininities in Barbados it is necessary to contextualise the Barbadian colonial regime, which so much affirmed white domination whilst simultaneously sublimating race.

Barbados experienced a long continuous period of British colonialism, which dated back to 1625. The colony maintained a stable white population to the extent that, unusually for colonial context, women sometimes outnumbered men during periods of its history, and the numerous white populace did not tend towards absenteeism as was the case in other islands.[11] The elite exercised monopolistic control over both planting and the merchant trade.[12] Barbados's geographical position, an easterly outlier of the string of the islands of the Antilles, made it strategically important to the slave trade and the British navy, and as a result Barbados was heavily militarised, making organised slave resistance more difficult.[13] Barbadian topography was probably also significant. The island's relatively flat and open landscape made slave escape and marronage harder still. Against this background of heavy militarisation and a large white community, slave life was dominated by the struggle for survival and self-preservation and rebellions, though they did occur, were infrequent and brutally repressed.[14]

Such was the economic domination of the Barbadian plantocracy that Barbados retained bicameral representative government after emancipation in 1838, and even after the Morant Bay Rebellion in Jamaica of 1865, which prompted the British to impose more restrictive Crown Colony government or similar elsewhere in their Caribbean territories. Whilst propertied whites in Jamaica and Trinidad willingly sacrificed their vote, rather than see a small but increasing number of free men of colour enter the propertied franchise, and risk that browns would ally themselves to free blacks, in Barbados such sacrifice was unnecessary because the wholly elected House of Assembly, was so completely dominated by white interests. Few people of colour ever qualified for the franchise before universal suffrage in 1950.[15]

Agrarian life was almost entirely dominated by the sugar crop. After emancipation planters grabbed any remaining Barbadian land, leaving freed persons only tiny patches of land rented from estates for use as 'subsistence gardens'.[16] There were no reserves of public land, known as Crown Lands, available for freed persons to buy. Thus Barbados lacked the conditions for a partially independent peasantry to develop as it did in Jamaica. Nor was indentured labour required in Barbados. In Barbados especially, labour was so abundant, and overcrowding so acute, that seasonal and long-term overseas migration, amongst both professionals and labourers, became the norm.[17]

However, Barbados did experience currents of radicalism and resistance against enslavement and colonialism. The most significant slave uprising was the 1816 rebellion led by Bussa, thought to be precipitated by the combined effects of revolution in Haiti, the abolition of the British slave trade in 1807 and the rise of the anti-slavery movement.[18] After emancipation, rioting against poverty broke out in the 1860s and 1870s. The elite responded by voting more money for religious and moral programmes to pacify the poor and increase their domination over them.[19] As conditions worsened with the long-term decline of sugar prices into the twentieth century, Barbadians of colour continued to organise. The UNIA reportedly had as many as eleven chapters in Barbados between the 1920s and the 1940s.[20] During the labour rebellions of the 1930s, Barbados experienced a sustained period of uprising from July 1937 that resulted in the formation of the Barbados Progressive League (later the Barbados Labour Party) in 1938, headed by future premier Grantley Adams. However, many agitators were deported or imprisoned in the aftermath of July 1937, and the path towards self-government continued with Adams securing dominant leadership over both the trade union movement and the constitutional reform movement.[21]

This radical activity was sustained in part by the effects of Barbadian migration within the Caribbean basin, especially to the Isthmus of Panama, where, in the first two decades of the twentieth century, West Indians met and organised in solidarity as they laboured on the American Panama Canal project. Migration itself, the act of asserting one's mobility, was a form of resistance against the Barbadian regime, and one that many took up. Historian Bonham Richardson describes migration as an established tradition amongst Barbadians, both middle and lower-class, by 1900.[22] Previous generations had exported their labour since the postemancipation era. Barbadians worked throughout the Caribbean as teachers, domestics and labourers. In Trinidad female Barbadian domestics were a highly politicised group at the forefront of the labour movement to the extent that the 'Bajan Cook' became its own Carnival masquerade.[23] Reputedly Barbadians were preferred for skilled and domestic work for their spoken English, which was less creolised with French and other languages than the Trinidadian vernacular. Barbadians were recruited in large numbers to the police service in Port of Spain. However, tellingly, they were also labelled insolent, litigious and given to criminality by elites who accused them of being greedy for high wages. Furthermore Barbadians' familiarity with the parliamentary system, their attempts to influence elections, even if they could not exercise a vote, saw them branded as socialist troublemakers. These reports not only reveal the ways in which elites tried to deter solidarity between subalterns based on notions of distinct national characteristics, they also trouble the picture of the passive black Barbadian, unconcerned with resistance or organising.[24] Thus, as cultural critic Linden Lewis has pointed out, formulations of the quintessentially 'English', orderly and compliant, character of brown and black Barbadians are obviously problematic. They reveal not only the success of colonial ideology in masking and suppressing dissent, but they also help to submerge the complexities of Barbadian colonial experience.[25]

Within this context there were few opportunities for social mobility, besides leaving the island, and in the main, an exceptionally rigid class-colour hierarchy thrived.[26] Even with outward migration, population density in Barbados was, at 1096 persons per square metre, five or six times the density of other British Caribbean islands in 1896 and remained the highest in the Caribbean at least until 1921.[27] Planter-merchant monopolisation of the economy continued unabated in the twentieth century. Gordon Lewis has remarked that it was highly anomalous for the brown Wilson family to finally breach in the 1940s the so-called 'Big Six' circle of six white families who controlled commerce in Bridgetown.[28] The 'Big Six', consolidated as the Barbados Shipping and Trading Company Ltd in 1921. They represented the wealthiest core of endogamous white families of the Barbadian upper-class.[29] This diverged from other colonies, including Jamaica and Trinidad, where a middling strata, made up especially of formerly indentured labourers of Chinese and Portuguese descent and similarly ostracised groups, such as Syrians, were gradually becoming influential in the retail industry by the mid-twentieth century. Instead in Barbados the middle-class were still largely concentrated in the lower strata of civil-service and professional work, especially teaching.[30] Lowly as it was, such non-labouring work in the Colonial Civil Service was still hard to obtain. As historian Mary Chamberlain has evidenced, expatriate and sometimes local whites were favoured for the running of the civil service, and black applicants with the Cambridge certificate of secondary education and excellent references could be casually humiliated in the search for a position.[31]

Antoinette Burton reminds us that colonial hegemonies are 'unfinished business'.[32] However, in the case of Barbados it is perhaps unsurprising that the typical instruments of colonial hegemony, the Church, education, sport, and especially mutual-aid societies and the masonic lodge, played a doubly important role. These institutions were used to reinforce hegemony from above, but they were also used by the disenfranchised to challenge this process: to assert solidarity, resist poverty and affect some meagre social mobility. In the first decade of the twentieth century, the Friendly Society movement was established with remittances from labourers on the Panama Canal. The societies, which were run and maintained by the working-classes, allowed for micro-savings, insurance against sickness, and funeral expenses. Societies also sought to establish land cooperatives, but in 1905 the Friendly Societies Act was passed by the colonial government, thus making it illegal for societies to hold more than one acre of land, which, as Hilary Beckles writes, immediately curtailed the potential of the movement for land redistribution. In spite of this, the Friendly Society movement grew, and had nearly 100,000 members by 1946.[33]

Another example of working-class organising was the Landship movement. Based on the classifications of naval hierarchy, the landships were mutual-aid associations formed by black working-class men and women, which emphasised dignity and competence and became renowned for their preoccupation with hierarchy, dress and composure. Though members were mocked for this fastidiousness, Richardson argues that landships represented a response to the depression of the 1920s and in general symbolised working-class strategies for acclimatising to proletarianisation.[34]

Aviston Downes's study of elite secondary education in Barbados reveals that schooling was designed to sustain the dominance of white ruling-class masculinity. For a minority of African-Barbadian boys admitted to secondary school, it helped shape them as 'boys of empire', developing in them an association between masculinity and socio-political dominance, of which paradoxically, they would not partake. Education, though posited by government as a 'meritocratic instrument of social justice, mobility and cultural "refinement"', in fact aimed to sustain class-colour hierarchy and to manufacture loyal colonial citizens.[35]

Within this context of the sublimation of race whilst being socialised into self-improvement and the myth of meritocracy, the significance of the Jaycees movement in Barbados is crucial. The Jaycees represented the spirit of self-help social-organising, and the promise of social ascription. Though the movement tended to target the lower-classes for its work, rather than welcome them into its ranks, for the determined few well-educated, middling young men of colour, the Jaycees represented a path to upward social mobility and respectability.

The Jaycees

The Jaycees movement sprang from the progressive reform movement in the early twentieth-century United States. It began in St Louis, Missouri, in the 1910s, as the Young Men's Progressive Civic Association and later became affiliated with that city's Chamber of Commerce. It was otherwise known as the Junior Chamber, or Junior Citizens, which became JCs or Jaycees. The Jaycees was a youth movement principally for men aged 21 to 40, though women also formed partner chapters of Jaycettes. Their core tenet was that young men (primarily) ought to participate in civic life for the greater good. In 1944 the Junior Chamber International (JCI) was established in Mexico City and spurred a proliferation of new Jaycees' chapters throughout the Caribbean. By 1964 there were ten chapters in the Anglophone Caribbean alone.[36]

The Jaycees operated as a benevolent society. Its members gained training for leadership by providing aid to the 'the indigent poor' and by fundraising for public works projects, through not-for-profit business initiatives.[37] In attending to the poor and underemployed in the Caribbean, the Jaycees not only engendered their own upward social mobility, but aimed to encourage so-called social uplift among the lower-classes. This good citizenship coalesced with contemporary development policy in the wake of the report of the Moyne Commission into West Indian poverty and malcontent in 1945. The Barbados Jaycees adopted the international movement's liberal creed:

> [T]o know a purpose to life, to find peace in brotherhood: to have
> a fair share of the material wealth of the world: to establish justice in
> the administration of government: to seek recognition of the intrinsic
> worth and dignity of each individual: and to achieve a sense of accom-
> plishment in their own personal lives.[38]

The Barbados Jaycees were founded with the help of Conrad O'Brien of the Trinidad Jaycees. O'Brien was prominent in the organisation and would later serve as the overall president of the international movement. As a mark of his affluent background, O'Brien had enjoyed childhood holidays in Barbados, and remained a regular visitor to the island. In 1957 he joined with Barbadian friends to form the Barbados chapter. The Barbados Jaycees exemplified civic pride and patriotism. They drew wide public admiration, as was reflected in the tributes heaped upon them in the upper-middle-class journal *The Bajan*. They were praised for organising a successful trade fair in 1962, donating $85,000 to the new University College, and founding a lottery, which by 1962 had donated funds to the disabled and provided for a refrigerated blood bank.[39] However, one of the Jaycees' first fundraising initiatives was the 'Carnival Queen' beauty competition, founded in 1958. It was a close copy of the Trinidadian beauty competition, which the Jaycees were bound to restore in Trinidad after its brief suspension by the new PNM government in the same year.

Not only did the Barbados Jaycees enjoy a soaring reputation for good work, but their 'Carnival Queen' competition was born at a time when the Jaycees were earning additional credit as the most competent managers of contentious beauty contests elsewhere in the West Indies and even beyond.[40] They appeared even-handed, and professional. The Jaycees claimed a special authority because they were an ideal alloy: they combined the commercial imperative of contest sponsors, and the respectability of middle-class audiences, who were prominently engaged by the question of fixing the national image, and therefore seemed to reconcile the disparity and potential for confrontation between the two. In Trinidad the Jaycees assumed the management of the 'Carnival Queen' contest, *after* the conflict between the boycotting artists, the new PNM government, and the *Trinidad Guardian*. In Jamaica, the widely admired Jaycees would oversee the running of the 'Miss Jamaica' contest *after* independence, when the colour-bar to the competition had ostensibly been lifted, a handful of brown winners had claimed the crown and the competition as a result was gaining wide approval, including that of government. The respectable, pro-commerce, patriotic Jaycees therefore seemed to offer steady stewardship after heightened moments of contention in the process of decolonisation, a stewardship that was (falsely) imagined as above politics and without conflict.

Parading the 'crème de la crème': how to run a beauty competition . . .

One of the founding members of the Barbados Jaycees was Marcus Jordan, a black man with a professional career as an insurance clerk.

Jordan helped to oversee the organisation of the first 'Carnival Queen' show in 1958. The competition was founded in the same year as the Barbados Board of Tourism, and was very likely encouraged by the new board. The first competition was won by a white woman, Sally Ann Mackie. The significance of Mackie's win was probably to establish the primacy and popularity of the beauty contest amongst a conservative middle-class. Before 'Carnival Queen', Barbados had very few beauty contests and no annual, national event on a par with 'Miss Jamaica' or the 'Carnival Queen' competition. Nor had it been a part of Webster's 'Miss British Caribbean' enterprise. Hence it lacked the public tradition of whites-only beauty competitions that had developed elsewhere. If Mackie's involvement, before a racially mixed audience, brought disavowal from the most conservative quarters of white opinion, in this most segregated of British colonies, it also signalled to the brown middle-class audience that the 'Carnival Queen' competition was a 'serious' affair.

At around the same time, other smaller beauty contests began to appear on the cultural scene. In 1958 the apparently short-lived 'Miss Tropics Figure' competition was won by 'olive-skinned' Margaret Skinner. Skinner worked as a clerk in a jewellery shop in Broad Street, the island's primary shopping street, which detail placed her near the top in the pigmentocracy of store-front employment in Bridgetown.[41] Later, in the 1960s the Barbados Civil Service Association, the trade union of public employees, would launch its own beauty competition, offering modest prizes to the generally darker Afro-Barbadian women who, in growing numbers, staffed the civil service as nurses and teachers.[42]

However, the tenure of white-identified 'Carnival Queen' winners was very short, lasting only a few years, before a 'watershed' in 1963 after which brown-identified winners became the norm and white participants, especially upper-class whites, were few thereafter. Linden Lewis has remarked upon the retreat of white Barbadians from public cultural institutions, especially in sport, the most obvious example being cricket, as they slowly, one-by-one, desegregated in the postcolonial era.[43] The scarcity of white participants in Barbados surely reflects the extent of snobbery and segregation in the island, but it also reflects the more subtle contours of the Barbadian racial and cultural conflict. White-creole identity, so assured in its primacy in 'Little England', had not produced a public beauty competition as in Jamaica and Trinidad, instead the job had been left to middle-class nationalism, though nationalists trod a careful path seeking white patronage for the competition in the form of commercial sponsorship.

Furthermore, the general lack of beauty competitions in Barbados also reflects Barbados's more muted experience of the cultural nationalism that was engaging other West Indian societies, fed by subaltern activism and artistic movements. Barbados also lacked a significant entertainment sector of the kind growing elsewhere in the region, for the pleasure of middle-class consumers and North American tourists alike. Like Trinidad and Jamaica, Barbados had experienced an American wartime presence of military personnel, and this had stimulated growth in a market for formal middle-brow entertainment. However, its tourism industry was little developed after the war, and was limited to a small number of very wealthy tourists who wintered on the island, and the inter-island movement of holidaying white-creoles.[44] In the late 1950s tourist-geared entertainment was limited to a handful of nightclubs and hotel bars, the foremost of these being Club Morgan and Coconut Creek. Notably these clubs attracted touring performers from islands better known for their cultural life, as *The Bajan* reported, almost apologetically, in 1964:

> [T]he night clubs in Barbados have never been able to attract or find within its own boundaries entertainers of the calibre to be found in Havana, Kingston, Port of Spain or San Juan, yet some of the 'discoveries' made by Frank Morgan at his nightclub and by Jack Teller at Coconut Creek have reached laudably high standards as entertainers and are still being warmly applauded at new nightclubs and hotels in Barbados.[45]

Deferential reference to the capitals of other Caribbean islands, from Cuba to Puerto Rico, and the relative success of those cities in sustaining paying audiences for cultural entertainment, reflects the greater confidence in these islands in formulations of 'national culture' that had their origins in abundant so-called 'folk' life. Elsewhere businessmen were able to exploit cultural products which were the result of the less successful suppression of racial and cultural identity, and the vivacity of the cultural revolution, renaissance and refinement led by middle-class nationalists and artists. Barbados's perceived failure to compete in the entertainment sector was the result of the lopsidedness of the creolisation process that made the public expression of African-Creole culture, let alone affirmative celebration of this culture, so rare in Barbados.

A sample of the club acts described by *The Bajan* reveals the prevalence of limbo, calypso, striptease, burlesque and novelty dance or comic acts, and a general lack of anything that celebrated Barbadian cultural originality. Instead they revealed the familiar flesh trade between black performers, male and female, often scantily clad, and white consumers.

This often repeated scene that played throughout the postemancipation New World, tells the story of the black body that has been racialised as primordially comic, hypersexed and athletic. For its part *The Bajan* reflected and validated this othering relationship, with front covers, which (until the 1970s), either glorified in the beauty and luxury represented by tanned blonde tourists or romanticised the Barbadian 'folk' as market traders and costumed performers. 'Carnival Queen', though no less derivative in its content than nightclub entertainment, was a rare and audaciously successful addition to a fledgling market for commercial entertainment in Barbados.

In 1964 Jordan ascended to the role of President of the Barbados Jaycees, making him their first black leader, albeit in an avowedly apolitical organisation that did not expressly target racial prejudice, but more opaquely prized 'brotherhood', and defused the question of racial solidarity by emphasising individual achievement. Nonetheless, Jordan's appointment seemed politically expedient, at a time when brown and black leadership in government, while constrained by the overwhelming power of white capital, was becoming essential window-dressing as Barbados neared independence from Britain.[46] Jordan was an anomalous figure. Not only was he employed in the private rather than the public sector, he was surrounded, within the Jaycees' leadership and patronage, by more socially assured whites and browns.

In an interview Jordan described how the organisation of the 'Carnival Queen' beauty competition involved selecting suitable candidates and pairing them with business sponsors. Jordan provided an image of an early beauty contest that relied on networks of influential and obliging white people from the business elite. The female contestants, according to Jordan, were guided and advised by their sponsors in the city, on the points of good conduct. The Jaycees solicited sponsors by carrying photographs of the prospective contestants around to city firms: 'The queens were to a great extent selected and advised by the companies in the city . . . They selected their queens, they had their photographs, everything. But they did not necessarily select only white queens. They selected coloured queens as well.'[47] Here Jordan uses the term 'coloured', as it was sometimes used, to describe a wider African-descended population, rather than to describe only the mixed-raced population more typically referred to as 'coloured'. In fact epithets of skin tone in Barbados extended to 'light skin, dark skin, brown skin, high brown, yellow, red, grey-goose and snuffy', and many more besides.[48] However, Jordan's application of the term coloured is also deliberately ambiguous. Of the African-descended women in the competition during Jordan's tenure, all were light-skinned, of mixed ancestry, and would have been described as brown or 'red', i.e. coloured in the mixed-raced sense, and certainly would not have been called dark-skinned or black-identified. In his description of the contest, therefore, Jordan is doubly denying the racial system in Barbados as reflected in 'Carnival Queen'; neither was his beauty competition racist, nor was there an absence of 'black' bodies within the competition. By denying the category of 'blackness' Jordan is then able to deny the missing dark-skinned women in the 'Carnival Queen' parade.

Fellow Jaycee Frank Hunte, a very light-skinned Barbadian of mixed ancestry, described to me how, as the contest became more established, he took over special responsibility for canvassing for contestants and liaising with businesses to secure sponsorship. Hunte emphasised the importance of networking in promoting the beauty competition as a viable advertising venture for firms:

> If you know people you try to sell them the idea that they are going to get something out of it, because . . . to attract sponsors you have to make sure that they are getting something out of it. So you go around to . . . various individuals . . . [Y]ou would have a network. Remember it's an organisation; I might have my network from a lot of members, some of the other members would have their networks and they would know business people. Actually my company did sponsor one of those two, I can't remember the year I think it was 1966 that my company sponsored one of the [contestants].[49]

In both accounts the beauty competition brought Jaycee members into contact with more powerful businessmen, and allowed them to ingratiate themselves as charitable workers, thus providing opportunities to gain respect and upward social mobility.

Interviews with former beauty contestants Marvo Manning CBE, Betty Hill, Claudette Pickering and Millie Small, helped to build a picture of the process of candidate selection. All four women described being pursued and cajoled by contest organisers to put themselves forward as beauty candidates. The contestants were required to deliver an accomplished performance of Barbadian femininity throughout the contest. This idealised performance was marked from the outset and enhanced through training as part of the competition. At the point of selection would-be contestants betrayed modesty rather than confidence, which would have seemed 'forward' and out of place with social convention. However, in Hill's particularly reserved narrative, the attentions paid to her by the Jaycees bordered on mild harassment. Hill was frequently called at home and advised that should she enter the competition, success might lead to her participation in the other regional competitions and beyond that, 'Miss World'. But, although she eventually agreed to take part, Hill, who was identified by another contestant variously as 'white' and 'near-white', was aware that her family disapproved of beauty contests, and during the interview she referred repeatedly to a general snobbishness and prudishness in society towards beauty competitions.[50]

In her interview Marvo Manning denied her own beauty queen credentials, but nevertheless was well-placed to be selected by the Jaycees. Manning had a friendly association and working relationship with Jaycees' members through her membership and one-time presidency of the female branch, the Jaycettes. Manning was also a dedicated member of a youth theatre group, in which she acted and danced, and her aptitude for confidence on stage leant itself to the 'Carnival Queen' spectacle. Manning was ambitious, confident and fortunate, in an island saturated with ready labour, to be light-skinned and grammar-schooled. She had held the full range of respectable clerical and sales jobs for a light-skinned middle-class young woman before taking her opportunity as a beauty queen. Manning had joined the civil service as post office mistress, worked in a Broad Street department store (Fogarty's) and was employed at the Bank of Nova Scotia in Broad Street, when she was canvassed by the Jaycees. Though understandably frustrated by these uninspiring job options, Manning nonetheless belonged to a relatively elite stratum of employed women, and enjoyed the sort of highly visible 'prestige' that was still reserved for light-skinned and white women. In contrast, the majority of Barbadian women were employed as seamstresses, domestics or in agricultural labour, with a growing secondary-educated minority finding respectable professional work as teachers and, in particular, as nurses.[51]

Manning described how she was visited at work on alternate days by the Jaycees' canvasser, armed with photographs of all the prospective candidates involved in the process, but Manning demurred time and again, insisting that she was 'too short'.[52] Eventually the manager of Fogarty's, her former employer and prospective sponsor, declared that he would not sponsor any of the other candidates showed to him by the Jaycees except Manning, and that if she would not agree, he would withdraw from the competition: 'And I said well, gee that's very nice, but I don't want to go. So then Timothy called me at the Scotia Bank, he said "Marvo", he was English . . . He was a very beautiful English [school] master. Anyway, he convinced me to go in so I went, and the rest is history.'[53] Key to Manning's narrative is the influence of the charming English schoolmaster, who by virtue of his status as a British national, had special purchase over standards of proper respectable conduct. Insular and overcrowded Barbadian society did not seem to reward confident, ambitious young women who stepped outside of the dictates of respect-ability. As Hill revealed, part of the reason for the dearth in beauty con-tests in Barbados was the general disapproval of more affluent families who did not consider them a suitable experience for their daughters. However, with the English schoolmaster's assurance that taking part in a beauty contest would not be outlandish or audacious on her part, Manning could go ahead confidently.

Evidently the process of making the beauty competition involved some careful calculations on all sides as to who best fitted the parade. The Jaycees' canvassing work revealed the dilemmas of the prospective female candidates, who were acutely aware of the censures against 'forwardness' within respectable femininity, and had to weigh these against the attractions of the contest, and felt obliged to affect demureness even as they accepted the invitation to take part. Then there were the city firms who seemed not to be concerned with asserting white-creole nationalism, but made tactical decisions over which woman to charge with represent-ing their organisation, and in the process bought advertising exposure for their brand. The dilemma of the business sponsor revealed the con-stitutive elements of idealised femininity, a matrix in which race was foremost but affected and altered by other determining factors such as family background, education and speech, social accomplishments and deportment. Not least there were the Jaycees themselves who portrayed not only the good citizenship which might ratify them as public men, but also a certain connoisseurship in facilitating the beauty contest, which revealed that they were on terms with contemporary, middle-class social standards of feminine desirability and good taste.[54] Reflecting on his role in this process Marcus Jordan returned to the theme of even-handed colour-blindness in the firms' selection of candidates:

> [T]he carnival queens were all sponsored by various firms in the city. And they were among the crème de la crème of society in that day. It had nothing to do with race. They were coloured and they were white and they were, oh just every race was represented, but they were certainly of the crème de la crème of society. We didn't have just any old person representing us in the beauty contest . . . She represented the nation. She represented Barbados in many respects.[55]

For Jordan and other Jaycees who acted in the making of the 'Carnival Queen', black political leadership and white business domination were not two elements in contention, but reconcilable forces that could be navigated with diplomacy for the good of national destiny. The 'crème de la crème' are mythologised, in Jordan's account, as a core multiracial cadre, but in effect were drawn from the middle and upper middle-classes, who were, almost by definition light-skinned. The few women who qualified for the performative standards of idealised femininity and were read by the Jaycees as beautiful were tasked with performing indispensable public relations work for the emerging nation. In the year of her win Marvo Manning undertook a publicity tour in the United States with representatives of the Barbados Tourist Board.[56] As fourth runner-up Claudette Pickering attended many formal evening receptions with other finalists, where she met public dignitaries and tourists, and enjoyed highly visible prizes, including a stay in an expensive hotel, normally reserved for visiting whites.[57]

According to Hunte the competition had wide appeal among audiences across the class-colour spectrum; it was popular with 'black, white, [the] in-between'.[58] Pickering described her popularity with people as she walked through the streets of Bridgetown after the competition, in which she finished fourth. They would shout 'you're still my favourite'.[59] This corroborates the notion of a wide audience for 'Carnival Queen' to some extent. However, it does not confirm that working-class black people purchased tickets for the show itself; rather that they may have been engaged by its wider publicity and fanfare, and took advantage of opportunities to view the contestants when they made glamorous public appearances as part of the extension of the ticketed 'Carnival'. However, Hunte was more willing to concede the middle-class bias in the selection of the female candidates. The image that emerges is of a decidedly bourgeois contest, in which the 'crème de la crème' of Jordan's account were the most esteemed 'young ladies' of middle-class society who could be persuaded to participate. Hunte emphasised certain competencies that a well-educated, accomplished young woman could bring to the contest:

> [Y]ou're out there in the public, it's not only a question of beauty . . . , it's a mixture of beauty, you have to do some talking when you go on stage. They'll ask you some questions and . . . you want to be intelligent, you want to give some intelligent answers. So I think that from that point of view it would have attracted [middle-class women]. And not only that, I think now, you'll find that shows *now* would attract people from all classes, in that you find that people are more aware, they can handle themselves better . . . maybe a question of education, over time you see these shows [changed], I'm sure you know that it would be a little different now. We didn't go along race lines or class lines or anything like that.[60]

Aside from seeking an assured, confident performance of cultured, modern femininity, which in spite of the repeated denials of organisers was class-bound and race-bound, the competition also brought with it a reciprocal element. Like Jordan, who suggested the candidates were tutored in good conduct by the firms themselves, Hunte suggests the contest had a role in *improving* the women involved:

> With a beauty show there are two things you're trying to achieve: [to] develop a young person, a young lady, because that's part of it too, you have to be a sort of relatively brave young lady to say you're going to join in a [beauty contest] ... because what you are doing, you're putting yourself before the public. So in that way you are sort of developing people too.[61]

Thus the women chosen for their accomplishments and eloquence in the bourgeois feminine mould would only become more so in the process of performing for the nation. The contest had a role in further constituting the female participants as ideal women worthy of national applause, and in turn improved by the national gaze. The black village headteacher in Lamming's *In the Castle of My Skin*, reflects upon delivering a class-bound ideal to his audience, a village of peasants whose surveillance of him conditions and directs his conduct: 'The village teacher represented an unattainable ideal. He had to live in a way they admired and respected but did not greatly care to follow. He had to think of them in any decision made.'[62] The headteacher's exemplary performance formed part of the diffuse, 100-year-old, civilising mission, but placed him in an impossible bind. Assigned, within the colonial state apparatus, to influence and guide the peasants through his behaviour, the headteacher was meanwhile being critically appraised by the villagers, for the quality of his respectable conduct, even though they were not minded to emulate it. This tension reveals a transcript of the colonial experience and how it situated differently raced, classed and gendered subjects within the hierarchy. This concept of being critically appraised (above, below or sideways) in representing a prescribed and yet largely unspoken ideal is the subject of exploration below, for the women involved in the beauty parade.

Performing the national standard for femininity

'Carnival Queen' crowned Hazel Eastmond in 1963. Eastmond was perhaps the competition's first brown-identified winner, the first winner to be widely considered 'coloured', rather than 'near-white' or 'pass-white', and certainly the competition's darkest winner to that point. Eastmond was widely popular both with organisers and with audiences.[63] Her win appeared as a 'breakthrough' moment for the iconic possibilities of the brown feminine image in Barbados. There followed a string of brown beauty queens, including Marvo Manning in 1964 and the former 'Miss Civil Service Association', Norma Chadderton, in 1966. Manning became the last 'Carnival Queen' before the competition was renamed 'Festival Queen' in 1965 and 'Independence Queen' in 1966, which it remained for some years thereafter.

'Independence Queen' was established as a fixture of the wider national celebration on 30 November, Independence Day. The transition to iconic brown beauty queens coincided with the transition to Barbadian independence, which followed the collapse of the British West Indian Federation in 1961, and Jamaican and Trinidadian independence in 1962. The new brown beauty queens seemed to represent a consensus between the Jaycees, judges, sponsors and audience as to the representative capacity of the brown woman as Barbados entered this new post-independence era. The female contestants, who were both consumers and co-producers of beauty competitions, were tasked with delivering idealised femininity on this national stage. Their commentary offered some insight into the constitutive elements of idealised Barbadian womanhood as prized by the competition.

Claudette Pickering entered the competition in 1966, the year of Chadderton's win. Pickering described her path to the beauty contest within a list of other daring decisions she made as a young woman in search of new experiences. Pickering was an active grammar school student, and served as head girl. Whilst at school she took part in a student exchange to the United States. After leaving school she became a débutante. This aristocratic tradition, historically a means of finding husbands for young women, was then being revived in Barbados amongst the upwardly mobile middle-classes as an ascriptive rite of passage for their own daughters, one that affirmed their accomplishment as feminine and respectable young ladies. However, being a débutante could also be an opportunity. In an interview Pickering recalled it fondly as her 'going out into the world'.[64] Pickering was inspired to enter the beauty contest by its 'breakthrough' icons, Eastmond and Manning:

> [T]hey were very polished women. And they were very intelligent women. They could mix, with any and everybody. And I consider myself an outgoing person. I'm a people's person. All of my jobs have been in contact with people. Like my first job before I was in the show, I worked at a travel agency. And then after a year I went to fly with Pan-Am. I was one of the first Barbadian girls. There was another girl, Dianne King. And we were the two first Barbadian girls to fly with

Pan-Am. . . . She married an Australian. . . . There were a lot of firsts in my life. I was head girl at [The] Foundation [school]. And I left school, and I was a débutante. Which was a big who-ha in those days.[65]

Pickering describes performative skills of the beauty contest that were an extension of skills acquired through grammar school and in the middle-class social world surrounding it. As with poet Una Marson, Marvo Manning, Claudette Pickering and Millie Small were the graduates of elitist colonial schooling that aimed primarily at 'making white ladies'.[66] Since this system socialised them into gender roles that had actually been prefigured as 'white', coloured and black girls at school had to accommodate, to find a means of resolving diametrically opposed gendered paradigms of whiteness and blackness. Pickering frames her experience of the beauty competition, as part of acquiring ladyhood, within the process of acquiring adult maturity, attended by a series of firsts. Race is not explicitly mentioned at this point in Pickering's narrative, but these 'firsts' are implicitly racialised as audacious bold moves for a young, brown woman, and further implied that the acquisition of exemplary femininity could be accompanied by certain freedoms.

In Pickering's account the beauty competition is compatible with other adventurous opportunities that took place both before and after, and probably as a result of, the competition. Her narrative bears similarities to Manning's. Manning had enjoyed a wide range of experiences from theatre and dance, to presidency of the Jaycettes, before the beauty competition. After the competition she had launched a successful career, becoming the first woman radio and TV broadcaster in Barbados. Pickering makes a figurative link between the débutante ritual and the social world of the beauty contest in the Caribbean, which was echoed by the early 'Miss Jamaica' competition, a virtual rite of passage for many upper-class white women, the so-called 'Daughters of Jamaica'. However, Pickering's reference to the débutante custom underscores the significance to the brown middle-class, of what Segal has described as acquiring respectability through 'achieved lightness'.[67] Eastmond and Manning, so admired by Pickering, not only represented exemplary femininity, but exemplary *brown* femininity. In following the path to exemplary brown femininity, Pickering occupied a leadership position in a multiracial school, undertook foreign travel at a young age, was feted for the beauty competition and eventually became an air hostess, which as Kathleen Barry has shown, was at the pinnacle of glamorous femininity, bettered only by Hollywood stardom.[68] Furthermore, exemplary femininity carried the promise of a modicum of freedom from the constraints of the colonial society. Diane King and Pickering were not only the first Barbadian women to join Pan-Am, they were the first *brown* Barbadian women to join the Pan-Am flight crew during its first attempts at desegregated recruitment after the US Civil Rights Act of 1964.[69] As we have seen the path to air hostess work was well-trodden for a limited few former beauty contestants in the Caribbean, including the much-lauded exceptional position of black Trinidadian Pearl Marshall, who became a BWIA air hostess in 1957, much to the delight of African American civil rights activists in the US. Pickering here illustrates the theme of audaciousness, and rare opportunity with reference to her (brown) colleague who married a (white) Australian and thereby circumnavigated the rigid racial hierarchy of Barbados, which positioned two such people as socially 'unmatched'.

The beauty contest stage provided moments that racialised and gendered the candidates differently. Significantly, however, all the women interviewed (if they mentioned race at all), told of racial confrontations which took place abroad, in the United States or in Britain, rarely at home in Barbados. Manning went on a four-week trip, two weeks of which would serve as her prize holiday, and the other two as a publicity tour with the Barbados Tourist Board. The tour was a fast-paced jaunt from city to city, including a visit to the Chicago World's Fair. Manning regularly attended evening receptions in her ballgown, and was required to talk to business executives, presenting, in her person, speech and conduct, a favourable image of Barbados. Manning recalled a travel agent executive from Texas who regarded her with racist fascination because she was so well-spoken, elegant and beautiful. Pickering described how she came under particular surveillance as a trainee air hostess in segregated Florida, and related the astonishment of her trainers that she could perform gracefully when serving customers and that she knew how to stand, walk and to gather fallen items from the floor, without drawing 'indecent' attention to her rear, a particular concern of her prudish supervisors. These were repertoires of feminine conduct, and the beauty candidates had long been schooled in them, and such conduct was closely tested in foreign venues. Yet, though the interviewees created narratives that migrated their experiences of racism abroad, the Barbados competition itself provided contexts into which they were placed as raced, classed, and gendered subjects. In the following passage Pickering describes herself relative to other women in the contest. It is significant that 1966 was the year of Chadderton's win, the year in which a former 'Miss Civil Service Association', typically a competition for darker women, and one that took pride in robust work-identities, made the unprecedented crossover into the pre-eminent national competition. This was also a year in which Pickering, a brown woman, was accompanied on the platform by a majority of other brown women:

> CP: One thing that came out of that show, I was one of the few blacks that had my natural hair.
>
> RR: In the show?
>
> CP: In the show, in *that* show. Norma [Chadderton] had a hairpiece. [Ruth] Collins had a hairpiece, Muriel [Sandford] had and Hazel Harper [also wore a hairpiece]. Betty Hill is a brownskin girl and Mary Hollis was white. Right, but this was false hair. So the night after the show I just went to my hairdresser and I said, cut it all off. I cut my hair when I left school at 17 to go on AFS (student exchange programme), cut it straight, and then I had grown it. When I came back home I had grown it and I was wearing it past my shoulders, in a little French twist. And after that show I just got so upset . . .
>
> RR: Because of the hair pieces?
>
> CP: Yes to me beauty, beauty to me is natural. Nowadays everybody has extensions, I don't know how they can cope because sometimes they are so itchy and everything. I know sometimes it helps, they say that it helps if you want to 'rest' your hair. I'm not really one of these people, although I had two wigs when I used to fly and they were very natural-looking wigs. I used to straighten my hair – right now sometimes I just go natural or if I straighten it I use the [gentler] children's straightener because my dad was, black, but my mum was 'Indian', y'know mulatto; white – black, that kind of thing. So I mean I am not fish or fowl as my friends would say, my brother is very Indian-looking, my sister . . . her hair is different from me, I say I have the bag fuzz, but my sister . . . But I stay with the natural look.[70]

In this passage Pickering describes herself explicitly as 'black' for the first time in the interview and within the same passage as mixed, 'neither fish nor fowl'. In her taxonomy of the women participants she is numbered among the 'black' entrants, and measures her own beauty alongside theirs in a trade-off for racial authenticity in beauty that problematises falsehood. Mary Hollis and Betty Hill are described as 'white' or 'brownskin' respectively, which, because of their phenotypical appearance and straight hair, renders them exempt from this critical appraisal of authentic versus fabricated beauty.[71] Pickering, on the one hand, 'enjoys' the rewards of having the sort of hair that is compatible with chemical straightening, and is therefore suitable for conversion into the elaborate styles of the day. She is privileged on the ever-shifting scale of 'blackness' by her ability to demonstrate beauty by her own long, straight hair. This, it emerges, is one of the competencies of 'black beauty'. The other 'black' women in the contest, who could not reproduce the contemporary trends for large up-swept hairstyles without additional hair pieces, are, to Pickering, fabricating a script of black beauty. This script determines that they ought to be judged according to each woman's ability to replicate contemporary styles authentically and without artifice. Pickering's assessment of beauty therefore is an interesting combination of these competing ideas. On the one hand, it is tinged with what sociologist Shirley Tate has called the 'anti-racist aesthetics' of the black-nationalist tradition. That is to say, that Pickering's account, shares a concern to affirm black (feminine) beauty, but also to create standards in black beauty that are ascribed and fixed as 'natural'.[72] Yet on the other hand, Pickering's assessment of black beauty nevertheless privileges traits such as long, straight hair, which she casts as not typically black, the gift of her mixed-raced heritage, and thus, while natural to her, unobtainable to the other 'black' women of the competition, without the use of hairpieces. Hence Pickering is combining lingering notions of blackness that is improved by whiteness, *alongside* notions of natural, unadulterated blackness in her assessment of black beauty, and the ideal representation of Barbadian womanhood.

The Jaycees' narratives suggested that the beauty contest both selected candidates for their display of ideal femininity that is the strength of their feminine credentials, and yet also played a role in their apprenticeship to proper femininity. This function of the competition was self-reproducing. Pickering had been inspired to take part in the competition by the displays of accomplished womanhood she saw from Eastmond and Manning in particular, brown women like herself. Pickering in turn cast the beauty contest as a staging post in her passage to proper womanhood. Yet, to perform the national standard for femininity, a standard that was paradoxically elusive, and always in process, one had to be trained. Manning credited her win, and later success in mature theatre and broadcasting, to her early childhood training in ballet. As a national broadcaster Manning acquired a certain competence as a feminine flag-bearer that extended beyond the reach of the beauty contest, but upheld the beauty contest's spirit of delivering exemplary femininity for the greater good, and continues, in her semi-retirement, to offer training in presentation and etiquette.[73] Similarly Pickering took to the skies in a 'representative' capacity, exemplifying Barbadian womanhood to thousands of international travellers and potential visitors to the island, as she worked American routes between New York in the north and Argentina in the south.[74]

Cultivation

Manning in turn served as a trainer of prospective beauty queens, pre-selected by the Jaycees, and as a broadcaster, was asked to interview them for television. In her training of beauty candidates Manning emphasised the importance of posture and 'good' presentation. Manning endorsed the Jaycees' notion of a beauty queen as having special competencies beyond good looks:

> [P]eople used to say 'you were a beauty queen!' I'd say no, it was called a 'Carnival Show', it wasn't just about beauty. They were looking for how you carry your posture, full presentation, and I went as a poinsettia . . . [I]n the early years it was not just a face, a pretty face, quite a few of the women had the top story [superior intelligence], and this was because the Jaycees were responsible. And I must admit, not [just] because I was involved with the Jaycees . . . they selected people, they *hand-picked* people.[75]

Manning here implies that the elegance, poise and charm required for the contest were uncommon qualities, not frequently occurring among 'ordinary' Barbadian women. Grooming, training and cultivation were the watchwords of a process that made ladies fit for the parade, even as that intangible, and subtly racialised quality of authentic Barbadianness remained essential.

The task of cultivating femininity in young Barbadian women of colour usually fell to expatriate white women. Historian Hilary Beckles's study of the women of the Fenwicks family of nineteenth-century Bridgetown is instructive here. Beckles's work was an initial exploration into the lives of enterprising single, white middle-class women in pre-emancipation Barbados who travelled to the island singly in search of a 'West India Fortune'. Beckles has called for more historical attention to these sorts of lives, which breach the 'plantation mistress' paradigm. The Fenwicks settled outside of the confines of the plantation house, and instead set up in business independently in the city.[76] This account of enterprising white women in the tropics resonates in 1960s' Barbados, which seems to have been home to a number of white women making an independent living in some branch of the beauty industry, some in the vague arts of female 'cultivation'. Alicea Taylor, originally from south Wales, taught 'movement' at the Lucy Clayton Model School in London's West End before becoming a school teacher at the Modern High School and later at Queen's College, both in Barbados, where she also taught extra classes in modelling and what was described as, 'develop[ing] poise, confidence and posture and improve[ing] grooming, and beauty preparation'.[77] From Taylor's first crop of thirty-six graduates came Patricia Barrow. Barrow went on to become an instructor in modelling at Skinner Business College, via the New York-accredited Nancy Taylor Charm and Modelling Course. The course included: '[T]he secrets of make-up, hair care, diet, body rhythms, movement like a model, wardrobe planning, the art of camouflage in make up and close care of clothes, speech, model manners, etiquette and memory training.'[78] According to these standards, femininity was demonstrated largely through the rituals of modern capitalist consumption, especially proper use of fashion and cosmetic commodities. The graduate in charm and modelling would be the ideal wife, decorative and conversant in esteemed company, the sort of able social mixer envisioned by Claudette Pickering.

Anna Adimira, also a native of Wales, with a background in theatre, described in interview how she prepared prospective beauty queens in Jamaica for the 'Miss Jamaica' competition and in Barbados for the 'Carnival Queen' show. Adimira had a background in theatre and used her skills mainly to teach a confident stage presence in candidates. She particularly taught candidates the correct way of walking, posing and speaking on stage. Adimira maintained a long involvement with Barbadian beauty pageantry, including, later the 'Miss Barbados' competition of the 1980s. Adimira orchestrated the 'Queen of the Teens' pageant of the 1970s, another elaboration on the débutante ritual, within which wealthy, mostly white, young women paraded in period-inspired costume.[79]

Though the Barbadian 'Carnival Queen' beauty competition was only dominated by white-creole winners for a short time, and thereafter increasingly looked for 'brown' 'visions of beauty', the competition institutionalised standards of hegemonic feminine performance, which were still invested in idealised notions of white femininity, and increasingly with the culture of capitalist modernity, associated pre-eminently with North America. Through the late 1960s and early 1970s brown and black 'Carnival Queen' candidates began to grace the pages of *The Bajan* in their alternate roles as 'cultivated' part-time models and graduates of charm school. The 'Carnival Queen' competition and its professionalisation of decorative Barbadian womanhood helped to produce a fledgling local modelling industry, which, as the following quote from *The Bajan* reveals, existed almost entirely for its tourism-boosting and quasi-diplomatic remit:

Although normally seen at the Holiday Inn during lunch time on Saturdays, Alicea Taylor's models have also appeared at fashion shows at the Hilton, Marine, and Sandy Lane [hotels], where they appeared before a high-powered group of Time Life executives and housing officials from across the United States. Colour photos of the girls taken around the Holiday Inn pool have been used by the [Swedish Airline] SAS in their programme of making the islands more attractive to Scandinavians. The photographers could not have asked for anyone more likely to make Barbados look beautiful.[80]

However, as changes were wrought in the 'Carnival Queen' competition through the 1960s, its credentials as a refiner of Barbadian women were sometimes at risk. Manning grew less and less satisfied with the performance of Barbadian femininity available at the national contest after the withdrawal of her generation of Jaycees around the mid-1960s who had managed the parade so competently. 'After a while you'd find that [standards fell]. I think they just wanted them to look good, they had a good body, and that's it'.[81]

Here were candidates who were apparently not nearly so accomplished, who seemed to lack the performative qualities, taught by professional white women, and accredited by North American beauty schools. These candidates had been approached on the street, proverbially, 'at the bus stop' and, by implication, threatened to embarrass the nation with their 'coarseness'.[82] The subtext was that in attempting to extend the representativeness of the beauty contest to dark women, the new Jaycees were losing the desirable and indispensable qualities of refinement, which could insult the national image. This dilemma exposed the core racial work of the Caribbean beauty contest, the attempt to deliver an exemplary cadre of refined ladies of colour, whose performance, it was hoped, could figuratively overwrite the racist past. It was a dilemma that was captured in the 'Miss Ebony' contest in particular.

'Miss Ebony'

In 1964, the year of Manning's memorable win, another beauty contest was launched. The 'Miss Ebony' competition revealed what could happen when the cultural remit of the beauty contest, to bolster the national image through the show of accomplished femininity, was seen to lapse. According to experienced beauty contest judge Cyralene Fields, the 'Miss Ebony' competition was a farce and breached those essential processes of refinement and cultivation described by the Jaycees, Manning and other trainers, in the search for exemplary femininity. The Barbados

'Miss Ebony' contest was probably inspired by a competition of the same name in Jamaica. Fields, though she had agreed to serve as judge, ultimately decried the Barbados 'Miss Ebony' contest as a 'misnomer': a dismal failure and an unworthy and troublesome experiment which should never have attempted to privilege blackness, let alone black feminine beauty. 'Miss Ebony', Fields warned, represented a dangerous threat to fragile Barbadian race relations: 'This is a community which is struggling to maintain racial harmony between its white minority and coloured majority, and segregation should be kept off the stage.'[83] Like Marcus Jordan, Fields uses the word 'coloured' in its alternate usage as the ambiguous and 'polite' referent for all Barbadians of African descent. Used here the term 'coloured' has a masking effect, denying the very real class-colour stratifications that divided and subdivided brown and black populations. In masking such effects the term is intended here to be politically mollifying. According to Fields, the effects of rising racial-consciousness in Barbados are unsettling, and she reveals her nostalgia for a mythic 'racial harmony', which would be better described as the culture of diffidence to whiteness that oiled the wheels of the Barbadian colonial system.

The contest was organised by entrepreneur Mr Shaw, and hosted at the Globe Cinema in Bridgetown. The chosen winner was dark-skinned nurse and sometime model Millie Small. Fields writes that: '[W]ith the exception of Millie Small, the contestants were not familiar with the essentials of stage appearance or stage deportment and one got the impression that they did not know whether they were coming or going. If someone had been hired to train the girls beforehand, this awkwardness would have been lessened.'[84] It is worthy of note that the 'awkwardness' of the sight of beauty contestants could only have been lessened, in Fields's view, not altogether eliminated. For Fields the embarrassment caused was a matter of national and economic significance, vital to the still fledgling entertainment industry in Barbados: 'Beauty contests are becoming quite popular with the Barbados public . . . If we are going to *cultivate* organised contests in this island, professional integrity must be the first necessity. We need entertainment but not at any cost'[85] [italics my emphasis].

Though little is known of Shaw's identity, it is safe to assume that Shaw was involved in some measure with the Jaycees' movement, and had been impressed by the success of the Jamaican 'Miss Ebony' beauty contest, part of the 'Ten Types' multi-competition, that had been so widely lauded. Manning and Jordan both betrayed a sense of alienation from the Jaycees after the first founding generation of members had elapsed in the mid-1960s. Though, in Fields's estimation, the 'Miss Ebony' contest seemed to have none of the credentials in good management and connoisseurship of the previous Jaycees' 'Carnival Queen' competitions, nevertheless it shared another hallmark of Jaycee involvement, namely that the finalists were sent to the regional Trade Fair in Suriname. The Barbados Jaycees had to great renown organised the Barbados Trade Fair in 1962, and it is unlikely that they would not have been involved in preparing Barbados's delegation to this fair in Suriname.

Five Barbadian women, led by winner Small, were chosen from the 'Miss Ebony' competition to represent Barbados at the Trade Fair Beauty Contest in Suriname. This was the sort of cultural ambassador role usually held by 'Carnival Queen' winners. Indeed the organisers of the Trade Fair had been sent a photograph of 1964 'Carnival Queen' winner Marvo Manning in advance of the competition, but the 'Miss Ebony' finalists arrived in her place and were met with rejection by a rowdy and affronted audience. Suriname, on the Caribbean coast of South America, sandwiched between British Guiana and French Guiana, with Brazil on its southern border, was in 1964, another New World plantation colony, with a history of (Dutch) colonialism, slavery and indentured labour. Like other emerging nations in the region, Suriname was struggling to fashion a harmonious multiracial future amidst African and Asian-descended brown and white communities, historically set against one another. Fields labelled the beauty contest a money-making sham and sympathised with contestants, whom she described patriotically as 'our girls' whilst also casting them as naïve children, innocent and misled by the villainous Shaw. This position allowed Fields to both sympathise with the undoubtedly 'humiliated' contestants, *and* with the racist, 'astonished Dutchmen' who booed their presence on stage shouting 'Nien, nien [No, no].' The five Barbadian contestants were first banned from the competition, and then allowed to participate, with some reluctance from organisers. In a mark of the importance to reputation of male orchestrators of beauty contests, the Barbardian delegation's involvement prompted the resignation of the secretary of the Trade Fair Foundation, Mr Bueno De Mesquito.[86]

Glaringly absent from Fields's account of the debacle is the subject of race, and what part race played in the women's exclusion from the beauty contest. Race is sublimated beneath Fields's indignant narrative. Instead Fields recurrently addresses what she sees as the key problem, the presence of untrained, uncultivated women who are thereby egregious to the beauty contest stage. Fields fails to directly address her own prejudice towards the idea of a celebration of black beauty as an affirmative gesture of race pride, or the racism of the audience and organisers in Suriname who booed and jeered the black women on stage. It is perhaps unsurprising, given that Fields has already betrayed her relative privilege in the racial system, by suggesting it protects racial harmony, that she refuses the radical imperatives behind the 'Miss Ebony' competition idea. Race looms large and unnamed in much of Fields's narrative, as submerged as the racial discourse in Barbados itself. It is implicit in her characterisation of the childlike, untutored contestants. It is also present in the alignment of her own views with that of the racist audience and organisers of the beauty competition who all affirmed that these were women who did not belong in the contest. Fields does not describe the women as beautiful or even attractive, and repeatedly confirms that they were not accomplished or refined according to institutional standards. Fields is unable to do this since the Trade Fair beauty contest ennobles as arbiters of feminine beauty, the indignant audience and the appointed judges who fail to make the Barbadian candidates their favourites.

For Fields, a considerable part of evaluating idealised femininity is a question of acquisition and training, a process hampered and complicated by assertive racial politics. Fields uses the question of training to mask race, and reserves most indignation for the idea that women with no special training should appear in an international beauty contest representing the nation of Barbados, though beneath this is evident alarm that black women were sent at all. The readers of the *Advocate* are left to draw their own conclusions from the significant differences between light-skinned Marvo Manning, the intended delegate, and the dark-skinned 'Miss Ebony' finalists, who arrived in Suriname. Fields concludes that the process of (racially) screening contestants must be restored, 'It cannot be too clearly emphasised that there is a need for aspiring beauty contestants to be selected for entrance by a committee.'[87] Millie Small's ordeal becomes a fable against the 'arrogance' of race pride. It warns other blacks against personal humiliation, and humiliating the new nation of Barbados: 'Millie was embarrassed, and her pride and self-confidence are sorely damaged. I too am embarrassed, not only for Millie's sake, but for Barbados' name.'[88]

In interview Small repeatedly and understandably circumnavigated the subject of the 'Miss Ebony' competition, but like Pickering and Manning constructed a narrative of opportunistic and adventure-seeking Barbadian womanhood. Small first became involved in beauty contests and then in sometime modelling opportunities for local fashion shows at hotels, which she regarded as opportune and potentially a means for travel. However, in Small's narrative these points were more strenuously made, with a particular emphasis on her own exceptionality as a black woman, time and again finding herself in contexts where she did not seem to belong. As with Honor Ford Smith's oral history of 'making white ladies', and Amy Bailey's caricature of uptight black womanhood, the dark-skinned Small was particularly attuned to her need to avoid 'vulgarity' of the black working-class woman in the Caribbean. Small told how she attended grammar school, and was socialised into a racial system that marked her out as exceptional and lucky, for instance in the seating system in class: 'White ones at the front, "clear" [light-skinned] ones in the middle, [those with] parents that were better off at the back, and blacks at the very back'.[89]

As a black scholarship child at grammar school Small was made very aware of the marginality of her position. The image she draws is a model of social ascription, and where the different colour-class groups are imagined on a scale of journey to respectability, a model reinforced by the colonial apparatus that made it.

Like the other contestants, Small described being courted and cajoled into the beauty contests, beginning with the Civil Service Association contest, in which she was placed first runner-up. Later Small entered the 'Miss Industry' contest. It is no coincidence that competitions featuring darker women, named 'Miss Civil Service Association' and 'Miss Industry', seemed to invest in affirmative work identities inhabited by respectable, professional black women, and reflected another dimension of the development of ideas of 'beauty for the national effort'. They affirmed respectable work identities even as they disrupted respectable values. Small risked social approbation and was admonished by the supervising matron at the Queen Elizabeth Hospital where she worked for her participation in beauty contests; Small's matron asked 'how dare' she reveal her body in public. Small regarded a nursing career as limiting, but knew it was one of the few opportunities open to her. She rejected the 'Florence Nightingale' paradigm that trainees were expected to emulate.[90] In preparation for beauty contests and modelling, Small was tutored in the essentials of how to 'walk and stand' as a model by the wife of a doctor at the hospital where she worked. Thus, of all the candidates involved in the doomed 'Miss Ebony' contest, Small, though tacitly excluded from the prestigious 'Carnival Queen' contest, had nonetheless served her apprenticeship in so-called feminine cultivation.

By way of conclusion, the Barbadian case reveals the racial work of a Caribbean national competition, its developmental and quasi-diplomatic portent, as well as its role in constructing idealised brown femininity and broadly shunning black femininity, in spite of the appetite for competitions with black women at their centre. The beauty competition in Barbados was affected by the local context: the suppressed discourse of racial consciousness, the extent of white dominance, and the related social conservatism. Unlike Jamaica, where the beauty competition had begun as an elite private party, or Trinidad, where white elites clung vehemently to control of the beauty competition even after it had made the transition to mass popular event, the Barbados competition was marked by a distinct lack of interest by the separatist white elite, who offered their sponsorship and patronage but typically very few beauty candidates. Instead the practice of beauty competitions was left almost entirely to the upwardly mobile men and women who used the competitions to assert themselves as successful persons.

More pronounced in Barbados than in other British West Indian islands, was the stress upon the beauty competition as a proper staging post on the path to capitalist modernity. This developmental effort would preferably take place in the absence of racial confrontation and would be soothed by an image that affirmed the civilisation of the Barbadian populace. The Barbados competition echoed an ongoing process of essentialising ideal British Caribbean femininity as brown and middle-class, respectable and accomplished, yet also exoticised for the tourist gaze. However, if the competition, like others in the region, projected an idealised brown femininity that supposedly resolved racial conflict through the body of the mixed-race woman, it also stimulated the making of racial definitions in the process of the beauty competition, as candidates reviewed and judged their peers using parameters of racial authenticity and natural versus unnatural racialised beauty. This race-making continued with the advent of new competitions. New on the scene were 'Miss Industry' and 'Miss Civil Service Association', both of which seemed to affirm robust work-identities for respectable black women. Additionally the short-lived 'Miss Ebony' competition attempted to affirm black femininity as a gesture of race-pride. The response to the 'Miss Ebony' competition and to the Jaycees' attempts to broaden beauty competitions, revealed not only fears of a black backlash in a postcolonial Barbados, but also the deeply ingrained and racialised investment in the black (female) body as the locus of primal Africanness, prone to vulgarity. This was the very image that new black beauty competitions attempted to rehabilitate. Crucially the process of *cultivation* spoke of the paranoia of middle-class audiences who craved affirmation through the contest and feared any traces of 'vulgarity' escaping onto the beauty contest stage.

Notes

1 Barbados's historic annual Crop Over season of festivities, which originated from the agrarian cycle of the sugar crop, went into decline in the 1940s and was revived in 1974 amidst a general cultural renaissance in Barbados.

2 Former Jaycee Frank Hunte estimated an audience of 10,000 for the competition in the early 1960s when it was hosted in the national cricket arena, the Kensington Oval, in Bridgetown. Interview with Frank Hunte, April 2007.

3 Gordon Lewis, *The Growth of the Modern West Indies* (London: MacGibbon and Kee, 1968), p. 226.

4 Ibid.

5 Ibid.

6 Mary Chamberlain, *Empire and Nation Building in the Caribbean: Barbados 1937–1966.* (Manchester: Manchester University Press, 2010), p. 105.

7 Jennifer Franco, *When the Ti-Marie Closes* (Franco: Port of Spain, 2000), p. 16.

8 Wenzell Brown, *Angry Men-Laughing Men: The Caribbean Cauldron* (New York: Greenberg, 1947), p. 300.

9 Ibid., p. 308.

10 Chamberlain, *Empire*, p. 101.

11 Hilary Beckles, *A History of Barbados: From Amerindian Settlement to Nation State* (Cambridge: Cambridge University Press, 1990), p. 41.

12 Linden Lewis, 'The Contestation of Race in Barbadian Society and the Camouflage of Conservatism', in Brian Meeks and Folke Lindahl (eds), *New Caribbean Thought: A Reader* (Mona: University of the West Indies Press, 2001), pp. 145–146.

13 Hilary Beckles, *Black Rebellion in Barbados: The Struggle against Slavery* (Bridgetown: Carib Research, 1987), p. 53.

14 Ibid.

15 Bonham Richardson, *Panama Money in Barbados, 1900–1920* (Knoxville: University of Tennessee Press, 1985), p. 23; Bolland, *Politics of Labour*, pp. 63–64.

16 Richardson, *Panama Money*, p. 6.

17 Ibid.

18 Beckles, *Black Rebellion*, p. 86.

19 Bolland, *Politics of Labour*, p. 88.

20 Lewis, 'Contestation of Race', p. 156.

21 Bolland, *Politics of Labour*, pp. 279–295.

22 Richardson, *Panama Money*, p. 8.

23 Franco, 'Dressing Up', pp. 65–67.

24 Bridget Brereton, *Race Relations in Colonial Trinidad* (Exeter: New Hampshire, Heinmann, 1981), pp. 60, 76, 114–115; Melanie Newton, 'Philanthropy, Gender and the Production of Public Life in Barbados ca. 1790–ca. 1850', in *Gender and Emancipation*, p. 241.

25 Lewis, 'Contestation of Race', pp. 154–156.

26 Lewis, *Modern West Indies*, p. 229.

27 Chamberlain, *Empire*, p. 27; Winston James, *Holding Aloft the Banner of Ethiopia: Caribbean Radicalism in Early-Twentieth Century America* (London: Verso, 1998), p. 361.

28 Lewis, *Modern West Indies*, p. 229.
29 Rosyln Lynch, *Gender Segregation in the Barbadian Labour Market, 1946–1980* (Mona: University of the West Indies, 1995), p. 25.
30 Lewis, *Modern West Indies*, p. 229.
31 Chamberlain, *Empire*, p. 102.
32 Burton, 'Introduction', p. 1.
33 Beckles, *Barbados*, p. 151.
34 Richardson, *Panama Money*, p. 224.
35 Aviston Downes, 'Boys of Empire: Elite Education and the Construction of Hegemonic Masculinity in Barbados, 1875–1920', in Rhoda E. Reddock (ed.), *Interrogating Caribbean Masculinities* (Kingston: University of the West Indies Press, 2004), p. 128.
36 'JCI in Barbados', *The Bajan* 2 (1964), p. 12; Barbados Jaycees Newsletter 1 (1996).
37 Interview with Marcus Jordan, April 2007.
38 'JCI in Barbados', *The Bajan*, p. 12.
39 Ibid.
40 Rebecca Chiyoko King O'Rain, *Pure Beauty: Judging Race in Japanese American Beauty Pageants* (University of Minnesota Press: Minneapolis, 2006) p. 11. The Honolulu Japanese Junior Chamber of Commerce founded 'Miss Cherry Blossom' contest, part of the Cherry Blossom Festival in Hawaii, in 1949.
41 'Queen in a Swimsuit', *Spotlight* 19 (1958), p. 30. A popular anecdote was that white women occupied front-of-house positions in banks and department stores of Broad Street, Bridgetown's main shopping thoroughfare, and brown-complected, or 'red', women worked as store clerks in Swan Street, the second street of Bridgetown. Darker professional women worked as nurses and teachers, jobs with far less prestige, but nonetheless hallmarked with modest respectability.
42 Barbados Civil Service Association, Monthly Newsletter, 1 (1965).
43 Lewis, 'Contestation of Race', pp. 147–148.
44 Edsil Phillips, 'The Development of the Tourist Industry in Barbados 1956–1980', in DeLisle Worrell (ed.), *The Economy of Barbados, 1946–1980* (Bridgetown: Central Bank of Barbados, 1982), p. 107.
45 'Entertainment', *The Bajan* 156 (1966), p. 20. At this point *The Bajan* altered its indexing system and began numbering by each issue and not by volume.
46 Lewis, 'Contestation of Race', pp. 149–150.
47 Interview with Marcus Jordan, April 2007.
48 Lewis, 'Contestation of Race', p. 180.
49 Interview with Frank Hunte, April 2007.
50 Interview with Betty Hill, April 2007.
51 Lynch, *Gender Segregation*, p. 30; Jocelyn Massiah, *Employed Women in Barbados: A Demographic Profile, 1946–1970* (Cave Hill: University of the West Indies, 1984), pp. 58–61.
52 Interview with Marvo Manning, May 2007.
53 Ibid.
54 Here I again use Mary Ryan's conceptualisation of a 'proliferation of publics' by which marginalised groups have constituted themselves as part of the centre, as cited in Melanie Newton, 'Philanthropy', p. 22.
55 Interview with Marcus Jordan, April 2007.

56 Interview with Marvo Manning, May 2007.
57 Interview with Claudette Pickering, April 2007.
58 Interview with Frank Hunte, April 2007.
59 Interview with Claudette Pickering, April 2007.
60 Ibid.
61 Ibid.
62 George Lamming, *In the Castle of my Skin* (New York: Schocken Books, 1983), p. 67.
63 Eastmond's wide popularity was reflected in the tones in which all other interviewees mentioned her.
64 Interview with Claudette Pickering, April 2007.
65 Ibid.
66 Ford–Smith, 'Making White Ladies', p. 55.
67 Segal, 'Race and Colour', pp. 91–93.
68 Barry, *Femininity*, p. 2.
69 Ibid., p. 119.
70 Interview with Claudette Pickering, April 2007.
71 Although it is important that Pickering excludes white women from the context in this way, it is particularly ironic because elaborate 'high' hairstyles of the 1960s were popular and hairpieces were widely used by women of different racial backgrounds. Popstars and models in the public eye, such as Dusty Springfield, helped to popularise this look.
72 Shirley Tate, 'Black Beauty: Shade, Hair and Anti-racist Aesthetics', *Ethnic and Racial Studies* 30 (2007), 300–319.
73 Interview with Marvo Manning, May 2007.
74 Interview with Claudette Pickering, April 2007.
75 Interview with Marvo Manning, May 2007.
76 Hilary Beckles, 'White Women and a West India Fortune: Gender and Wealth during Slavery', in Howard Johnson and Karl Watson (eds), *The White Minority in the Caribbean* (Oxford: James Currey, 1998), pp. 1–16.
77 'Models', *The Bajan* 197 (1970), p. 10.
78 Ibid.
79 Interview with Anna Adimira, May 2007.
80 'Models', *The Bajan*, p. 12
81 Interview with Marvo Manning, May 2007.
82 Ibid.
83 *Barbados Advocate*, 24 October 1964.
84 Ibid.
85 Ibid.
86 Ibid
87 Ibid.
88 Ibid.
89 Interview with Millie Small, May 2007.
90 Ibid.

4

Fashioning 'Ebony Cinderellas' and brown icons: Jamaican beauty competitions and the myth of racial democracy, 1955–64

Jamaica, which not only by her own boast, but by world acclaim has long ago shown the right concept which enables peoples of diverse races to live and move together as one, has struck the final chord in a unique contest – TEN TYPES–ONE PEOPLE.[1]

I N 1955, Jamaica celebrated a national festival, 'Jamaica 300', which commemorated 300 years of Jamaica's history as a British colony. A highly visible part of the year-long celebration was the 'Ten Types–One People' beauty contest, which attracted 3000 participants and ran in the national tabloid, *The Star*, from May to December.[2] The contest comprised ten separate competitions, each of which represented a category for a specific skin tone. 'Ten Types' produced ten winners, one from each competition, who would all 'reign' as beauty queens with no overall winner presiding. The titles euphemistically described race, ethnicity and skin-shade, including, 'Miss Appleblossom', 'Miss Allspice', and 'Miss Ebony'. The ten categories, expressed through the female entrants' bodies, were paraded alongside each other to suggest a racially harmonious Jamaica. Thus as the islands of the British Caribbean grappled with the problem of how to stabilise the national image, out of Jamaican cultural nationalism, a solution, a multiracial, multi-competition with an audacious experimental air, was proudly put forward.

Since their inception in 1929, beauty contests in Jamaica had emerged as deeply political ventures which staged idealised performances of femininity that were pointedly racialised and class-bound. Jamaica had seen the prewar 'Miss Jamaica' contest, dominated by white-creoles and nurtured by Herbert de Lisser, who identified strongly with the creole upper-class. After the war, Jamaica had witnessed Aimee Webster's attempts to transfer idealised femininity to brown women in both the

'Miss Jamaica' and 'Miss British Caribbean' inter-island competitions. But the latter was short-lived and following Webster's short management of the 'Miss Jamaica' contest, the pageant fell briefly into a lapse and was later revived once more by the Body Builder's Association in 1954, a private health society managed by the brown businessman Keith Rhino. The Jamaica Tourist Board, a government-funded body, partnered the Body Builder's Association to sponsor the pageant. Together they invested more money into the contest than previous franchise holders and professionalised the role of 'Miss Jamaica' as both a national representative and a cultural ambassador.[3] 'Miss Jamaica' titleholders now won lucrative prizes, foreign trips and began to attend 'Miss World' and other international beauty competitions within the region. In this format the brown participants who had been singled out by Webster's contest lost status, no longer able to compete with white Jamaicans nor rise above the occasional place in the final line-up. As Barnes points out, this was an ironic state of affairs in which white-creole winners toured North America garbed in romantic 'native' costumes intended to impart the 'exotic appeal' of the woman of colour.[4]

Within this context the 'Ten Types' beauty contest was exceptional for its time, and provides the opportunity to examine the spectacle of the racialised feminine body in the construction of a multiracial modern Jamaican identity. Though the nationalist planners of the 'Jamaica 300' commemorations sought to circumnavigate overt references to British conquest and domination, the beauty contest would nevertheless invoke a legacy of inventing and objectifying racialised female bodies that had begun with the colonial encounter. While nationalists plotted a path to postwar modernity through political and economic development, they in fact drew upon the European project of expansion that had launched the age of (European) modernity and had been reliant upon reading difference onto African and Amerindian female bodies.[5] The 'Ten Types' beauty contest symbolically called upon the history of (en)gendering race through the bodies of Caribbean women. Thus, nationalist enthusiasts would mobilise an inheritance of racialised and gendered constructs to imagine a new Jamaicanness, even as they proposed a multiracial society that had overcome 'race'. Furthermore, they would use gendered constructs to renegotiate race, specifically African-descended racial identities, to infer Jamaica's departure from colonialism and entrance into the modernity of new nations. This chapter explores the path of the 'Ten Types' multi-competition and its impacts, including the 'Miss Jamaica Nation' competition, a black-nationalist intervention to rival 'Miss Jamaica'.

Jamaican cultural nationalism and the origins of 'Ten Types'

The 'Ten Types' contest sprang from the cultural nationalist impulses accompanying the Jamaican and larger West Indian independence movements. While the mass political activism of 1938 had provided the initial spur for the formation of new political parties in Jamaica, by the 1950s, the two foremost political parties that had emerged, the People's National Party (PNP), and the Jamaica Labour Party (JLP), were dominated by middle-class, urban, educated men of colour and reflected middle-class proprietorship over the transition to self-government. Radical black-nationalism, including Marcus Garvey's Pan-Africanist programme, failed to secure a place in formal representative politics. Instead, the PNP, the party of Jamaican nationalism, promoted a gendered ideology of respectability and modernity. The PNP celebrated a masculine image of the industrious black peasant as the wellspring of a decent black citizenry that would mature gradually through the political process. Though much of its membership was originally radicalised by Garveyism and black religious nationalism, the PNP primarily invested in a model of harmonious racial democracy that separated racial consciousness from national consciousness. The party engendered cultural creolisation and both promoted and pronounced a Jamaican racial paradise.

The idea of a commemorative tercentenary festival originated in 1954 with the JLP administration. Minister of Finance Donald Sangster proposed the festival as a means of expanding a long-term economic agenda to combat severe unemployment and underemployment with foreign, specifically North American, investment and tourism. Jamaica's population was still predominantly rural, surviving through seasonal employment, smallholding cultivation and with little formal welfare provision. Though the economy had grown progressively in the preceding decade, unemployment remained high and was projected to worsen with population growth. Large-scale outward migration had for generations been one of the few outlets for people seeking work, and eased pressure on the economy, still characterised by a concentration of wealth amongst the planter and merchant oligarchy.[6]

The JLP initially proposed the celebrations as the commemoration of Jamaica's 300 years as a British colony. However, they were quickly embarrassed by an outcry from the press and political opponents who thought the festivities should celebrate the emergent Jamaican nation rather than the departing British rulers. The PNP, who took office in January 1955, promptly revised the tenor of the celebratory plans, from a commemoration of 300 years of British rule in the colony, to a celebration of

Jamaica's 300 years as a national entity with a distinctive history, culture and people. Such a celebration would serve the PNP's programme of cultural nationalism, which had thus far included founding welfare associations aimed at community uplift and a cultivation of the 'folk' arts.[7] For the PNP, the 'Jamaica 300' event provided an opportunity to extend the nationalist spirit beyond its narrow middle-class following to the mass of working people, and to encourage them to accept the sentiment of a united Jamaican identity.[8]

As part of 'Jamaica 300' the 'Ten Types' contest was designed to express the idealised model of a plural Jamaica. It reiterated an amenable historical record, what Howard Johnson has described as the selective 'amnesia' of the national Jamaica project.[9] The contest would indicate to both domestic and foreign audiences that Jamaica had resolved the 'race problem', thereby establishing Jamaican modernity. Much like Brazil's official myth of racial democracy and the 'melting pot' rhetoric of the United States, 'Ten Types' would serve as a metaphor for Jamaica's successful assimilation of once disparate peoples in democratic harmony. Theodore Sealy, the first black editor of the leading national newspaper, the *Daily Gleaner*, was appointed chair of the 'Jamaica 300' organising committee and wrote of 'Ten Types':

> Jamaica by its climate and geographical position, its past trading and history, has over the centuries become one of those focal points where peoples of diverse races meet and merge. It is from this merging that has developed that consciousness of nationhood reflected in this great modern contest not hitherto conceived in any other country.[10]

However, given the history of the Caribbean as a place where racial hierarchy was sustained over centuries, from the colonial encounter, to enslavement and empire-building, with female bodies at the centre of the process of race-making, the model of a plural Jamaica and its agent the 'Ten Types' pageant was an attempt to mask and contradict the reality of the Jamaican social environment.

Immediately after the war, Aimee Webster's *Caribbean Post*, 'Miss Jamaica' and the short-lived 'Miss British Caribbean' competitions had linked Caribbean modernity to representations of mixed-raced femininity. However, the 'Miss Jamaica' competition, now under the management of Keith Rhino and the Body Builder's Association, continued to represent the ideals of a white Jamaica. In 1955, Theodore Sealy used his editorial in the *Gleaner* to reproach 'Miss Jamaica' organisers for appointing yet another white 'queen' in Marlene Fenton. Sealy called it irresponsible to encourage foreigners to associate the better part of

Jamaican society with whiteness and refinement at the expense of the wider population, whom he feared were still imagined as backward. As organiser of the 'Ten Types', Sealy set about creating a Jamaican ideal that would challenge the social caché of whiteness.[11]

Ten Types: 'uncovering a wealth of feminine charm'[12]

The *Star* launched 'Ten Types' in May 1955 as an exceptional beauty contest, the first of its kind, with a plural political message and cleverly implied critique of the all-white 'Miss Jamaica' contest summarised in the 'Ten Types' slogan, 'Every lassie has an equal chance.'[13] While it is important to distinguish 'Ten Types' from the exclusive 'Miss Jamaica' contest, both pageants represented the interests and tactics of the establishment, relying as they did upon commercial sponsorship, press exposure and the involvement of the Jamaica Tourist Board.

Publicity for 'Ten Types' appeared regularly in the *Star* and the *Gleaner*, and revealed the grand scale of the contest and the organisers' commitment to demonstrating its national scope. The published rules suggested that the competition was open to 'all girls' aged between 18 and 25, though in practice, married women and mothers were probably barred from the beauty contest, particularly the finals, as was customary. The 'Ten Types' competition would tour the island; almost scouring the countryside for Jamaica's hidden beauties. There would be seven months of preliminaries between the launch of the contest in May and the final unveiling of the winners at Christmas. To do this work the *Star* staffed a caravan with its representatives, including a photographer, a reporter, and members of the Jamaica Federation of Women (JFW) to act as chaperones and to encourage participants to enter. The JFW had absorbed the core of middle-class Jamaican feminists into their ranks, but in effect nullified feminism and pursued instead its mandate to encourage the nuclear family as a means of encouraging development and better standards of welfare. To this end they organised mass weddings and formal registration of fathers.[14] The Federation's involvement in 'Ten Types' not only lent respectability to the contest's proceedings, but also dovetailed with the racialised and gendered project of 'uplift' that was the professed aim of the nationalist project.

The press published the schedule of the 'Star Beauty Caravan' for visits to Jamaica's villages and towns and employed local correspondents to distribute leaflets. As a rule, judging panels had to include some members drawn from the colour-group they were assigned to judge. Throughout the competition, the public were invited to vote for their favourites on the basis of the photographs published of entrants in the paper. 'Prizes will be based on attractiveness of face, figure and personality in the opinion of the judges and the general public', the *Star* announced.[15] Final judging took place in Kingston – willingness to come to Kingston was one of the stated rules of the competition – but in private, not before an audience, contrary to the beauty contest custom.[16] Overall £1300 in prizes was offered, to the female competitors and to *Star* readers who voted for their favourite contestants.[17]

The result was ten separate beauty queens, each one crowned alongside her fellow 'queens' as a national representative:

Miss Ebony – A Jamaican girl of black Complexion.
Miss Mahogany – A Jamaican girl of Cocoa-brown Complexion.
Miss Satinwood – A Jamaican Girl of Coffee-and Milk Complexion.
Miss Golden Apple – A Jamaican Girl of Peaches and Cream Complexion.
Miss Apple Blossom – A Jamaican Girl of European Parentage.
Miss Pomegranate – A Jamaican girl of White-Mediterranean Parentage.
Miss Sandalwood – A Jamaican Girl of Pure Indian Parentage.
Miss Lotus – A Jamaican Girl of Pure Chinese Parentage.
Miss Jasmine – A Jamaican Girl of Part Chinese Parentage.
Miss Allspice – A Jamaican Girl of Part Indian Parentage.[18]

'Ten Types' attempted to universalise a feminine standard by showing that women of differently raced bodies could conform to a recognisable

Miss Ebony   Miss Mahogany   Miss Satinwood   Miss Allspice   Miss Sandalwood   Miss Golden Apple   Miss Jasmine   Miss Pomegranate   Miss Lotus   Miss Appleblossom

A spectrum of Jamaican beauty displayed before a cannon of Fort Charles, Port Royal. 'Ten types; one people' was the heading of this contest, run in 1955 as part of the 'Jamaica 300' celebrations

4.1 'Ten Types – One People'

Western ideal. The selected beauty queens were all, unsurprisingly, slim and petite in frame. In the photograph they are posed in a row, tiptoed, hands on hips, heads turned to face the camera. The array of slim-figured women in identical poses, reframed discourses of racialised othering. It suggested instead a universal beauty standard to which all Jamaican women could conform, and furthermore that the differently raced ethnic groups of Jamaica could assimilate to modernity.

The imagined colour categories of the 'Ten Types' parade appeared to decimalise the Jamaican demographic profile. That is, they appeared to give some measured proportionality to the division of Jamaican society into tenths, as though each category represented a tenth of the diverse whole of the population. In the process, they confined the perhaps most numerous skin shade – the dark brown skin of prominent African descent – to only one of these categories. Moreover, the visual array gave primacy to the categories that referenced racial mixes, those that reflected the ethnic composition of the coloured middle-class. In the parade of feminine beauty, brownness was imagined expansively and occupied a number of the given categories. The array of light brown beauty queens suggested the pre-eminence, in the Jamaican social landscape, of light-skinned brownness as a social category in the ascendancy, worthy of broad national representation. The 'Ten Types' panorama of feminine beauty, which had attempted to deliver a multiracial model of modern Jamaica, was, therefore, weakened by what it revealed about the persistent unease with the place of blackness in the new political order at this heightened moment of cultural nationalism.

Miss Ebony: imagining black femininity in modern Jamaica

Although the categories provided an array of Jamaican identities that seemed to spell out the project of a plural Jamaica, the most striking element of the 'Ten Types' contest to contemporary audiences was the novelty of a category for dark-skinned Afro-Jamaican women. In 1959, 'Ten Types' was relaunched as an annual competition for each of the colour categories. The 'Miss Ebony' contest, now renamed as a competition for 'coal-black or cool-black girls,' was placed at the head of the proceedings and allocated the first year, with 'Miss Mahogany' to follow in 1960, and so on through each category.[19] Again the competition would trawl through each county of the island. The *Star* beauty caravan was required to make two stops a day, from Hanover in the west to St Thomas in the east, between May and September, for the 'Miss Ebony' and 'Miss Mahogany' competitions, which together attracted the most prospective contestants. This time the rules explicitly stated that only 'unmarried girls' could participate, and offered the winner £250, plus an all-expenses-paid prize trip to Carnival in Trinidad.[20] The exceptional attention paid to 'Miss Ebony' makes it worthy of further exploration in this discussion.

Dark-skinned women had remained largely absent from beauty contests in the Caribbean to this point, just as they were invisible as figures of feminine desirability in newspaper advertising, glossy publications and cinema.[21] African-descended women seeking glamorous careers were restricted by the confines of racialised binaries that had always accompanied their presence in the 'New World'. Black and brown women were typically called upon to perform the polar opposite to the ideal of chaste white femininity: the libidinous and primal Other. Those women who did manage to achieve some success as actresses, models and entertainers were celebrated for their ability to break through these racial barriers. The Jamaican press closely followed the rise of the 'brownskin' model in US advertising, and proudly reported on the smattering of light-brown actresses, such as Eartha Kitt and Lena Horne, who had breached Hollywood.[22] However, most women of African descent working in the entertainment industry, whether dark or light-skinned, seldom appeared in the press and, when they did, were typically nightclub dancers in Caribbean resorts or in North American and European cities.[23] The 'Miss Ebony' contest raised the possibility of a desirable and respectable black femininity that an entire community of dark-skinned, black-identified Jamaicans, both male and female, could invest in and were expected to aspire towards. Moreover, the 'Miss Ebony' contest attempted to position black women as figurative symbols of Jamaican blackness, and as 'exemplar(s) of social, sexual, and racial parity.'[24] As part of the PNP's project of cultural nationalism and 'uplift' among poor black people, the 'Miss Ebony' contest also served as a particularly important symbol of blacks' capacity for dignity and progress: to show that a black woman could perform ably in a 'white' space. Through 'Miss Ebony,' the *Star* inferred the promise of progression for the black race itself. It was a bold departure, and yet also a necessary fixture, showing that all were happily accommodated within the Jamaican nation. The 'Ten Types' panorama, with the novelty of 'Miss Ebony' attached, was essentially a gesture at fair play, and was intended to be especially affirmative of black (male) political designs on leadership.

Black male middle-class leaders were the primary public discussants of the 'Miss Ebony' contest and their commentary is particularly revealing of a gendered ideology of colour – the symbolic path to Jamaica's progression – under construction. There is some evidence that black women supported the 'Ten Types' contests, not least the many women who entered the competitions, yet whose voices are missing from the historical record. Furthermore there is some indication that nationalist-minded women shared in the political rhetoric of cultural nationalism articulated through feminine beauty. However, the prewar taboo-breaking feminist commentary on black women's exclusion from idealised femininity had been silenced with the postwar submergence of black-nationalist feminism. Lady Allan, widow of black politician Lord Allan, was assigned to judge the 'Miss Ebony' category and praised the contest for its attention to black women, saying, 'it brings out some of our really good-looking Jamaican girls – if I use the term natives they might not like it, but that is what I mean – it brings out the girls who would otherwise not get a chance.'[25]

Publisher Evon Blake, editor of the *Spotlight* and *Newday* news magazines, seized upon the slim evidence of brown women's successes in beauty contests as a sign of wider social improvements in Jamaica and elsewhere in the British Caribbean. At the same time Blake championed the 'Ten Types – Miss Ebony' contest as a lesson in Jamaican racial democracy for other, less advanced, West Indian audiences. Blake considered the presence of the winner of 'Miss Ebony' 1959, Doreen Bryan, at Trinidad Carnival alongside the white 'Carnival Queen' competition, as clear evidence of this, noting that 'a "black" queen is totally unknown in Trinidad, where racial lines are so sharply drawn it appals visiting Jamaicans.'[26]

Blake subscribed to the project of a plural Jamaica and praised the 'Miss Ebony' contest as a progressive social project delivering self-respect to black women. Like Sealy, his seniority as a black professional made him a rare figure whose career breached a world dominated by white businessmen and coloured professionals. A self-made man who had overcome considerable odds, Blake posed himself as both a 'Race Man,' a 'champion' of antiracist campaigning, and yet a disciplinarian of the 'Negro element.' He challenged racism, such as racist employment policy, but rejected black-nationalism. Blake endorsed the plural project as one that imbibed liberal meritocracy.[27]

Spotlight celebrated the 'Miss Ebony' competition and all it stood for. Doreen Bryan, 'Miss Ebony' 1959, was featured on the front cover of its December issue. Blake praised the contest's 'sociological import,' its ability 'to give black girls a firm consciousness of their own beauty.' He suggested that black women were 'victims of post-slavery propaganda that projected "whites" as superior and "blacks" as inferior', and thus, had a particular susceptibility to a racial inferiority complex. Blake reproduced an account, apparently from a contest organiser, of the diminished racial pride of the 'typical' black 'office girl,' a 'type' whom, it was alleged, had avoided the contest in droves: 'The coal-black Civil Servant girl would consider it an insult if you called her ebony. She tries desperately to lighten her shade and will not face up to the fact that she is wasting her time for

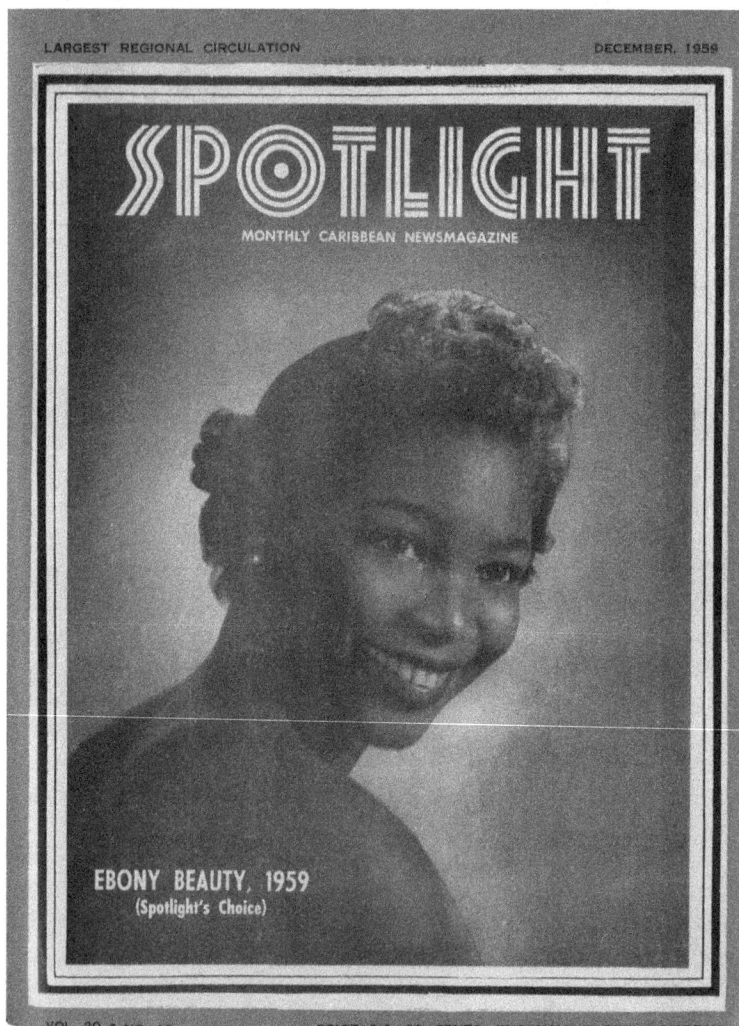

4.2 Doreen Bryan, 'Miss Ebony', 1959

her best bet is to cultivate her own type of beauty.'[28] This comment is more important as a figurative rhetorical anecdote than as the verbatim account of an organiser, or indeed as a reflection of any black women's responses to the contest. Blake used this example to underline what he regarded as the psychological victimisation of the black woman, who as a result, bore a pathological denial of her essential self, which would, by implication, eventually inhibit the progress of the race.

Blake's attack on the figure of the black woman haunted by her colour echoes Fanon's gendering of the black struggle. Lola Young has shown that Fanon denied the black female subject in *Black Skin, White Masks*, relying instead on fictionalised accounts of black women to cast them as complicit in the potential annihilation of the 'black race' through their own misplaced desire for whiteness. Michelle Wright has identified this silencing of the black female subject as consistent in a trajectory of black intellectual thought in which black women appear as caricatures.[29] Similarly, in his characterisation of the black struggle, Blake constructs an allegorical 'choice' for black women: as symbolic figures of either progress or paralysis. Either they willingly cast themselves as proud black women or languish in a state of self-hatred that inhibits the wider (male) progress of the black race, imagined as a whole.

While Blake chastised the un-proud 'office girl', an allegory for the black middle-class woman, he praised instead the transformation, with the aid of 'brush and comb', of 'country girls' into beauties fit to be seen in a national contest. Blake revelled in the novelty of the 'Cinderella-like transformation' of the black finalists now stepping into the limelight. He embellished the *Star*'s account of searching the country for beauties. The 'Miss Ebonies', he suggested, were 'unsophisticated country girls' from the 'humblest' backgrounds, buried deep in the countryside. In fact the eventual winner, Bryan, was a secretary and a resident of Mountain View, St Andrew, a new development in the suburban hinterland of Kingston. First runner-up Dorrett Pinnock, who featured in *Spotlight* alongside Bryan, was also a resident of St Andrew.[30] Though neither were in fact the 'country girls' that the *Star* Beauty Bus set out to find, the 'country girl' label would continue to be associated with black women involved in competitions.

Blake's praise for 'country girls' who became beauty contestants reveals something of the appetite among the ambitious black, male-dominated, middle-class leadership, to place a specific kind of black feminine icon at the service of the cause of black advancement; one that was respectable, but above all non-threatening, an image that vanquished narratives of the emasculating black woman.

Black welfare organisations welcomed the 'Ten Types' competition and 'Miss Ebony' in particular. With it they embraced the beauty contest format as a new means of challenging racial discrimination. The Afro-West Indian Welfare League petitioned the Body Builder's Association to alter 'Miss Jamaica' along the lines of 'Ten Types,' so that black women would be included in the contest. They even offered to sponsor 'dark-skinned' candidates 'of beauty, poise, and intelligence', and to provide two black-Jamaicans for the judging panel. In 1960, the local UNIA proposed its own socially conscious beauty competition. In aid of the UNIA's aim, the 'social and economic uplift of the coloured peoples of the world to a status of respectability and responsibility', this contest would offer prizes geared towards educating and training lower-class women out of poverty.[31]

So important were beauty contests to symbols of power that in 1961 Millard Johnson, a radical black nationalist and an embarrassment to the new political establishment, picketed the rounds of 'Miss Jamaica'. From 1959, the 'Miss Jamaica' competition had begun a glacial pace of change by crowning very light-skinned brown winners. Johnson protested the contest's racial discrimination against the black majority with placards reading, 'Jamaica is Black,' 'Who do these girls represent?,' 'Down with Colour Discrimination' and, 'Beauty is Black'.[32]

As a response to Johnson's campaign, acerbic *Spotlight* columnist, Sylvia Slade (perhaps a pseudonym), endorsed Johnson's argument against 'Miss Jamaica' for its continued exclusion of darker Jamaican women. Slade agreed this was a potent metaphor of exclusion at a vital moment of political transition when independence was imminent. Jamaica elected by referendum to leave the British West Indian Federation in 1961 and was set to pursue political independence alone. Slade listed the remaining problems with the 'Miss Jamaica' contest, but unlike Johnson, did not critique the project of plural nationalism or praise black-nationalism. Instead Slade heaped praise upon 'Ten Types' as the worthy alternative to 'Miss Jamaica' and suggested that nationalising the latter contest would secure a fairer deal.[33]

In 1962, black *Gleaner* sports writer Alva Ramsay suggested in a public letter that in the year of Jamaican independence, a dark-skinned black woman should be crowned 'Miss Jamaica': 'I suggest either we go into the *hedges and byways* and select a Negro girl as 'Miss Jamaica' for the independence year or we adopt a modified Star ['Ten Types'] pattern and have four queens, – one a negro girl, one a white girl, one a Chinese and one an Indian'[34] [italics my emphasis].

Thus, like Sealy and Blake before him, Ramsay suggested only country women, apparently dwelling in the 'hedges and byways', could provide an untainted image of black femaleness to be moulded and elevated to the level of national feminine icon of blackness. Ramsay not only drew upon an intellectual tradition in Jamaican nationalism that favoured the peasant as a symbol of independence, but also upon an image of virginal black femininity, the 'country girl', which male black nationalists had consistently preferred to the figure of the urbanised, professional woman since the inception of the black nationalist and feminist movements.

Two years later, Ramsay and his organisation, the Council for Afro-Jamaican Affairs, began its own 'Miss Jamaica Nation' contest to rival 'Miss Jamaica'. The 'Miss Jamaica Nation' contest combined imagery of an upright peasantry, respectable rural black femininity and new gendered articulations of blackness linked to Africa. Black winners of this competition were again described as unadulterated country dwellers even as they delivered an accomplished performance of femininity through the groomed appearance, measured deportment and mannerisms that were predicated on their consumption of Western beauty culture and their identification with middle-class life-ways. These articulate, dark-skinned black women were to be sent to Africa as unofficial cultural ambassadors and agents of mutual learning as new African nations emerged independent from the British Empire. The first winner, Yvonne Whyte, came from a middle-class professional background but was praised at her crowning by Senator Kenneth McNeill as 'the first real country girl to win a beauty contest', demonstrating absolutely that 'country girl' had by then become a euphemism for respectable, dark-skinned femininity.[35] Whyte, who had a large following amongst black Jamaicans, made a visit to the independence celebrations of Malawi. Thus Whyte represented a figurative link between decolonising Africa and blacks emerging from colonial Jamaica. The 'Miss Jamaica Nation' pageant therefore mobilised Africa as a 'symbolic referent' of what Thomas has called 'modern blackness,' which both 'engaged and rejected Western visions of progress and development.'[36]

Black middle-class men took varying positions on nationalism, on a scale from the plural model, which attempted to mask racial inequality and prescribed uplift as a social leveller, to those concerned about a crisis of black disempowerment. Yet in spite of their ideological differences they all sought and helped to create iconic imagery of black femininity. They regarded the black beauty queen as an essential allegory of black advancement but revealed lingering unease about how this gendered and racialised figure of modernity should look and perform. This vein of black thought, which mobilised black femininity as a political tool, had a legacy in Jamaica and beyond. It echoed Robert Love's call for the betterment of black women who would become the cultured wives of a new generation of black male leaders towards the end of the nineteenth century. It reverberated with Garvey's romantic poetry on ideal black womanhood.[37]

Paradoxically, the sought-after black feminine icon would not, unlike the 'office girl,' succumb to normative values for feminine desirability, by 'mimicking' 'white beauty.' The ideal black woman would somehow embody these normative values, which were the very essence of the beauty contest format, but not appear ashamed of her African features. Although 'Ten Types' did not overtly make references to the supposed 'coarseness' and 'vulgarity' of lower-class women, extra emphasis was placed upon the transformation of such women in readiness for the beauty competition. As the figure of 'Miss Ebony' marked a dramatic transformation from country girl to beauty queen, so too would the mass of Jamaican people be transformed in time. The iconic black woman acquired modernity and sophistication, just as she had acquired 'beauty, poise and charm,' and she did so on behalf of the nation. The allegorical black femininity of the 'Miss Ebony' contest found a welcome reception within the black leadership, who saw it less as an agent for the project of plural Jamaica, and more as a symbol of black progress in Jamaica.

Responses to 'Ten Types' from the United States

'Ten Types' soon aroused the interest of media voices from overseas. Journalists were enthralled by questions of race in the 'New World' at this transitional moment of civil rights activism and anti-Apartheid struggles. For US journalist Edward Scott, writing for the *Havana Post* in Cuba, the 'Miss Ebony' competition most exemplified the essence of the 'Ten Types' message of non-confrontational racial politics and black political ambition. Scott described 'Ten Types' as a model of racial tolerance and reserved particular praise for the humility shown by 'Miss Ebony':

> I do not know who made up that list of ten names, but it is a masterpiece of poetry, dignity and good taste. The various qualifications are beautifully prepared and I find myself admiring particularly the little Jamaican girl who does not protest that it is undemocratic to have a class for 'Miss Appleblossom,' but who readily admits that she is 'a Jamaican girl of black complexion' and proudly enters her name in the competition for 'Miss Ebony.'[38]

Scott's response engaged with the subtext of containment in the model of plural Jamaica, the ethos of the 'Jamaica 300' festival. As with the 'office girl' who should learn to cultivate her own type of beauty, black claims for full democratic representation ought to be managed and contained. Black political ambition threatened the status quo. Scott's praise for the 'Ten Types' contest reveals that its work, to decimalise the Jamaican racial profile in this way, was to suggest the sublimation of blackness, where blackness signifies a dangerous presence that threatens to overturn white privilege.

In contrast, resident South African writer Peter Abrahams viewed the competition differently and was intrigued by its careful design. He asked wryly whether an overall national representative was to be chosen from the 'Ten Types' array of women:

> [W]ith fine subtlety, the contest was both *racial* and *multiracial* ... Black girls competed amongst themselves; Chinese and Chinese-coloured amongst themselves; the fair competed only against the fair ... I wondered and asked, whether the organisers would, after they had chosen the winners from the ten types, choose a reigning queen from one of the ten. No one knew. People tended to shy away from this[39] [italics my emphasis].

The North American press audience found in the decimalisation of the Jamaican demographic profile an appealing message. *Time* and *Life* magazines, both with million-strong circulations, emphasised the mythology of racial democracy. *Life* reproduced its 'Ten Types' feature in its international edition. *Time* informed its readers that 'because of the tangled racial mixture of the island colony's population of 1,500,000,' ten beauty queens would be chosen 'for each of ten racial-colour groups.'[40] To some commentators, 'Ten Types' was so successful in dispersing the threat of black political power and in calming racial conflict that it was also interpreted as the visual display of the end of racism.

Unlike those who looked for reassurance of a black political threat quelled, African American society magazine *Ebony* instead sought proof of a racial paradise that might offer hope for a US black bourgeoisie. *Ebony* sent both its chief photographer and its managing editor to Jamaica to cover the finals of the competition. The *Ebony* team was hosted by a Jamaica Tourist Board eager to show off the 'Ten Types' success story. Marshall Wilson, *Ebony*'s white photographer, took 'Ten Types' as a model of Jamaican racial harmony with the power to convert racists as it provided tangible proof that people of colour could attain the heights of 'white' culture, refinement and respectability:

[Jamaica is] making an invaluable contribution to the development of better race relations in the United States . . . Travellers coming to the island from the United States . . . are very much interested to find that discrimination does not exist in Jamaican hotels or night clubs. Those Americans who believe in equality of races are able to point to the island as an example of how various peoples can live together in harmony. Those who are in favour of segregation are at first amazed – and often converted. By mixing on a social level with *cultured* coloured persons, even the most die-hard believer in segregation begins to have doubts about his convictions[41] [italics my emphasis].

Ebony frequently looked to the Caribbean for evidence of racial harmony and black advancement. If there was a crisis of 'race' in the United States then at least elsewhere in the African Diaspora, specifically the Americas, race, and implicitly, blackness, was not only happily accommodated in society but, also, apparently represented in democratic leadership.

Following its 'Ten Types' coverage, *Ebony* produced an article on Dutch-controlled Suriname. Aptly, here was another postemancipation, post-indentureship American society, with a diverse population and rival nationalisms. *Ebony* featured an array of Surinamese beauty queens drawn from different ethnic competitions, declared Suriname a racial paradise and pondered whether the country welcomed African American migrants. That *Ebony* sought a utopia for a black bourgeoisie indicates not only a wider diasporic concern for the future path of a modern black race, but also that the solutions were to be found within the 'New World' African Diaspora itself.[42]

Clearly, the 'Ten Types' competition had done much to popularise the notion of a plural Jamaica abroad. But despite its ability to represent a racial democracy, the contest also revealed both a persistent unease with the African female body, and an attempt to contain the political energies of the black population. Ultimately, the overriding image of 'Ten Types' was an expansive representation of brownness that suggested brown identity as the natural representative symbol motif of Jamaica. However, the memorable images of the 1955 multiracial array of 'Ten Types', and its 1959 reprisal, captured the imagination of the press and advertisers, especially those representing government-backed corporations, who saw potential for further use of 'Ten Types' as a model of fairness.

Institutionalising the 'Ten Types' model in public discourse

Certain elements of the *Star*'s 'Ten Types' enterprise had far-reaching consequences, whilst others were quickly forgotten. One that was quickly forgotten was the temporary visibility of decorous images of dark-skinned women in commercial advertising that 'Ten Types' had briefly brought about. The competition was sponsored by Dream Toilet Soap and Pluko Hair Pomade. During the course of the ten competitions this sponsorship accompanied the campaigns to find candidates for the mid-toned to darker-skinned categories of 'Miss Sandalwood', 'Miss Allspice', 'Miss Mahogany' and 'Miss Ebony'. These categories featured entrants from the countryside 'search' for beauties through the villages, and perhaps won the most exposure for the two brands in these new markets. In 1956, following the first 'Ten Types' competition of 1955, 'Miss Sandalwood' appeared in an advert in *Spotlight* accompanied by the phrase, 'Beautiful girls everywhere use fragrantly perfumed Dream beauty soap'.[43] From 1959, when the competition resumed with 'Miss Ebony', Dream Soap's sponsorship returned with more finessed advertising. Regional finalist Dorrett Pinnock appeared in an advert as an 'An Ebony Dream Girl': 'Yes, lovely Dorrett Pinnock uses Dream Toilet Soap! You too can enjoy a youthful radiant complexion. Follow the example set by Jamaica's beautiful Ebony Girls . . . Bring out your hidden beauty'.[44] The campaign associated natural beauty and cosmetic preparation with dark-skinned women of African descent, which was unprecedented, though it of course suggested this beauty was somehow submerged, *uncultivated*. The commercial incentives for sponsoring such a large and long-running competition were self-evident, and yet this image-making was striking and unique. Previously, images of black women in advertising at best featured the respectable domestic. The campaign for Guinea Gold laundry soap featured two black domestics; a heroine called Winnie, with neat, 'pressed and curled'[45] hair, and a glowing white uniform, and her raggedy, sweating counterpart who had coarse, swollen and 'unfeminine' hands. The part of the uncouth washerwoman was perhaps posed by a man. 'Whew! Look at me 'ands . . . washing and me jus don' agree', says the harassed, washerwoman. 'Mine keep dainty because I use Guinea Gold', replies a serene Winnie.[46] Winnie's relative refinement is underscored by her use of enunciated English, while her associate's creole or patois speech represents stubborn coarseness.

In another 'Guinea Gold' ad, the ragged washerwoman says, 'Winnie, I wish washday could-a-neva come', to which Winnie replies, with a smile, 'That's because you don't know about Guinea Gold'.[47] The uncouth washerwoman raises the spectre of the emasculating, mannish black woman, vulgarised by the sweat and rigour of labour. This was the 'vulgar' black woman who represented, in the view of the Moyne Commission, an obstacle to the nuclear family and to development. She was therefore a subversive, problematic figure, and an important target for ridicule. By contrast Winnie represents the most sanctioned image of black working-class femininity appearing in the press, prior to the 'Ten Types' competition, the black woman dutifully engaged in honest, gendered and suitably humble work. Ironically, however, Winnie delivers this promise by presenting with elements of understated polish, most likely to be practised by black professional women rather than toiling labourers; the neat clothing, coiffed hair, and 'dainty hands'.

However, the unprecedented Dream Girl image of black beauty disappeared with its commercial incentive. With the end of the 'Ten Types' competition, positive commercial images that presented black femininity as desirable ceased to exist in the Jamaican press until much later. However, images of desirable *brown* femininity in advertising began

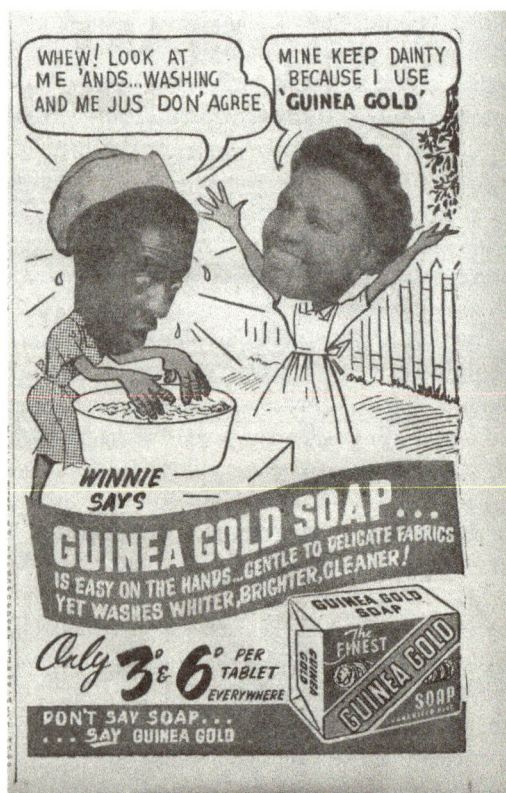

4.3   Guinea Gold Soap

to appear with more frequency at around this time and became especially visible in the 1960s.

The 1959 'Miss Ebony' winner Doreen Bryan made at least two further public appearances in beauty competitions. However, Bryan did not appear as a contestant, but as a presiding 'goodwill' figure; once as a judge in a local competition in the new suburb of Harbour View, and later to crown the winner of the 1961 'Miss Chinese Jamaica' competition.[48] Yet, in the main, images of black women candidates quickly disappeared from view, and in contrast the lasting legacy of the 'Ten Types' competition, as seen in Bryan's occasional public appearances, was to provide a new vernacular of fair dealing. 'Ten Types' was often cited, especially by black nationalists, as the ideal template for all subsequent national competitions. However, this did not immediately materialise, and its more significant lasting effect was in providing a visual shorthand for equality in the press, and in press advertising.

Presumably buoyed by the praise from abroad, the Jamaica Tourist Board used the approach and influence of 'Ten Types' to answer, as though on behalf of elite Jamaicans, persistent criticism of racial and colour discrimination in high-visibility, respectable work, in banks, hotels and shops. It announced in *Spotlight* that it had recruited a new batch of female clerical staff:

> Typical Jamaican staff greet visitors to Jamaican Tourist Board head-quarters in Kingston. Ranging in shade from mahogany to pale pink, each is a honey – and a clipper in efficiency. To get this eye-filling cross-section Chairman Abe Issa and Secretary Phillip Barker-Benfield last year fine-screened 400-odd applicants. Said Abe: We could easily have filled the jobs with all fair-complexioned girls. But we wanted none of that. As an agency spending public funds, we felt obligated to set an example of drawing our staff from all the various colour shades represented in the islands, because efficiency is no respecter of race or colour.[49]

The *Gleaner* revelled in opportunities to reproduce the imagery of 'Ten Types'. In 1962, Jamaica's independence year, it effectively staged a beauty contest between the wives of international heads-of-state. As with the 'Ten Types' competition, the array of feminine 'types' presented was in fact most striking for its standardising effects rather than its intended show of diversity. Notwithstanding that, by dint of the imperial legacy, many of the worldly 'first wives' presented were white women; it was also the case that all the women, from Princess Grace of Monaco, to Queen Farah of Persia, were young and slim and similarly styled. All the women of the array conformed to a standardised Western register of ideal feminine appearance. And, as with 'Ten Types', exceptional fuss was made of a single 'black' presence, which was filled by the 'exotic beauty and cultured elegance' of Madame Houphouet-Boigny, second wife of the Ivory Coast premier. Madame Houphouet-Boigny, like 'Miss Ebony', readers were told, had undergone her own Cinderella-like

4.4   Reigning beauties

transformation, having lived and been educated in France. Houphouet-Boigny, like 'Miss Ebony', was also figuratively marginalised within the expansively imagined parade of standardised beauty, in that her photograph barely revealed her face.[50]

The core message of harmonious plurality of the 'Ten Types' competition recurred in local advertising campaigns for American and British products. In February 1959 an advert for 'New Yorker Shirts' appeared in *Newday* featuring a handsome Afro-Jamaican man in smart formal attire, arms folded in the sober contemplative pose of one shouldering significant responsibility. On his wrist is a smart leather-strapped watch. The modern man of colour wears a serious expression, and looks outward toward a bright future. Smiling at him admiringly are three, ethnically diverse, attractive women, one east Asian, one south Asian and one European. The models are stacked above each other, only their heads and upper torsos appear, with arms folded, like the mythical genie who emerges from Aladdin's lamp. Each model has her hair swept to her right over her shoulder, which emphasises the focus of her gaze on the modern man to her left. The byline, 'You can see the difference', puns on the array of racial difference represented by the models, and their irresistible attraction to the man distinguished by his smart corporate attire, 'designed to make heads turn your way everytime . . . everywhere'.[51]

The orientalisation of the models' pose as pleasing and servile genies underscores the presence of 'difference', the burden of which is represented by exotic femininity of the mystic East. This is required because the alpha (white) male, in this instance, has been displaced by a modern black man. To affirm the primacy of black masculinity, difference is diverted away from him. The models symbolise the orient, and the black man, by contrast, becomes more properly a modern Western man. However, the presence of the white female model is key. Though orientalised as a pleasing, placid genie, she also acts as a mark of heteronormative standards. Evidently the local marketing men did not consider that the Western modernity and the universal appeal of the black man would have been adequately affirmed by the presence of a black model as the third admiring female. Much like the 'Ten Types' competition itself, white femininity, historically the adjunct to a liberal, patriarchal ideal of white masculinity, is so much bound to the accentuation of consummate modernity that it cannot be altogether removed from the array of worldly beauty.[52]

A similar advert appeared for the British Overseas Airways Corporation (BOAC). BOAC served British Empire routes, part of which had recently

4.5 'You can see the difference'

formed the subsidiary airline BWIA, famously the first airline to employ a black stewardess, Pearl Marshall, in 1956. The BOAC advertisement similarly affirmed the 'Ten Types' template of an array of worldly beauties. Entitled 'Your B.O.A.C. Stewardesses, Sir', the advert featured three differently costumed models, representing BOAC's trade in the 'Orient, Europe and the East'.[53] Jamaica had entered the modern age of jet travel. BOAC boasted that the intercontinental Boeing Rolls-Royce 707 could reach London in 6 hours and 20 minutes. The executive male who could afford the luxury of air travel, marked by the attentiveness of glamorous female staff, is not pictured in the advert. Instead he is addressed as 'sir' in the text. As with the New Yorker shirts' advertisement, the consumer's manliness is affirmed by his 'choice' of worldly beauties.[54]

In Trinidad and Barbados the impact of 'Ten Types' was also accentuated by this marriage between beauty competitions and the glamour

4.6 'Your BOAC stewardesses, sir'

of modern air travel. Both of these revolved around selling images of feminine beauty as an abundant national product, which was seemingly different and exotic, and yet standardised. The impact of 'Ten Types' was marked by calls for similar, 'fairer' national competitions in each island. In Trinidad, before the eventual demise of the 'Carnival Queen' competition in 1971, letters to the editor appeared in the *Guardian* and the *Port of Spain Gazette* respectively: the first suggested that judging be replaced by a lottery among the finalists, and the second proposed that five queens from five nominated racial groups 'Negroes, East Indians, Chinese, Pure Whites and Mixed Blood,' be selected.[55] In the competition's last year, the Jaycees assembled a multiracial panel of female contestants for the 'Carnival Queen' competition, and then organised sponsorship by raffle draw, apparently to avoid sponsors' preference for only the light-skinned candidates. It was reported that this new approach, which delivered the competition's first and only 'Afro Queen', had caused a reduction in ticket sales.[56] There followed in both islands brief experiments in multi-competitions, in the 'Ten types' mould. In Barbados, the attempt at a 'Miss Ebony' competition in 1964 became an infamous national controversy, but towards the end of the decade, the parade of finalists in the 'Independence Queen' competition began to resemble the 'Ten Types' multiracial array.

The 'Ten Types' model continued to dovetail in particular with the task of selling the modernity of a national commercial airline carrier in the Caribbean. The Trinidad government acquired BWIA, with its mostly North American and inter-island traffic, in 1966. By 1971 Barbados had its own 'national airline' International Caribbean Airways (ICA), which operated charter flights between Luxembourg, London and Barbados.[57] Both BWIA and ICA appointed local models and former beauty contestants to their hostess staff, and revelled in the functionality of the multiracial template of 'Ten Types'. The ICA stewardesses served as cultural ambassadors in Europe. They were pictured meeting the Governor General of Barbados at the exclusive Claridge's Hotel in London, as part of a glamorous publicity trip, not unlike a beauty queen's prize holiday. BWIA used multiracial stewardesses, 'beautiful West Indian girls', prominently in its glossy advertising for its Sunjets fleet of aircraft. Their captions reflected the shift to the overt sexualisation of air travel, and female cabin crew, from the early 1970s: 'Here, temptingly displayed, is a selection of our island beauties'.[58]

In another BWIA advertisement, harmonious creole culture was paired with consummate modernity, the emphasis being that both were equally at home in Trinidad. The advert offered a 'split-screen' of two contrasting images, the multiracial women dressed in Afro-Creole costume, illustrating Trinidad's cultural vivacity, and the multiracial uniformed air stewardesses representing professional service, and racial harmony, of BWIA, underscoring the modernity of Trinidad itself. Customers were promised 'laughing eyes and beautiful smiles'.[59]

'Ten Types' provided a useful framework for selling moderation and glacial political change, disguised as 'fairness' and meritocracy, to Caribbean audiences, particularly in the definitively modern industries of air travel and mass tourism that would so much determine the economic fate of the islands. Just as the 'Ten Types' model, Sealy's gift to the 'Jamaica 300' festival, was covered in civic pride, so too were these new modern industries. Advertising for new state airlines revelled in exemplary multiracial femininity. 'Ten Types' was institutionalised as *the* symbol of equality in the visual repertoire of modern West Indianness.

'Miss Jamaica' and brown femininity as national motif

Though the 'Ten Types' competition stimulated accusations of racial discrimination in the older 'Miss Jamaica' competition, 'Miss Jamaica' nonetheless continued as the most prestigious and lucrative of beauty contests in the island. Dark-skinned contestants of 'Ten Types' competitions did not fare well in the 'Miss Jamaica' contest. In 1959, the first of a slew of light-skinned women triumphed, following the previous year's competition, which was dogged by persistent rumours that in fact 1958 was to have been the year of the first brown winner, but that this event was hampered by the Chamber of Commerce's commitment to sending the winner to a regional business fair, the Festival of the Americas, in Miami where 'Jim Crow' conventions of racial segregation prevailed.[60] 'Miss Jamaica' 1959, Sheila Chong, was celebrated in the now-familiar language of harmonious

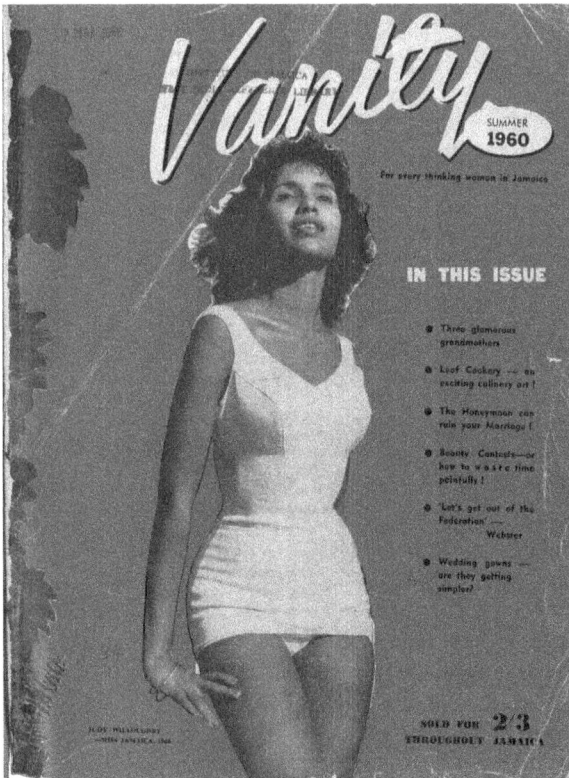

4.7 *Vanity* celebrates 'Misses Jamaica'
Judith Willoughby, 'Miss Jamaica', 1960

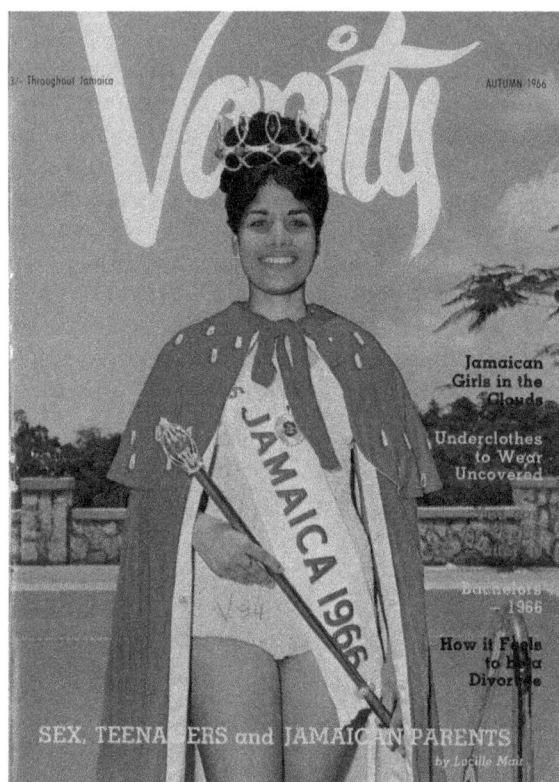

4.8 Yvonne Walter, 'Miss Jamaica', 1966

race-relations exemplified in feminine beauty. Chong was of Chinese and coloured parentage. Her diverse racial heritage appeared foremost in press coverage; she was cast as the literal embodiment of Jamaicanness. As *Newday* put it, 'This is the first time the queen seemed to please everyone. Sheila Chong is a typical Jamaican girl. A Negro-Chinese-Syrian composite.'[61] Ultimately this process would be cemented in 1963 when the light-skinned Carol Joan Crawford achieved what was regarded as the unprecedented feat of winning 'Miss World', thus establishing a standard for light-skinned 'Miss Jamaica' queens in the years that followed, and affirming the political and economic efficacy of Jamaica's investment in hybrid beauty in the process. The light-brown 'Miss Jamaica' type combined an image of femininity that met with dominant aesthetic values, and offered some exotic appeal to white tourists besides, and yet satisfied calls for typicality and cultural authenticity in a national representative.

Proof that brown femininity had become *the* glamorous leitmotif of Jamaican identity abounded. The new women's glossy press, *Vanity* and *Jamaican Housewife*, featured brown cover girls almost without exception. They glorified in the 'honey-brown' skin-tones of aspiring models, actresses and singers.[62] Evidently the brown woman had become sufficiently iconic to attract sustainable commercial sponsorship through advertising, some of which explicitly targeted a brown and black middle-class market, with bleaching crèmes and hair straighteners. Alongside glamorous brown women, other content included Hollywood gossip, short fiction, and instruction on feminine etiquette. *Vanity* was founded in 1958 by Chinese-Jamaican Amoy Kong Quee, to serve the 'West Indian family and in particular the West Indian woman'.[63] It recruited the experienced feminist publisher Aimee Webster to deliver 'very strong and independent views'.[64] Alongside this it included conduct advice, such as an article entitled 'Pretty Ways Make Pretty Girls': 'Not married? Then remember that your manners towards your family are what those visiting boy friends always notice. Married? Then treat him as if he were the most important person in your world. He probably is!'[65] The *Jamaican Housewife* combined content on female firsts, policewomen and pilots, with articles that stressed personal grooming and male perspectives of feminine desirability, including one article entitled, 'You'd be so nice to wake up to . . . with a little extra care'.[66] The new glossy press, whose appearance in the late 1950s coincided with the shift to brown 'Miss Jamaica' winners, fed the discursive and visual construction of ideal Jamaican femininity as heterosexual, mixed-raced and betraying a precise register of refined manners, deportment and personal grooming. One *Vanity* travel writer in Africa, grasping for a reference to counterpose against the beauty of Senegalese women, summarised the now iconic role of brown femininity in Jamaica, 'The Jamaican woman of mixed blood is the most beautiful I know in the Caribbean'.[67] Jamaica, the largest of British Caribbean islands, had refined the template for pre-eminent femininity in the body of a brown woman.

On the eve of independence the *Gleaner* heightened its rhetoric of Jamaican racial harmony and fixed this to mixed-raced identity. In August 1962, *Gleaner* columnist Frank Hill suggested Jamaica's brown population were the only people that were truly indigenous to the island, 'The only group created out of the Jamaican environment'.[68] Fellow columnist WOB Aitcheson claimed racial democracy was not so much an aspiration as a 'fait accompli'. Jamaica, Aitcheson claimed, could speak with the authority of the 'World Council of Nations for we exemplify a national character of the best of human attributes, racial equality and impartiality of justice that is unsurpassed.'[69] In a reversal of nineteenth-century

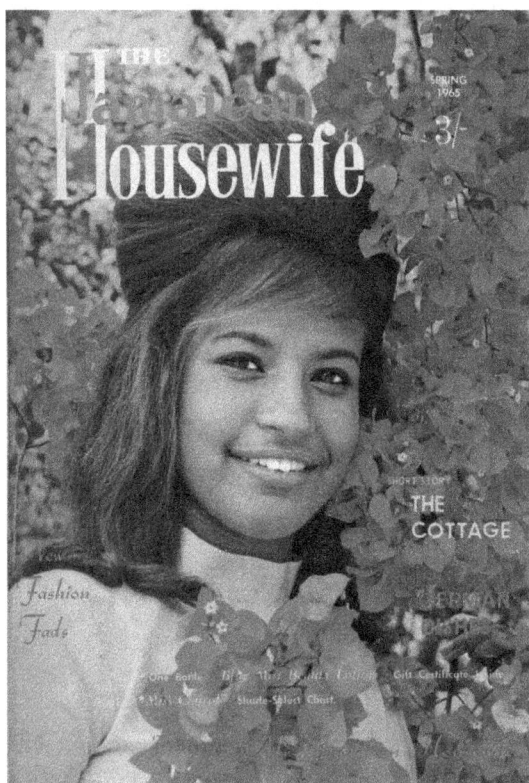

4.9 *Jamaican Housewife* cover, Spring 1965

biological racism that claimed mixed-raced people were degenerate and mentally feeble, Aitcheson suggested Jamaican schooling and its ultimate annual prize, the Rhodes scholarship (a place at Oxford University), were both evidence of Jamaican meritocracy and proof that racial mixing bred intelligent people: 'The children exhibit the fact that the blend is indissoluble, a chemical mixture, and not a physical one. As a result [of impartiality in allocating scholarships] our Rhodes Scholarship holders have all been typically Jamaican'.[70] Aitcheson provided his spurious evidence of racial equality thriving in Jamaica, and reduced the dissident activism of the likes of Millard Johnson, and the tradition of black-nationalism, to, 'little pockets of occurrences here and there; now and then [that] . . . try to mar the unification of the people.'[71] Added to this, *Newday* published an article extolling Jamaican sporting prowess entitled, 'Mixed Blood is Sporting Blood'.[72]

Nationalists who promoted a plural Jamaica unconsciously revealed the weakness of the model for delivering their essential message; that the critical harmonising element of racial democracy was in fact the presence of mixed-raced people, and the sublimation and gradual assimilation of the 'un-mixed' people, imagined in distinctive groups. Where plural Jamaica was the official message, one that masked racism, the trope of 'hybridity', the seemingly natural realisation of racial democracy, was increasingly literalised through the body of the brown woman of mixed racial heritage.

Fittingly, the 'Ten Types' contest assumed pride of place in projecting the mythology of Jamaican racial democracy into the post-independence era. Sealy won a lead role in organising another national event, the celebrations to mark Jamaican Independence on 6 August 1962. Sealy took part in formulating the new national motto announced as 'Out of Many – One People.' He later tentatively acknowledged the role of the 'Ten Types – One People' beauty competitions in shaping the motto. He recalled, 'The contest . . . was so popular that the concept entered the public consciousness and it was probably by force of habit that the members of the Legislature in 1962 chose the expression, "Out of Many, One People" '.[73]

In spite of the large impact of 'Ten Types', Sealy's assessment here is not entirely accurate. The Legislative Council was not in session when the national motto was announced in April 1962. Rather, the phrase was urged on by the Working Committee who needed a motto for publication on promotional material, which suggests a more direct input from Sealy as the 'Ten Types' organiser and Committee Chair.[74] In his handwritten unfinished manuscript, outgoing Chief Minister Norman Manley at first suggested the national motto was his own idea, but later corrected this assertion to write that he was only 'part-author'.[75] Just as 'Ten Types' had crowned a first Jamaican national festival, 'Jamaica 300', so too had 'Miss Jamaica' entered the national embrace, becoming the glamorous centrepiece of the government's new annual 'Jamaica Festival' from 1963 onwards.

The Festival beauty competition became a three-pronged event. Borrowing from the 'Ten Types' template, it crowned three queens, 'Miss Jamaica', 'Miss Festival' and 'Miss Farm Queen', for several years. The 'Miss Farm Queen' category seemed to echo the idealised 'country girl' image behind 'Miss Ebony' and 'Miss Jamaican Nation'; here was a category for 'unadulterated' rural woman to be transformed and assimilated into modern Jamaica. This competition was sometimes won by darker-skinned women, such as Karlene Wardell, in 1967, a woman who might, under the 'Ten Types' stratification, have been offered the 'Miss Allspice' crown, due to her mixed African and Indian heritage. Unusually Wardell made the transition from the lesser crown of 'Farm Queen' to the greater prize of 'Miss Jamaica' in 1968. Sealy again took the opportunity to announce the end of racism, with an editorial entitled 'Black Beauty', in which he praised the arrival, at last, of a 'Jamaican type' as 'the fairest of them all'. Sealy also admitted Wardell's win might have been influenced by the political moment, what he described as the rise of the 'Black is Beautiful' slogan amongst 'coloured-Americans' and the 'political awakening of Africa'.[76] Unsurprisingly, however, Wardell's win was followed by a return to the status quo. Nonetheless it illustrated the political and temporal context of ideals of feminine beauty, and, once again, the circulation of racial ideologies within the African Diaspora. Wardell's different racial mix was temporarily permissible for the premier

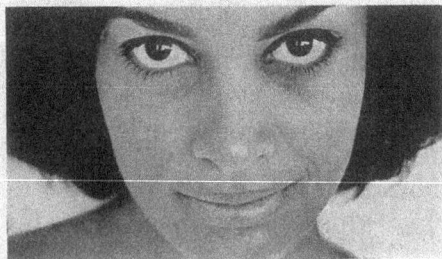

*Her ancestors were
African, German, Welsh, Indian,
French and Costa Rican.
She's pure Jamaican.*

4.10 'Pure Jamaican'

title, and this was made possible by the exceptional circumstances of the political moment. However, in the same year the Jamaica Tourist Board cemented the institutionalisation of light-skinned mixed-raced feminine beauty as the national standard, with a tourist advert for Jamaica featuring former 'Miss Jamaica' Judith Willoughby, which made their message explicit and read, 'Her ancestors were African, German, Welsh, Indian, French, and Costa Rican. She's pure Jamaican.'

Conclusion

The 'Ten Types' competition replaced race with a gendered ideology of colour in which brownness symbolically desensitised racial confrontation and blackness was marginalised. Black leadership engaged with the national project took up the beauty contest as an anti-racist campaigning tool, but struggled to reconnect racial and national consciousness through the body of the idealised black beauty queen. 'Miss Ebony' represented the transformative power of assimilation by so-called refinement. Yet it also spoke to contingent of the audience for 'Miss Jamaica' who would never be satisfied by the standardisation of the beauty represented in the competition. As evidence that the brown competition would always have its detractors Jimmy Cliff released a hit record in 1962, the year of Jamaican independence, entitled 'Miss Jamaica', which proclaimed 'You're my "Miss Jamaica"' and praised the beauty of a woman not fitting the standardised 'Miss Jamaica' type but at odds with it.[77] From the decimalising array of 'Ten Types', however, brown femininity, expansively represented, emerged as the figurative shorthand for modern Jamaica.

Notes

1 *Star*, 19 November 1955.
2 Theodore Sealy, 'How We Celebrated Our First Independence: A Personal Recollection,' *Jamaica Journal* 46 (1982), pp. 2–13. The 'Ten Types' competition began in 1955 and resumed in 1959 until its demise in 1963. The *Gleaner* claimed that 6000 women had their photographs taken for entry into the competitions ('LaYacona Takes Top Award in Photo Competition,' *Gleaner*, 29 July 1985). It is likely that the figure of 6000 participants relates to the amount of women attracted to the pageant over its entire lifetime from 1955 to 1963. Hereafter, the 'Ten Types – One People' beauty contest is referred to as 'Ten Types'.
3 Barnes, 'Face of the Nation', p. 358.
4 Ibid., p. 289.
5 Eudine Barriteau, 'Theorising Gender Systems and the Project of Modernity in the Twentieth-Century Caribbean', *Feminist Review* 59(1) (1998), p. 186.
6 Munroe, 'Constitutional Decolonisation', pp. 102–105.

7 Deborah Thomas, *Modern Blackness: Nationalism, Globalization and the Politics of Culture in Jamaica* (Durham, NC: Duke University Press, 2004), p. 52.

8 Howard Johnson, 'The "Jamaica 300" Celebrations of 1955: Commemoration in a Colonial Polity,' *Journal of Imperial and Commonwealth History* 26 (1998), pp. 120–37.

9 Ibid., pp. 123–124.

10 *Star*, 19 November 1955, p. 1.

11 *Gleaner*, 5 December 1955. Sealy took issue with the image of the peasant 'woman on the donkey', the market woman of colonial imagery that had been popularised by the United Fruit Company on postcards as an emblem of a non-threatening and compliant black peasantry. This image of the black peasantry contended with nationalist ideology that saw the peasantry as foundational to Jamaican society; with independence, not colonial subjection. For further discussion of the 'woman on the donkey' imagery see Krista Thompson, 'Black Skin, Blue Eyes: Visualising Blackness in Jamaican Art, 1922–1944,' *Small Axe* 8 (2004) pp. 1–31.

12 *Star*, 29 July 1955.

13 *Star*, 1 September 1955.

14 French, 'Colonial Policy', pp. 50–53.

15 *Star*, 1 September 1955.

16 This decision probably had to do with the non-confrontational basis of the competition and the desire of organisers not to see one overall winner emerging as the favourite of any assembled crowd. Not only would it have been very expensive to host ten separate public finals before an audience, but to have brought the finalists of each of the ten competitions together in one public meeting might have led to particular favourites emerging that would have contravened the plural, non-confrontational professed ideal of the competition.

17 *Star*, 16 July 1955.

18 *Star*, 23 July 1955.

19 *Star*, 19 May 1955. In fact only five of the intended ten competitions took place after the re-launch in 1959: 'Miss Ebony' in 1959, 'Miss Mahogany' in 1960, 'Miss Satinwood' in 1961, 'Miss Golden Apple' in 1962 and 'Miss Appleblossom in 1963'.

20 *Star*, 9 May 1959.

21 This is with the notable aforementioned exception of the PNP's earlier attempts at organising local Kingston competitions.

22 Laila Haidarali, 'Polishing Brown Diamonds: African American Women, Popular Magazines, and the Advent of Modelling in Early Postwar America,' *Journal of Women's History* 17 (2005) pp. 10–37. 'Brownskin' was the African American euphemism for light-skinned women, used to describe the women who increasingly appeared in the postwar era as models and occasionally as actresses, including Dorothy Dandridge and Lena Horne.

23 The *Star*, racier than its sister paper the *Gleaner*, reported the success of 'Abu La Fleur,' a topless Jamaican dancer named Jeeni Sherman who, while working in London, had managed to secure the role of lead dancer in a popular variety show, Toujours l'amour (*Star*, 15 May 1959).

24 Haidarali, 'Polishing Brown Diamonds,' p. 10.

25 'Black Beauty', *Spotlight* 20 (1959), p. 32.

26 'The Black Queen', *Spotlight* 21 (1960), p. 30.

27 'Black Beauty', *Spotlight* 20 (1959), p. 33; 'Black Shadow over "Paradise Isle",' *Newday* 5 (1961) pp. 19–21; 'A Man Called *Spotlight*', *Spotlight*, December 1956, pp. 32–35.

28 'Black Beauty', *Spotlight* 20 (1959), pp. 12, 33.

29 Lola Young, 'Missing Persons: Fantasising Black Women in Black Skin, White Masks' in Alan Read (ed.), *The Fact of Blackness* (London: Institute of International Visual Arts, 1996) pp. 87–97; Michelle Wright, *Becoming Black: Creating Identity in the African Diaspora* (Durham: Duke University Press, 2004) pp. 124–135.

30 'Black Beauty', *Spotligtht* 20 (1959), pp. 12, 33.

31 *Star*, 5 September 1955; UNIA (Jamaica Chapter), press release 10 October 1960, National Library of Jamaica.

32 'Ten Strikes Against the "Miss Jamaica" Contest', *Newday* 5 (1961), p. 36.

33 Ibid.

34 *Gleaner*, 13 July 1962.

35 *Gleaner*, 8 June 1964, p. 20; *Gleaner*, 31 July 1964.

36 Thomas, *Modern Blackness*, p. 266.

37 Marcus Garvey, 'The Black Woman', reprinted in *Jamaican Housewife*, Spring 1965, p. 17.

38 *Gleaner*, 10 August 1955.

39 Peter Abrahams, *Jamaica: An Island Mosaic* (London: HM Stationery Office, 1957), pp. 198–199.

40 'Jamaica – Skin Deep', *Time*, 28 November 1955.

41 *Star*, 30 November 1955.

42 'Suriname: Multiracial Paradise at the Crossroads', *Ebony*, February 1967 www.buku.nl/ebony.html (accessed 13 October 2006).

43 *Spotlight* 19 (1958), p. 12.

44 *Star*, 19 November 1959.

45 The 'press and curl' hairstyle involved straightening tightly curled hair with a hot-comb, heated on the kitchen stove, before curling it with heated tongs. Amy Bailey's discussion of urban working-class women's concern for beauty (featured in Chapter 1) and coverage of the 'Ten Types' competition, with its emphasis on transformation, both suggest that hair treated in this way was more of an 'urban' identity.

46 *Star*, 11 November 1955.

47 *Gleaner*, 5 December 1955, p. 16.

48 *Star*, 8 August 1962; 'Time of the Chinese Beauties', *Newday* 4 (1960), p. 75. In this latter appearance 'Miss Ebony' was praised for being 'poised, charming and demure'.

49 'Travel News', *Spotlight* 16 (1955), p. 6.

50 *Gleaner*, 24 June 1962, p. 13.

51 *Newday* 4 (1959), p. 12.

52 *Newday* 3 (1959), p. 20.

53 Ibid.

54 Ibid.

55 *Trinidad Guardian*, 30 January 1970, p. 7; *Chronicle and Port of Spain Gazette*, 26 January 1958, p. 6.

56 *Sunday Guardian Magazine*, 21 February 1971, p. 8; *Trinidad Guardian*, 21 February, p. 1.

57 'Travel', *The Bajan* 224 (1972), p. 28.

58 'Welcome Aboard', 'Trinidad Carnival: The World's Most Colourful Festival'; Barry, *Femininity in Flight*, pp. 175–209.
59 *The Bajan*, 217 (1971), p. 5.
60 'Women: Beauty Contests are a Bad Business', *Newday*, July 1958, p. 47.
61 'Sheila's Big Break', *Newday*, 3 (1959), p. 73.
62 'Cover Girl', *Vanity* 1 (1958) p. 1.
63 Editor's letter, *Vanity* 1 (1958), p. 1.
64 Ibid.
65 'Pretty Ways Make Pretty Girls', *Vanity* 1 (1958), p. 47.
66 *Jamaican Housewife* 1 (1962), pp. 27, 43; *Jamaican Housewife* 3 (1964), p. 45.
67 'Senegal', *Vanity* 9 (1966), p. 41.
68 *Sunday Gleaner*, 28 July 1962.
69 *Sunday Gleaner*, 17 June 1962.
70 Ibid.
71 Ibid.
72 'Mixed Blood is Sporting Blood', *Newday* 7 (1962), pp. 47, 61–62.
73 Sealy, 'Our First Independence', *Jamaica Journal* 46 (1980), p. 4.
74 *Gleaner*, 4 April 1962, p. 1.
75 National Library of Jamaica: (MS 2035) Norman Washington Manley, 'Second Autobiography' (unpublished manuscript), 6 June–21 July 1969.
76 *Gleaner*, 18 August 1968, p. 6.
77 Cooper, 'Re-fashioning Beauty', pp. 399–400.

5

'Colonisation in Reverse': Claudia Jones, the West Indian Gazette and the 'Carnival Queen' beauty contest in London, 1959–64

Wat a joyful news, Miss Mattie,
I feel like me heart gwine burs
Jamaica people colonizin
Englan in Reverse

By de hundred, by de tousan
From country and from town,
By de ship-load, by de plane load
Jamica is Englan boun.

Dem a pour out a Jamaica,
Everybody future plan
Is fe get a big-time job
An settle in de mother lan.

What an islan! What a people!
Man an woman, old an young
Jus a pack dem bag an baggage
An turn history upside dung

Excerpt from 'Colonisation in Reverse',
Louise Bennett, Jamaican poet and folklorist, 1966[1]

I N 1959 Trinidadian-born Claudia Jones, a communist leader exiled from the United States, formed a partnership with an illustrious band of West Indian artists, to organise the first Caribbean Carnival in Britain. The idea for Carnival sprang from the new *West Indian Gazette*, which Jones edited, and its supporters. This progressive and farsighted group sought a defiant and unifying response to the racial violence of the Notting Hill and Nottingham riots of the summer of 1958, when sporadic attacks on Caribbean settlers grew into mob violence.[2] Carnival was intended to illustrate the proud heritage and cultural vivacity of the new West Indian settler community; to assert dignity, personhood and solidarity in the face of hostility and neglect from the British government and the more direct violence done to them by the rioters. Carnival was staged at the St Pancras Town Hall in central London in February, to coincide with the timing of the Lenten carnival in the Caribbean, the most famous and spectacular of which was the Trinidad Carnival. A central attraction of the festivities was a black beauty competition to crown a 'Carnival Queen'.

In London, Jones used the *Gazette*, Carnival and 'Carnival Queen' to affirm a Diaspora Caribbean culture and identity. Central to this programme was her determination to bring more visibility to black women's experiences, not least by challenging racist beauty politics that marginalised black women. Jones sought to bring black women from the periphery to the centre.

At first glance Jones's vision of West Indian nationhood might appear to mirror the programme of cultural nationalism that nationalists had adopted in Jamaica, Trinidad and Barbados. However, Jones's background as leftist black feminist shaped her very different work among Caribbean settlers in Britain. As a communist Jones valued Caribbean nationalism as a means of resisting imperialism, both the European legacy and North American neo-colonial advances in the area. To her mind nationalism should promote international friendship between a 'community of nations' and, most pressing in the Caribbean case, raise oppressed people's awareness of their common history and culture. Nationalism in Jones's view could unite West Indian peoples, regardless of their location, in a consciousness of their shared heritage in the anticolonial struggle.[3]

Through the *Gazette*, Carnival and 'Carnival Queen' Jones extended and refashioned the project of Caribbean cultural nationalism for a new British context. In Britain, as Jones appreciated first hand, Caribbean people faced new challenges. Immigrants from the Caribbean now interrogated the ideology of the British Empire *at the metropolis*. They settled in the postwar urban squalor of British cities and had no choice but to engage the anti-racist effort in their daily lives. This process, as evidenced by Louise Bennett's poem 'Colonisation in Reverse', was chronicled by contemporary Caribbean writers living in Britain, including Sam Selvon and George Lamming, and not least by Jones herself, writing in the *Gazette* and other leftist journals. In the words of literary critic and cultural historian Bill Schwarz, the West Indian arrivals were 'living on the unofficial front line of [the] larger struggle for decolonisation'.[4] Schwarz and Jones's biographer Carole Boyce Davies, who has done a great deal to restore Jones to the historical record and bring her writings to light, have provided important analysis of the *Gazette* and Carnival as agents for the creolisation of Britain. Following these inroads, this chapter considers the cultural work of the 'Carnival Queen' beauty contest, at first glance an unlikely project for a communist feminist, to affirm black femininity in Britain as a mark of cultural and racial resistance. It examines Jones's steerage of the *Gazette*, Britain's first commercial black newspaper, to deliver a pronounced celebration of black womanhood. Through the *Gazette* Jones supported, and was supported by, a burgeoning black beauty culture, which provided uneven opportunities to extend this well-intentioned work.

The beauty contest in the Caribbean had advanced cultural nationalism through the image of an idealised light-skinned 'brown' woman, as a means of challenging British cultural supremacy. However, this male-dominated middle-class movement had, as it tried to imagine a standard for modern Caribbean femininity, betrayed an antagonism towards the women of colour who must somehow fit the ideal mould. It displayed particular unease over the proper image of dark-skinned women in the quest to define a modern black femininity. In contrast the *Gazette*'s black British beauty contest attempted to challenge the 'multilayered pigmentocracy' at the heart of Caribbean society, striking at the inner workings of the racial system of British colonialism in the process.[5] Claudia Jones's radical political vision affirmed black womanhood as a cornerstone of its anti-racist and community-building work.

Claudia Jones: a unique career in public life

Until recently accounts of the life and work of Claudia Jones had been uneven and few in number. A series of attempts had been made at recognising Jones for her political contribution, in the decades since her premature death from heart disease in London in 1964. Whilst these reflected the esteem within which Jones was held in a broad range of communities, they tended to be preliminary in nature, focusing either on her American activism or her time in Britain.[6] However, Carole Boyce Davies's political and literary biography *Left of Karl Marx*, published in 2008, has provided the most thorough treatment of Jones's political, intellectual and literary life to date, taking in her global perspective and prescient feminism on both continents. Following *Left of Karl Marx*, Davies edited *Claudia Jones: Beyond Containment*, which makes available many more of Jones's intellectual and creative works. This treatment has dramatically improved the landscape for scholars wishing to explore Jones's multifarious contribution to efforts at imagining and elucidating radical sensibilities within the African Diaspora.

Using Jones's writing, the *Gazette* and the recollections of Jones's friends, this chapter builds on Davies's works, and Schwarz's recognition of the *Gazette* as a deeply original publication, to focus on a particular impact of Jones's political and cultural vision; her attention to black femininity. It adds to the ongoing reclamation work, to consider the originality of the black beauty competition in London. It argues that Jones's childhood in colonial Trinidad and immigrant New York, her maturation in bustling Harlem, made her a carrier and innovator of radical ideas of the anti-racist effort that singled out gender and affirmed black femininity as a priority, and delivered innovative methods to the postcolonial community in London.

Before she arrived in London in 1958 as a deportee of the McCarthy communist witch-hunt in the US, Jones had already built an exceptional career of activism within the US Communist movement. Jones had risen to the rank of leader of the National Women's Commission in 1945. Prior to that Jones had served on the *Daily Worker*, become director of youth work in the Communist Party, and later edited *Negro Affairs Quarterly*. Her campaigning and organising work addressed race, gender, class and imperial oppression. She wrote a regular column entitled 'Half the World' in the *Daily Worker* to raise the race-gender consciousness of women and men in America. She challenged the neo-colonial strategies of American capital in the Caribbean.[7] Often Jones's standpoint necessitated challenging blockages to female leadership within the Communist movement itself, and articulating the theoretical limitations that bound the party's ideology.[8] Uniquely, Jones articulated the need for greater race-gender consciousness in the path of the Communist Party's work, especially in her article, 'An End to the Neglect of the Problems of the Negro Woman', which took as its representative example the plight of the New York domestic worker. As Davies describes, this piece:

> [O]ffered, for its time, the clearest analysis of the location of black women – not in essentialized, romantic, or homogenizing terms but practically, as located in the US, and world economic hierarchies . . . To develop her argument, Jones contended that if all workers are exploited because of the usurping of the surplus value of their labour, then black women – bereft of any kind of institutional mechanism to conquer this exploitation, and often assumed to have to work uncountable hours without recompense – live a life of superexploitation beyond what Marx had identified as the workers' lot.[9]

Jones was born Claudia Cumberbatch (she later adopted the *nom de guerre* of Jones) in 1915 in Port of Spain, Trinidad, to a family with Trinidadian and Barbadian origins.[10] The experience within her family, as educated blacks moving between Caribbean locales and then to the US, was representative and, for the young Jones, formative. Migration to the US had become more common when regional pulls within the Caribbean basin abated. Migration was encouraged by depressed wages and scarce opportunities for professional work amongst what historian Winston James has called, the 'dark-skinned bright children of the peasantry' who formed the aspiring professional class.[11] James cites West Indian 'pigmentocracy' as chief among the motivations for migration to the US for the black poor, as was recorded by black intellectuals Claude McKay and CLR James.[12] Between 1889 and 1932 the favoured destinations of West Indian migrants shifted from Central America to the US and within the US shifted away from agricultural Florida towards the industrial north and especially New York City.[13] By the 1920s New York was attracting the most migrants, 26,000 (over 58 per cent) between 1920 and 1926.[14] Jones's parents left Trinidad in 1922 and she followed with her three sisters and aunt in 1924. Like many blacks the family settled in Harlem, the bustling, overcrowded centre of black life in New York, then being swelled with migrants from the south, but from the Caribbean especially.[15]

Jones's father is reputed to have edited a West Indian newspaper in Harlem, the *West Indian American*. Very little is known about Jones's early life, but the newspaper is probably a good indication that the family sustained a sense of racial and cultural identity and, in the words of Davies, a sense of Caribbean Diaspora, which would continue in Jones' work in Britain.[16] West Indian migrants were predisposed to join radical social movements in the US, and ultimately made a disproportionate contribution to organised left politics in interwar New York. Among the factors that encouraged their radicalisation were: prior experience of organised politics; comparative perspectives of black oppression acquired through inter-island and international migration; military service during the First World War and their 'protected status . . . as subjects of the British Crown'.[17] However, the mass of West Indians were more colour-conscious than race-conscious upon arrival in the US and underwent their radicalisation – their transformation into race-conscious 'blacks' willing to organise around racial solidarity – under the privations of life in the US and the humiliations of Jim Crowism. Garvey's UNIA had its largest chapter in Harlem, and of the blacks represented in interracial left politics, West Indians dominated.[18]

The Cumberbatch family lived in poverty in Harlem. Jones's mother found work in the garment industry but died prematurely of associated ill-health and exhaustion. Jones's father held a range of low-status jobs and eventually took work as a caretaker in an apartment block. Jones contracted tuberculosis from the damp in their flat, and missed a year of school. Her childhood ill-health continued to plague her through adult life and was exacerbated by a period of internment during the McCarthy campaign.[19]

Jones grew up in Harlem at a time when black beauty culture, that is the industry and social world surrounding cosmetics and grooming specifically for the black body, represented a new market and social space that offered material gains and perceived social advancement to black people, especially women. Black beauty culture provided a focus for the entrepreneurial zeal of the African American community. Harlem in the 1920s had seen two decades of consolidation of new black arrivals and when other work proved hard to find, not to mention exploitative and low-paid, the new community was sustained in large part by the thriving industry in cosmetics and grooming. This was in turn fuelled by the strategic emphasis of black leadership upon 'self-improvement' as a resistance strategy.[20]

The mass beauty industry in the US was a new market at the start of the twentieth century. The potential for attracting black consumers was quickly apprehended, especially by white entrepreneurs who professed to offer 'fixes' for supposedly 'ugly' black appearance, primarily to straighten hair and bleach skin.[21] However, by the 1920s, alongside this reality, it also appeared that black beauty culture could function in a new, socially affirmative, capacity to its participants, both as workers and as consumers. Here was an independent source of income for both women and men, who could work freelance as beauticians and travelling salespersons, or as proprietors of salons and barbershops. This allowed black women in particular more work opportunities and the chance to avoid exploitative domestic and garment labour, of the kind railed against by Jones.

Furthermore through hair-straightening, make-up application and paradoxically through (the especially harmful) skin-bleaching products, the use of cosmetics opened up a path to feminine respectability. Beauty products promised to deliver the prevailing feminine ideal of the elite black leadership, the *New Negro Lady*, a paradigm of cultured, light-skinned black femininity, preached by the socially conservative National Association for the Advancement of Coloured People (NAACP) and modelled after the Gibson Girl.[22] Straightened hair was coded as middle-class, refined, feminine and urbane, and undergoing this process became a mark of adult maturity for women of colour with hair that was naturally tightly curled. Just as Jamaican migrant women arriving in Kingston were expected to undergo hair treatments, as was decried by Amy Bailey, so too were migrant women in New York City expected to make this show of modern grooming. A polished image provided a psychic defence against Jim Crow humiliations, and the mass of racist imagery, especially in Hollywood film, animation and blackface minstrelsy.

Beauty products also created new spaces for radically repositioning discourses of the 'diseased' and pathological black body of the racist imagination. Black women entrepreneurs, most famously Annie Turnbo Malone and Madame CJ Walker, made their fortunes from black beauty culture. As scholars have underlined, these women were distinct in their attempts to downplay the problematisation of black physiognomy in their advertising and cosmetics, and refused to manufacture skin bleach, but did offer hair-growing remedies and face powder with such names as 'Hi-Brown' which seemed to make desirable 'brown' appearance accessible to all black women. Thus they negotiated prevailing racist standards alongside black self-improvement discourses and emphasised their products as grooming aids that offered social mobility, pride in appearance and economic independence.[23]

Not only was Jones reared in Harlem amongst this culture of pride in appearance as an act of resistance, but at around eighteen she began writing for a black newspaper in Harlem.[24] Throughout her New York career Jones navigated a black world, especially the black press, that roundly embraced the economic and political uses of beauty culture, for all its complexity. Even the UNIA was compromised by its need for advertising revenue from these sometimes dubious sources. Amy Jacques Garvey, UNIA activist and second wife of Marcus, wrote angrily about the black cosmetics industry in the UNIA paper, *Negro World*, in 1926:

> Negroes use laboratories, not to discover serums to prevent disease . . .
> but to place on the market grease that stiffens curly hair, irons that
> press the hair . . . and face cream that bleaches the skin overnight.[25]

Yet still the publication, which like the wider UNIA was suffering financially, took advertising from such companies offering to rid consumers of 'kinks' in their hair.[26]

Indeed the association between the African American press and beauty culture had been long in the making. The first black paper to invent and sponsor a beauty pageant was the Chicago-based *Appeal* in 1891. Many followed suit, including the *New York Age*, which began its own contest in 1915. Beauty pageants became the favoured countercultural performance of race-pride by black leaders, who themselves were often newspapermen. Soon they spread to black institutions such as all-black university campuses. Sociologist Maxine Craig has named this race-pride work 'racial rearticulation'; the attempt to visually and psychically recast blackness in the popular imagination, to affect prevailing racist stereotypes and nurture black self-image.[27] Claudia Jones was immersed in the culture of resistance and racially conscious grooming that thrived in Harlem. In her tributes to fellow race campaigner Ben Davis, Jones referred to his practice of visiting beauty and barber shops to mobilise the captive audiences of waiting black consumers who were to be found there.[28] In London Jones continued to target beauty salons, as she no doubt had done in Harlem, seeking to capture the attention of an audience of black women and men devoted to the routines of grooming, for 'self-improvement', respectability and style.

In her farsighted essay 'An End to the Neglect of the Problems of the Negro Woman' Jones foregrounded black female experiences. Jones exposed the propagandist machine of the New York press in its attempts to encourage black women to resume domestic labour after the relatively liberating conditions and higher wages of factory work during the Second World War. She openly discussed the threat of exploitation and sexual abuse in domestic service. Jones also revealed her sensitivity to the power of mass culture to produce enduring stereotypes, what black feminist Patricia Hill Collins has called 'controlling images', of black women, which affected their perceived status as well as their social reality:

> In the film, radio and press, the Negro woman is not pictured in her real role . . . but as a traditional 'mammy' who puts the care of other children before her own. This traditional stereotype . . . which to this day appears in commercial advertisements, must be combated and rejected as a device . . . to perpetuate the white chauvinist ideology that Negro women are 'backward', 'inferior', and the 'natural slaves' of others.[29]

Jones contended that these stereotypes which so caricatured black women were visibly at work even in the social world of the progressive Communist Party. She argued that not enough black women were helped into the party, and once there could be casually ostracised:

> Some of the crassest expressions of chauvinism are to be found at social affairs, where, all too often, white men and women, and Negro men, participate in dancing, but Negro women are neglected. The acceptance of white ruling-class standards of 'desirability' for women (such as light skin), the failure to extend courtesy to Negro women and to integrate Negro women into organisational leadership, are other forms of chauvinism.

> Another rabid aspect of the Jim Crow oppression of the Negro Woman is expressed in the numerous laws which are directed against her as regards property rights, inter-marriage (originally designed to prevent white men from marrying Negro women), and laws which hinder and deny the right of choice, not only to Negro women, but to Negro and white men and women.[30]

Here, Jones connected racist imagery with racist legislation as dual forces that attempted to degrade black women. Jones aired these attitudes as a means of making explicit the links between the personal and the political. Boldly, Jones chose to write about the intimate zone of life, such as standards of desirability, *alongside* the public anti-racist campaign. Crucially Jones was prepared to suggest that these standards were internalised and acted upon by both blacks and whites. She challenged radicals to confront their own prejudice and to foreground the black female struggle in the leftist progressive agenda. By illustrating the core feminist adage, the 'personal *is* political' Jones illuminated the *process* of racial and sexual oppression, rather than giving credence to oft-repeated reductionist theories of pathological black self-hatred. In so doing Jones provided a contrasting perspective to those who vilified people of colour, especially women, for their supposed mimicry of whites, or like Fanon, overlooked the black female subject altogether.

Jones was criminalised and deported as a result of the US government's anti-communist, anti-foreign strategies that had begun during the Second World War with the Alien Registration (Smith) Act of 1940. These were followed by the Internal Security (McCarran) Act of 1950 and the Immigration and Nationality (McCarran Smith) Act of 1952. This legislation disproportionately targeted Caribbean people for deportation.[31] Jones was sentenced to a year and a day in Alderson Prison, West Virginia, followed by deportation under the terms of the Smith Act, and thus became the first black female prisoner of conscience in the US.[32] Prison exacerbated her ill health and she spent time in hospital during her sentence. On her release the colonial British government in Trinidad was unwilling to accept Jones and, as a British subject, she was instead sent to Britain in December 1955, after the failure of rounds of protests from communists and Harlem residents alike.[33] Before internment, at her sentencing, Jones made a defiant speech addressing the invisibility of black women in public life. She said in defence of her writing, that prosecutors were afraid to read her work aloud during the trial for fear that this would force them to recognise that, 'black women can think, speak and write'.[34]

Jones's radical world-view, her willingness to tackle oppression on many fronts and in particular her attention to black womanhood made her a prescient and insightful figure as she settled among London's West Indian community, where she emerged as a leader and spokesperson. As a Trinidadian-born, US-raised, new black Briton her life now spanned what Paul Gilroy has theorised as the 'black Atlantic', both in her intellectual vision and in her quotidian experience, as she theorised a way forward for the new black British community and embarked on pragmatic activism.[35]

West Indian settlement

The arrival of the *Empire Windrush* at Tilbury Docks with 492 Jamaicans aboard on 21 June 1948 is renowned as the beginning of large-scale West Indian migration to postwar Britain. In the early 1950s West Indian immigration was between 1000 and 2000 annually, but rose to roughly 10,000 in 1954. Claudia Jones's own research, using statistics from the former West Indian Federation Office, put the figure resident in Britain in 1962 at over 300,000.[36] However, migration was then curtailed by the Commonwealth Immigrants Acts of 1962 and 1968.[37] This legislation essentially restricted arrivals of 'coloured' people, from the former Empire, from the West Indies, Africa and the Indian subcontinent. Jones helped lead the campaign to protest this act and wrote a seminal article, 'The Caribbean Community in Britain', which appeared in US Communist journal *Freedomways* in 1964.[38] By far the largest number of migrants had come from Jamaica, and migrants were not only settled in the Notting Hill and Brixton areas of London, but throughout the Midlands and northern cities as well.[39]

Historians Bob Carter and Kathleen Paul have challenged previously dominant arguments which suggested a benign government response to West Indian postwar immigration, and have revealed instead that the state led the agenda to politicise and racialise West Indian, as well as African, Indian and Pakistani immigration, from its inception. The state helped to construct the arrival of 'coloured' people as problematic and undesirable for British social relations. This has dissolved notions of a pre-political 'honeymoon' period of black immigration to Britain permitted by '*laissez faire*' government policies.[40] Carter *et al.* have shown that the government used illegal strategies to limit colonial immigration to Britain. Officials were advised to stop issuing legal documents that proved British nationality including the British Travel Certificate, which was intended for travel between British and French West African territories, and to reject these documents when they were used to attempt to enter Britain; to refuse passports to would-be West Indian migrants while they were still in the colonies; and to withhold passports in India and Pakistan if applicants had no firm prospect of a job in Britain.[41]

Paul has shown that contradictory policies ran alongside each other. Government actively recruited in large numbers from Ireland and Europe, to supplement labour-poor industries, and subsidised British migration to the self-governing 'white' Dominion territories of Australia and Canada. At the same time, the state attempted to deter and prevent 'coloured' immigration into Britain, by issuing advice in the colonies that reports of labour shortages in Britain were false. Ministers were particularly surprised by the autonomy shown by West Indian migrants who arrived in Britain seeking work without being directly recruited as they were for temporary work schemes during both world wars.[42] West Indians it seemed, with their passage to the US barred by the McCarran Act, were interpreting the British Nationality Act of 1948 as an invitation to settle in Britain. The act created British citizenship for people formerly defined only as colonial subjects. However, colonial immigration to Britain was an unforeseen effect. The act had been intended to quell indigenous nationalist movements, following Indian independence in 1947, and was not intended to be used as a literal entitlement to residency in metropolitan Britain. While the act had created black British citizens in principle, these were imagined remotely; people who dwelt in far-off tropical locales, and were still reassuringly loyal to the Empire. It was only the prospect of mass voluntary immigration that raised, for the government, the unsettling spectre of a growing number of black Britons legally resident in the UK.[43]

Both Labour and Conservative governments monitored West Indian settlement with rising alarm. In the early 1950s, the Conservative government commissioned reports on settler communities designed to prove their unsuitability for British life, in the areas of housing, employment and criminality. These investigations ultimately failed to deliver the proof of negative impacts they were expected to provide. However, they did reveal the circulation of racist stereotypes, for instance in the report of a Sheffield policeman who described black men as perfumed dandies with too much money, which they spent charming (white) women.[44]

Meanwhile West Indians adjusted to daily life. Common amongst them was a feeling of deep alienation captured by a new genre of West Indian settler literature, which included such works as Barbadian George Lamming's *The Emigrants* of 1954, and Trinidadian Samuel Selvon's *The Lonely Londoners* of 1956.[45] Jones's protégé, aspiring Jamaican writer Donald Hinds published *Journey to an Illusion* in 1966.[46] This was a collection of memoirs compiled and shaped by Hinds to reveal the theme of alienation from the fabled 'Mother Country' and a growing racial aware-ness. An account offered by 'Ken', an Indo-Trinidadian, is representative of the transformation many underwent. 'Ken' was hugely enthused on his trans-Atlantic crossing and came to Britain seeking opportunity and adventure, but on arrival shocked by the rejection he experienced. 'Ken' made an inward vow, to 'groom himself for social intercourse in Britain', but was wounded by daily insults and hostility.[47]

Critically, Britain's race and class system provided a contrast to Caribbean colour-class structures, as is also reflected in *Journey to an Illusion*. 'Devon' revealed that though he had not been conscious of open discrimination in Jamaica, he was 'inhibited by colour', that is, aware of the racialisation of power, by the age of fifteen.[48] Thus he accepted that the majority of the authority figures he encountered were 'white or very nearly so'.[49] 'Myrtle', from British Guiana, recalled that she aspired to office work 'but never dared tell anyone, for working in an office meant a pale skin'.[50] 'Ken' described the racist prejudices that were preserved between groups in colonial Trinidad, 'that Indians possess vast sums of money and are mean . . . While Negroes . . . squander money on clothes and entertainment.'[51]

However, the British race and class system often provided contexts that nullified the learnt Caribbean pigmentocracy the migrants brought with them. Although it did not force the total collapse of ingrained shade distinctions and inter-ethnic mistrust between West Indians, in practical terms the British environment imposed homogenising strictures on immigrants that began to bind them together in one socio-economic category. Relatively middle-class West Indians were the exception and not the rule, if they managed to retain their social standing in Britain. Professional and skilled workers found they were often barred from the same level of work in Britain. For instance Hinds recalled anecdotally:

> At one time two London Transport garages in the south-west had the following sample from West Indian professional life: a bank clerk from Barbados working as a bus-driver; a journalist from British Guiana working as a driver; a teacher from Dominica working as a driver; and a teacher from Jamaica working as a conductor.[52]

The effect of this shift in status was to begin to erode the mechanisms of British colonial stratification of class, colour and even island loyalties, as Jamaicans, Barbadians and Trinidadians were forced to band together as 'West Indians' in the British environment.

The official neglect of new immigrants helped to provide the condi-tions for the riots of 1958. Unlike the European labourers, West Indians were not helped into housing and jobs. It was government's attention, or lack thereof, to housing in particular, that worsened conditions by allowing resentment and anger to build in inner-city bomb-damaged slum areas. In 1951 there were 500,000 more households in London than homes, and the incoming Churchill government pledged to build 300,000 houses annually.[53] Many West Indian tenants paid exorbitant rents to slum landlords, who let subdivided rooms in dilapidated houses, such as the notorious Peter Rachman, whose exploitative practices in Notting Hill coined the term 'Rachmananism' in the press. However, West Indians were scapegoated and accused by politicians of *creating* ghettos, 'New Harlems'.[54] Also fuelling intolerance were some quarters of the press who ran a discourse airing British psychological anguish at the decline of Empire, helped by the representations of the colonial wars in Malaya and Kenya. Historian Wendy Webster has shown that these violent conflicts abroad were used to further construct colonial immigration to Britain as the ultimate 'violation of domestic sanctuaries'.[55]

Eyewitness testimony accords that the riots in Notting Hill began with smaller skirmishes which led to open harassment and eventually four days and nights of violence, including fire-bombs thrown into black homes. In Nottingham white crowds said to be 4000-strong converged on the city centre.[56] After the riots tension continued to build, and Notting Hill became the focus of two fascist groups, Oswald Mosley's Union Movement and the White Defence League.[57] In May 1959, Antiguan Kelso Cochrane was murdered in Notting Hill. Few eyewitnesses came forward and no one was ever charged. Over 1000 people attended his funeral. The continued violence marked a watershed moment for many West Indian settlers. 'It was our awakening', remarked Ivan Weeks, who had been present at Cochrane's funeral.[58] The *West Indian Gazette*, founded as a monthly journal in the spring of 1958, had almost immediately to respond to the violence of the summer rioting, and in the following year, to the death of Cochrane. Jones showed her capacity for organising and forging political partnerships, by establishing a fund with visiting Jamaican premier Norman Manley to aid those West Indians arrested during the riots.[59] Against this tumultuous backdrop the Caribbean Carnival was born.

The *West Indian Gazette* and Caribbean Carnival

Although Jones was initially welcomed by the Communist Party, and assisted by individual comrades, it quickly became clear that she was not to be given a meaningful role in the party's work in the UK. Likewise, in the 1950s, the party lacked a concerted anticolonial and anti-racist campaign involving partnership with Caribbean activists either in the West Indies or in Britain, in spite of directives from the international movement in the 1930s that the British party ought to develop these relationships.[60] Jones was merely offered junior clerical work.[61] Given the party's lack of involvement with the black community, it is unsurprising that Jones emerged as a leader of West Indian immigrants in London, in spite of being marginalised by British Communism. As editor of the *Gazette* Jones waged anti-racist campaigns, supported the fledgling British West Indian Federation and reported worldwide news concerning the anti-imperial struggle. The paper also sponsored arts and community events, such as music recitals, fashion shows and talent contests, aimed at drawing the community together and affirming a shared cultural heritage.

The *Gazette* was founded out of the auspices of its leftist predecessor, the *Caribbean News,* which had a small audience.[62] Jones reputedly ran the *Gazette* on a shoestring with the help of volunteers, aspiring writers whom she trained and mentored, including Hinds and Guyanese writer Jan Carew.[63] Jones intended that the *Gazette* should be a popular, commercial paper. She decided it would take advertising and appear on the newsstands in the hope that it would reach as many West Indian settlers in Britain in 1958 as possible. It was to be explicitly anti-racist and anti-imperialist in its outlook, and as Davies writes, revealed itself 'feminist in its leadership and in its concern for women'.[64]

The new *Gazette* aided identity-formation in Britain. The paper's full title was the *West Indian Gazette and Afro-Asian Caribbean News.* Jones referred frequently to the 'Afro-Asian-Caribbean' community. This reflected, on the one hand, her commitment to imagining anti-imperial resistance globally, and on the other, the actual diversity of colonial settlers, not least the West Indians themselves. This group was broadly labelled in Britain as 'coloured', sometimes as 'Negro', 'Indian' or 'Half-caste', and typically as 'immigrant'. The *Gazette* and Carnival began the process of recasting this hostile, lumpen categorisation in Britain, and often articulated more innovative or affirmative racial-cultural configurations; 'West Indian', 'Afro-Asian', 'Afro-Asian-Caribbean', 'black'. The *Gazette* employed such terms inclusively and in this way began to imagine a postcolonial formulation of 'blackness' as a political category that would include Afro and Indo-Caribbean, African and Asian subjectivities. This political 'blackness' was unique to Britain and differentiated from political formulations of 'blackness' in the US, for example.[65]

However, though it was politically inclusive in outlook, and upheld positive representations of inclusive 'blackness', the *Gazette* did foreground the West Indian experience and its Caribbean readership. As Schwarz has shown, the *Gazette* had a central role in imagining a West Indian community in Britain. It sustained a notion of the West Indian nation that extended the entity beyond its Caribbean shores, and furthermore, belonged to an African Diaspora. Though, with its meagre resources, domestic reporting and social organising tended to be focused on London, the paper engendered a sense of a global African community. It placed reports from South Africa, the Deep South of the US, and Jamaica, side by side on the printed page. This proximity effected a 'simultaneity', drawing connections between world events relevant to the new black Britons. Jones intended this as a radicalising, awareness-raising force for her readership.[66] As Schwarz writes, the *Gazette* engaged an 'intellectual culture that explicitly drew upon Frantz Fanon, WEB Du Bois, Kwame Nkrumah, Jomo Kenyatta, Martin Luther King, Paul Robeson, Nelson Mandela and James Baldwin.'[67] Jones was herself a part of this culture, mentored by Du Bois and befriended by Robeson.

Similarly when it came to organising the Caribbean Carnival the committee boasted an illustrious band of Caribbean-descended artists, writers and performers, willing to volunteer their time to the cause, thanks in no small part to Jones's charisma and influence. These included acclaimed performers Nadia Cattouse, from British Honduras, Trinidadians Edric and Pearl Connor (founders of the first black theatre agency in Britain), London-born, Jamaican-English actor and jazz singer Cleo Laine, and Trinidadian musician and painter Boscoe Holder. In its first year, 1959, the Carnival Programme hosted acts including Trinidadian calypsonian, 'The Mighty Terror', the West Indian Students Dance Band and Holder's dance troupe, as well as a steel band and numerous singers. The souvenir programme contained a photographic tribute to the 'mother of Trinidadian dance', Beryl McBurnie OBE.[68] In the following years Jones attracted leftist English folk-singers Peggy Seeger and Ewan McColl to Carnival, Jamaican writer and dramatist Sylvia Wynter as compere, and the famous Trinidadian calypsonian the 'Mighty Sparrow' performed.[69] In 1961 Carnival drew a crowd of around 1800, and amongst them, as the *Gazette* reported, were representatives from twelve embassies and twenty Members of Parliament.[70] Carnival was televised in 1959 by the BBC (though no recordings survive) and subsequent broadcasts were also aired in the Caribbean thereafter. Thus within this Carnival programme Jones achieved probably the first televised black beauty competition on British television.

Within the souvenir programme Jones included an address entitled 'A People's Art is the Genesis of Their Freedom', which clearly related Jones's Marxist stance on the radical portent of culture, but also underlined her commitment to Caribbean cultural nationalism itself as a political force driving decolonisation. As Davies writes, Caribbean Carnival in London would illustrate the radical nature of Carnival, the act of 'taking space', even amidst the hostility and privations of black life in Britain.[71] Jones was not only born in Port of Spain, where Carnival flourished but witnessed the founding of the first New York Caribbean Carnival in 1946.[72] The London Carnival set forth a political course for unified anti-racist activism and cooperation in Britain. Jones wrote:

> A pride in being West Indian is undoubtedly at the root of this unity: a pride that has its origins in the drama of nascent nationhood, and that pride encompasses not only the creativeness, uniqueness and originality of West Indian mime song and dance – but is the genesis of the nation itself.[73]

The riots, Jones argued, were formative in the building of a West Indian identity, bonding West Indians together beyond island loyalties. Furthermore, she pointed to West Indian 'multiracial culture' as the expression of advancement every bit as essential to Western civilisation as 'the conquest of Space'.[74] In an ironic twist to the cultural battles for Carnival still raging between elites and middle-class nationalists in Trinidad, the London Carnival provided an opportunity for a pristine incarnation of Carnival as blended folk culture. Unlike in Trinidad, this expression was directed by creole artists who shared a consensus and single purpose. However, in a satisfying turn of events, the artistic directors of Carnival, Jones included, found themselves powerless to resist the truly autonomous and unpredictable and unruly spirit of the Caribbean festival. As an actor and friend of Jones, Corinne Skinner-Carter, recalled:

> In the 1950s there was a TV programme called 'Six-Five Special' . . . similar to 'Top of the Pops' . . . it looked as though it was chaos . . . it was the first of that kind of programme where people from all walks [of life] used to go . . . and do their thing. So Claudia decided that that's the way she wanted carnival to be. The BBC was coming to film it like 'Six-Five Special'. I remember Edric [Connor] saying 'Claudia, that chaos you see on that stage is organised chaos, it's not what you think.' But Claudia thought she'd be able to keep all these people in harness. We had all these well-known people, people who ordinary people in the street thought of as untouchables, people like Paul Robeson . . . And on the night . . . we had all these people, all these cameras and everything, and people were prancing and trying to get up on the stage and touch people they had never touched before. And I remember Edric [trying to calm people]. But nobody was taking any notice, they were just pushing and making a *real* Carnival out of it[75] [italics my emphasis].

Within this context the black beauty competition appeared. Whereas in Trinidad 'Carnival Queen' was at the centre of attempts to morally upgrade Carnival, in London it spearheaded anti-racist work directed at both a black and white audience.

Affirming black femininity in the *West Indian Gazette*

Pearl Connor recalled that Jones was always keen to politically mobilise black women into activism.[76] Jones joined forces with pan-Africanist Amy Ashwood Garvey, first wife of Marcus Garvey, who was now resident in London and ran her home as the Afro People's Centre, a place to meet and organise within the black community: '[Jones] established the Black Sash[77] movement at the Africa Student Centre in Earls Court and presented awards for special achievements for black women . . . Her wishes were to build up black women leaders in the community.'[78]

In London as in Harlem Jones used trips to the beauty salon as a campaigning pitch. When having her hair done she would talk to other women about the problems facing the black community and attempt to invigorate them with political awareness.[79] To this end Jones used the *Gazette* to support the black beauty culture networks that were developing in London, but also to make use of them, just as she had done in New York.

The Madame Rose Academy of Beauty Culture (here the term 'beauty culture' literally meant the *cultivation* of beauty) trained black women as hairdressers and beauticians. Madame Rose set up business in East Ham, London, but had been trained in the United States. Rose adopted the 'Madame' title, like her famous African American predecessor, Madame CJ Walker. The 'Madame' title was intended to stress specialised knowledge, and professional accomplishment, and to garner the respectability and dignity so deeply associated with well-groomed appearance in black communities at this time. Jones attended Madame Rose's regular graduation ceremonies, which became meeting places of the London-based black social elite, such as it was. In May 1961, it drew the diplomatic representatives of Haiti, Nigeria and Gambia, together with representatives of the British Caribbean Association, the Coloured People's Progressive Association and the Standing Conference on West Indian Organisations. More than an awards ceremony, this was an opportunity for political organising. Furthermore, the training itself to some represented an act of defiance. The trainee acquired the means to prosper as a beauty professional *within* the black community, where other esteemed work outside its boundaries was hard to obtain. 'There is a world of knowledge here', said the only male graduate, 'not merely to learn but to employ usefully and lucratively to one's own advantage. This is a field in which you shine by merit alone and it transcends all racial barriers'.[80]

At another Rose Academy awards ceremony later in the same year Jones presented prizes to the best trainees and used the opportunity to raise awareness of the mooted Commonwealth Immigration Bill: 'This Bill might jeopardise your very right to practice your skills so earnestly fought for and merited. Your fight to practice your skill must be extended to your fight for full equality, dignity and citizenship'.[81]

Jones remained enthusiastic about promoting beauty culture, seeing its potential to assist black women in acquiring the markers of femininity and dignity. Indeed Jones herself was strikingly elegant and well-spoken, and in spite of her straitened circumstances in Britain, retained a wardrobe of beautifully tailored clothes from her life in New York, as Donald Hinds recalls, 'Claudia reminded me of one of those famous black American singers. She dressed magnificently, and at the microphone she poured her heart out'.[82]

In the *Gazette* Jones employed one of her protégés, David Roussel-Milner, son of beauty salon-owner Carmen England to write a column posing as his expert mother, to advise women on beauty tips. 'Carmen' wrote about fashion, beauty, and maintaining an attractive appearance on a small income and in harsh British weather, and it was implied, under the stresses and strains of life in Britain (adverts for a hair-loss specialist regularly appeared in the *Gazette*). This column was important in the composition of the *Gazette* as a popular commercial paper. Jones wanted to appeal to female readers, and not to exclude those not yet radicalised into leftist politics. When Jones left the paper under the charge of her partner and activist Abhimanyu Manchanda, to take up an invitation to the USSR, she was alarmed by the dogmatically political tone and lack of varied content he delivered in her absence, especially the missing book reviews and beauty column.[83]

Such woman-oriented content also appeared in the form of an intermittent 'Woman's World' page. Inez Davidson-Lakhan, who sometimes served as Woman Editor, wrote in December 1960 a piece entitled 'Your Appearance Gets Close Scrutiny', which essentially determined smart, groomed appearance as race-pride work. Smart West Indian women drew 'favourable comment from Londoners' wrote Davidson-Lakhan. She advised on hat-wearing, the choice of stylish yet inexpensive clothing and the correct shade of lipstick and face powder. The tone generally praised black women, 'Much effort is not needed to show to advantage the soft texture of dark skin', but became awkward in its attempts to achieve the correct political register for combatting racism whilst affirming West Indian and African cultures simultaneously: 'I have been recently asked about the "grass skirts" worn by our "native" women. I showed absolutely no annoyance, since I was convinced that the questioner was untravelled and unread'.[84] This sort of anecdote became infamous among migrants who, though they were reared on knowledge of Britain, faced a barrage of questions about their person, their bodies, their homelands, ranging from genuine curiosity and ignorance to more hurtful remarks intended to patronise and denigrate. Indeed, colonial migrants quickly became renowned as sharp dressers, and the influence of migration on British fashion has only recently begun to be explored, as in curator Carole Tulloch's 2004 exhibition *Black British Style* at the Victoria and Albert Museum. Davidson-Lakhan rebutted the query by boasting of the famous elegance of the women of Port of Spain, Trinidad. However, at the foot of the article she delivered a disclaimer, 'Mention must be made of the graceful way in which some African Women wear their native costumes. They present an attractive picture.'[85]

Here the extent of Jones's challenge in fostering a sense of solidarity not only between West Indians but between West Indians and Africans was revealed. As her friend and collaborator Trevor Carter commented, 'Claudia was able to see very quickly above the small island and continental chauvinism that was an element of our young British Black communities'.[86] Davidson-Lakhan creates an image of West Indian modernity which foils received notions of black backwardness, but then (perhaps persuaded by the editor) attempts a rearguard action to resist caricatures of supposedly 'traditional' and 'backward' African cultures, as seen through feminine dress. The matter of confronting and examining such embedded racialised precepts of modernity and backwardness was an integral part of the process Schwarz has called interrogating Britishness from the margins which fell to migrants.[87]

As part of this woman-oriented content the *Gazette* also publicised Caribbean beauty queens on tour in England. It celebrated the glamour of beauty queens, and though controversy still reigned in the Caribbean about the exclusion of most women of colour from these competitions, the *Gazette* emphasised beauty queens' currency as positive cultural ambassadors. 'Miss Jamaica' 1959 Sheila Chong was interviewed by Hinds, who boasted 'She Does Us All Proud', reporting that Chong had visited the Clapham Inter-Racial Club and unofficially become 'Miss West Indies' as she charmed the cosmopolitan audience. By the same token Jones herself took the opportunity to be photographed with 'Miss Jamaica' and 'Miss World' of 1962, Carol Joan Crawford. Nevertheless in close proximity, also on the 'Women's World' page, was an 'Appeal to Women' to join the cause for a federal West Indian Nation.[88]

In keeping with the cosmopolitan ethos fostered in the pages of the *Gazette* and the talented mix of the Carnival Committee itself, the judges for the 'Carnival Queen' beauty competition annually comprised artists, intellectuals and notable persons. These individuals could win favourable public notice for Carnival and the anti-racist cause. A representative selection drawn from the lifetime of the competition included: Eslanda and Paul Robeson (the couple supported Jones's work when in London); writers Andrew Salkey, Jan Carew, Samuel Selvon and George Lamming; artist Althea McNish; English politicians Nigel Fisher MP and Marcus Lipton MP; and from the West Indian Commission, Public Relations Officer, Patsy Payne. From the theatre world came English playwright John Osborne and English theatre-director Joan Littlewood. In 1960 the High Commissioner for the West Indies in the United Kingdom, Mr Garnet Gordon, agreed to crown the beauty queen.[89] Hinds later recalled this moment as a mark of Jones's political nous:

> [I recall a photograph] of [beauty contestants] Marlene Walker, Beryl Cunningham with the High Commissioner. We got everybody in, the High Commissioner was there to meet *them* . . . Nowadays I don't know how it would be handled but here [together] we ha[d] Claudia Jones and 'Miss Jamaica' [1962] Carol Joan Crawford[90] [italics my emphasis].

Hinds reserved the most admiration for Jones's ability to capture the notice of an important public figure and have him honour a black beauty competition that crowned black women. In truth such a photo opportunity revealed Jones's talent for consummate public relations. If placed in the Caribbean context, let alone the British context, the public crowning ceremony bridged an expansive social gap, that of the senior colonial official and working-class black woman. Within the context of Jones's activism on behalf of black women and her concern for combatting racist caricaturing, a beauty competition, a public ritual that conjured glamour and prestige, was in this respect, an affirmative act for black femininity.

While the Caribbean beauty competitions slowly began to crown very light-skinned mixed-raced women, 'Carnival Queen' in London revealed itself to be a different sort of beauty competition. Insofar as any beauty competition can be said to be accessible to any but the few, the *Gazette* aimed to make its contest relatively open for the women amongst its diverse, mostly working-class 'West Indian' readership. The competition shared in many of the usual conventions; contestants were all young and slim, required to be 'single' (though notably not 'unmarried'), paraded in swimsuit and ballgown, and were rated for 'beauty, charm and intelligence'.[91] However, the procedure for joining the competition was relatively transparent and, the evidence suggests, did not operate an unspoken 'colour-bar'. Contestants were required to submit photographs with details of their vital statistics to enter, and the paper itself offered to help if sponsors could not be found. In careful wording it emphasised 'confidence' in beauty and the other qualifications and underlined that it wanted to encourage as many 'Caribbean beauty entrants as possible'.[92] It reiterated this by publishing photographs of hopefuls under the heading 'Our Beauties Compete for Caribbean Queen Prize'.[93] Significantly these were images of black women who ranged widely in skin tone, facial features and hair textures. That is not to suggest that the competition had the power to erase ingrained shade prejudice, but that the paper was conspicuously attempting to resist the patterns of Caribbean social stratification.

5.1 'Carnival Queen' contestants, London 1959

However, even in this work, contradictions and challenges were evident. Carmen England, who was the owner of a beauty salon and a key organiser of the beauty contest, also advertised her own brand of bleach cream in the *Gazette*, which claimed 'not only [to] generally lighten your skin but [to] help you rid [yourself] of those nasty dark patches when you have not taken the right precaution against the wind and rain'.[94] Here perhaps is an instance in which Jones's political agenda of race-pride was compromised, as was Garvey's in Harlem, by the need for advertising revenue to be gained from such cosmetic producers, even as Jones determined to affirm black womanhood and alter racist attitudes.

Actor and organiser Corinne Skinner-Carter recalled her surprise at the finals of the first year of the beauty competition, 1959:

> [T]his was before the Black Power days. This was before we all knew that we were beautiful. We might not have known that we were beautiful but [Claudia] knew that we were beautiful and she started this beauty contest. And the first year there was a girl called Fay Craig that won this beauty contest, and I'm telling you, Fay Craig was Black, I mean really Black. But pretty. But without Claudia we would not have known that, because then we used to judge everybody's beauty by the European standard.[95]

In fact it was Fay Sparks, not Fay Craig, who was the overall winner in 1959; nevertheless the impression Craig left with audiences is noteworthy, if Skinner-Carter's exclamation is representative.[96] Like Hinds, Skinner-Carter reveals her admiration for Jones's political foresight in affirming black femininity, and that it was a surprising process for her to witness. Hinds recalls that Craig, a charismatic aspiring actress was very popular with the crowd. Craig later won a bit-part as one of Elizabeth Taylor's attendants in *Cleopatra*.[97]

In the following two years the competition was won by Jamaicans: lightskinned Marlene Walker, and brownskinned Indo-Jamaican Cherry Larman. The beauty competition did not proclaim itself a black competition any more than Caribbean competitions had openly declared themselves the domain of only 'white' or 'high-brown' women. However, the *Gazette*'s competition made efforts to encourage black women to take part within an atmosphere that celebrated an inclusive formulation of West Indianness and blackness. Unlike the 'Ten Types' beauty competition of Jamaica, for example, this competition attempted a celebration of cosmopolitanism that did not marginalise blackness or tokenise ethnicity. Here Jones's immersion in Harlem's black beauty culture scene revealed itself in her creative orchestration of black cultural events in London. The subtly race-conscious beauty contest was her cultural import.

5.2   Claudia Jones, Marlene Walker and Carmen England

During Carnival's five year tenure the *Gazette* offered attractive prizes to finalists of the queen competition alongside the 'Best Dressed Band' and 'Best Individual Costume'. In 1959 the *Gazette* sought sponsors to support future trips for the 'Carnival Queen' to 'one of our new African states, Ghana, Guinea or Nigeria'.[98] Here Jones pre-empted the Jamaican Afro-Welfare League who sent Yvonne Whyte 'Miss Jamaica Nation' to Malawi's independence celebrations in 1964. First prize of the London 'Carnival Queen' was a Caribbean cruise, courtesy of sponsors the Grimaldi-Siosa shipping line, with whom many a migrant had sailed from the Caribbean into English ports. Second prize was typically a trip to Paris, or another European destination. In 1961 this prize was won by Grenadian Helen Fleming. In accordance with convention, appointed glamour reporter Hinds loaded Fleming with epithets of 'natural charm', loveliness and grace. Fleming, a qualified nurse, had found work as a model in London, and was hoping to achieve a break-through into 'show-business' and acting.[99] Along these lines the third prize winner in 1961, Pat Bryce, was awarded a year's training at the London Charm School.[100]

The *Gazette* closely followed the progress of former contestants, eagerly seizing upon evidence that black women could pursue viable careers in the performing arts and entertainment. Indeed Hinds recalled that many a contestant was an aspiring actress, given her first start in showbusiness by the *Gazette* and Carnival. Pat Bryce, readers were told, was highly popular at the charm school, where she was instructed in 'deportment . . . good dress sense, manners, hair care . . . speech and sensible eating'.[101] The *Gazette* boasted that Bryce seemed to be heavily in demand as a clothing model, and had hopes of securing a contract. Bryce was celebrated as a rare example of 'breakthrough' success: '[Bryce] is one of the few West Indian girls to step out in beauty'.[102] In a similar vein former beauty contestant Beryl Cunningham, who was also a law student and aspiring actress and who won the beauty competition on her third attempt, became the subject of the *Gazette*'s occasional 'Women's World' feature and garnered special mention for gaining a small part in a film:

> An object lesson in how to use one's opportunities in life has just been given by Beryl Cunningham . . . At the time of the Carnival Beryl was working as a clerk with the London County Council but, with brain and beauty . . . a dramatic change has occurred in her career. Under the skilled guidance of Madam Seignon, one of Europe's leading model trainers, she is known as Lucinda and has appeared in a small part in a Rank Organisation film series.[103]

Former beauty finalists were engaged as dancers in talent shows, or as models for the *Gazette*'s own 'Afro-Asian-Caribbean Fashion Show'.[104] The *Gazette* publicised dance events with beauty competitions included, which were organised on the basis of interracial friendship and cooperation, and encouraged its readers to take their share of the limelight.[105] These developments were perhaps inspired by the success of Carnival and its televised black beauty competition. In November 1960 the *Gazette* called for its readers to enter a similar dance and beauty competition to decide 'Miss Blue Beat' (Blue Beat was a contemporary strain of Rhythm and Blues) under the heading, 'Girls! Have Your Chance'.[106] Furthermore, using conventions of the popular press, the paper featured an attractive Caribbean woman, often a woman with a fledgling career in entertain-ment, modelling or the theatre, on each front cover.

In January 1962 the *Gazette* featured a retrospective of former beauty queens and runners-up in its annual appeal to find new contestants. The piece marked the efforts and successes of these select few black women in attempting to launch careers as actors, singers and dancers. The first 'Carnival Queen', Fay Sparks, had joined a cabaret in Europe, runner-up Fay Craig had become a nightclub dancer, subsequent winners were said to have begun dancing and modelling careers, though this was likely to have been embellished somewhat, and Marlene Walker, winner in 1960, had married and emigrated to the US.[107] The *Gazette*'s campaign to champion black women in entertainment ought to be contextualised here. Film historian Stephen Bourne has documented, in *Black in the British Frame*, a significant black presence on British stage and screen in the 1960s. However, interest in black actors was sporadic, trend-driven and tended to be short-lived. As actor Carmen Munroe reported, black actors were often used to 'dress the set'.[108] Though opportunities for professional work were scarce, black performers in Jones's midst formed a thriving amateur community, organising themselves through the West Indian and African Student's Union in particular. In addition, Jones's friend Pearl Connor, who with her partner Edric, had already formed the first black theatre agency, to represent underused actors, added a black modelling agency to its remit.[109] A compressed London edition of the Jamaican *Gleaner* newspaper, the *Jamaican Weekly Gleaner*, appeared on newsstands from 1962 and gloried in small evidence of black women making inroads in modelling, acting or singing.[110] Similarly the short-lived glossy publication of the Jamaica Overseas Family and Friends Organisation (JOFFA), edited by friend of the *Gazette* Theo Campbell, performed a similar role, producing copious images of glamorous black women hoping to become performers.[111] However, opportunities remained scarce. Aside from a few notable exceptions including singers Trinidadian Winifred Atwell, and Britons Shirley Bassey and Cleo Laine, the most sought-after black performers were African Americans on tour in Britain. To this end Jones's efforts in securing a televised black beauty competition are all the more remarkable. The *Gazette* heralded black women entering the arts and entertainment, not to overstate the bleak reality, but rather to encourage and motivate hopefuls, and to effect an improvement in the prospects of black performers.

The 'Carnival Queen' beauty competition in London represented a progressive and pragmatic response to Caribbean cultural nationalism transplanted into the new context of a West Indian settler community. In the Caribbean predominantly male middle-class nationalists had seized upon the beauty competition as a political tool, an allegory of hybridity and modernity. There the middle-class had fought to control white-dominated beauty competitions and used them instead to produce images of national identity heavily invested in an idealised brown femininity and generally marginalised black femininity, though occasionally the transformation of black women into modern beauties was celebrated and offered as a model for development. Overall the process was attended by much agonising and soul-searching over women's proper role in 'lifting the race' and embodying modernity. In London by contrast, Jones proved to be a carrier of a Harlem culture in which West Indian identity thrived and black beauty culture was central to economic life and to race-pride strategies; the means of accommodating black migrants to American life. Jones regarded the beauty competition as a pragmatic tool to help build an inclusive West Indian identity, and within this, showed a particular concern to affirm an inclusive black femininity. Jones understood blackness as a political category, a basis for common identification and resistance. Here, Jones's communism, in particular her concern with group solidarity amongst the poor, was central. Jones challenged the legacy of British imperialism with its emphasis on liberal meritocracy that encouraged separate identifications, and urged the individual towards upward identification and downward distancing. Jones effectively picked up where Caribbean feminists of the 1930s, especially Una Marson and Amy Bailey, had left off, by seeking to politically awaken black women, to affirm black womanhood and to draw attention to the ways in which black women were marginalised from the 'prizes' of femininity. The London 'Carnival Queen' competition retained the typical features of female beauty competitions in that it placed emphasis on refinement, cultivation and beautification. However, these gauges of idealised femininity were applied to subtly different effect and with unspoken racial and colour barriers removed. Women were encouraged into the competition, and an attempt was made to affirm a multiracial polity with less of the tokenism than the 'Ten Types' competition, its nearest Caribbean equivalent. Furthermore the burgeoning black beauty culture of London was imagined, through the *Gazette*, in similar terms to that of New York, as a pragmatic means of acquiring the respectable appearance that was 'race-pride' work.

Notes

1 Louise Bennett, 'Colonisation in Reverse', in James Proctor (ed.), *Writing Black Britain: An Interdisciplinary Anthology* (Manchester: Manchester University Press, 2000), pp. 16–17.
2 Donald Hinds, 'The West Indian *Gazette*: Claudia Jones and the Black Press in Britain', *Race and Class* 50 (2008), p. 92.

3 Claudia Jones, 'The Caribbean Community in Britain', in Carole Boyce Davies (ed), *Claudia Jones: Beyond Containment* (Banbury, Oxfordshire: Ayebia Publishing, 2011) pp. 180–181.

4 Bill Schwarz, 'Claudia Jones and the West Indian *Gazette*: Reflections on the Emergence of Postcolonial Britain', *Twentieth Century British History* 14 (2003), p. 267.

5 Gordon Lewis quoted in Winston James, 'Migration, Racism and Identity Formation: The Caribbean Experience in Britain', in Winston James and Clive Harris (eds), *Inside Babylon: The Caribbean Diaspora in Britain* (London: Verso, 1993), p. 243.

6 The most notable of those focusing on Britain include: Jennifer Tyson, *Claudia Jones Woman of Our Times 1915–1964* (London: Camden Black Sisters, 1988) and Marika Sherwood, *Claudia Jones: A Life in Exile* (London: Lawrence and Wishart, 1999). An edited collection of Jones's own writings was compiled by Buzz Johnson in 1985; '*I Think of My Mother': Notes on the Life and Times of Claudia Jones*, Buzz Johnson (ed.) (London: Karia Press, 1985).

7 Carole Boyce Davies, *Left of Karl Marx: The Political Life of Black Communist Claudia Jones* (Durham: Duke University Press, 2008), pp. 1–5, 54.

8 Ibid., pp. 45–50.

9 Ibid., p. 2.

10 Johnson, *My Mother*, p. 2. Jones's father was of Barbadian origin.

11 James, *Holding Aloft*, p. 38.

12 Ibid., pp. 39–41.

13 Ibid., p. 368.

14 Ibid., p. 358.

15 Ibid., p. 12.

16 Davies, *Left of Karl Marx*, p. 92.

17 James, *Holding Aloft*, p. 50.

18 Ibid., pp. 69–72.

19 Johnson, *My Mother*, pp. 5–7.

20 For further discussion of black beauty culture as a means of employment, empowerment and exploitation within the African American community in the twentieth century, see Kathy Peiss, *Hope in the Jar; The Making of America's Beauty Culture* (New York: Metropolitan Book, 1998); Julia Kirk Blackwelder, *Styling Jim Crow: African-American Beauty Training During Segregation* (College Station: Texas A&M University Press, 2003); Noliwe M Rooks, *Hair Raising: Beauty, Culture and African American Women* (New Brunswick: Rutgers University Press, 1996); Susannah Walker, *Style and Status; Selling Beauty to African American Women* (Lexington: University Press Kentucky, 2007); and for particular attention to Harlem in the 1920s see Richard Pearce, 'Toni Morrison's Jazz: Negotiations of African-American Beauty Culture', *Narrative* 6 (1998), pp. 307–311.

21 Kathy Peiss, *Hope in the Jar*, pp. 211–213; Rooks, *Hair Raising*, pp. 30–33.

22 Peiss, pp. 213–214.

23 Rooks, *Hair Raising*, pp. 42–43; Peiss, *Hope in the Jar*, p. 113; Walker, *Style and Status*, pp. 11–46. See also Davarian L. Baldwin's 'From the Washtub to the World': Madame C.J. Walker and the Re-creation of Race Womanhood 1900–1935' in Weinbaum *et al.* (eds), *The Modern Girl Around the World: Consumption, Modernity, Globalisation* (Durham: Duke University Press, 2008) pp. 55–76.

24 Johnson, *My Mother*, p. 9.

25 Quoted in James, *Holding Aloft*, p. 149.

26 Ibid., pp. 149–150.

27 Maxine Leeds Craig, *Ain't I a Beauty Queen Black Women, Beauty, and the Politics of Race* (Oxford: Oxford University Press, 2002), p. 47.

28 Johnson, *My Mother*, p. 184.

29 Jones, Claudia, 'An End to the Neglect of the Problems of the Negro Woman', in Johnson (ed.), *My Mother*, p. 112.; Patricia Hill Collins, *Knowledge, Consciousness and the Politics of Empowerment* (New York: Routledge, 2000).

30 Ibid. Jones was briefly married to Communist Party member Jewish-American Abraham Scholnick.

31 Davies, *Left of Karl Marx*, pp. 131–139; Sherwood, *Claudia Jones*, pp. 21–27.

32 Davies, *Left of Karl Marx*, pp. 107–109, 141.

33 Elizabeth Gurley Flynn, *The Alderson Story: My Life as a Political Prisoner* (New York: International Publishers, 1963), pp. 78–80.

34 Claudia Jones, 'Black Women can Think, Speak and Write', *Beyond Containment*, p. 8.

35 Paul Gilroy, *The Black Atlantic; Modernity and Double Consciousness* (London: Verso, 1993).

36 Claudia Jones, 'The Caribbean Community in Britain', *Freedomways* 4 (1964), p. 340.

37 Bob Carter, Clive Harris and Shirley Joshi, 'The 1951–1955 Conservative Government and the Racialisation of Black Immigration', in Winston James and Clive Harris (eds), *Inside Babylon*, pp. 57–59.

38 Jones, 'The Caribbean Community in Britain'.

39 Ibid., p. 340.

40 Carter *et al.*, 'Conservative Government', p. 56. See also Clive Harris, 'Images of Blacks in Britain, 1930–1960', *Race and Social Policy* (London: Economic and Social Research Council, 1998) for discussion of government's prewar strategies against 'coloured' immigration directed at colonial seamen and led by 'moral' arguments based on the spread of venereal disease and degeneracy of mixed-raced children. Kathleen Paul has also addressed this period with brief discussion of the Coloured Alien Seamen Order of 1925; Kathleen Paul, *Whitewashing Britain: Race and Citizenship in the Postwar Era* (Ithaca: Cornell University Press, 1997), p. 113.

41 Carter *et al.*, 'Conservative Government', pp. 57–58.

42 Paul, *Whitewashing*, p. 121.

43 Carter *et al.*, 'Conservative Government', p. 57.

44 Ibid., p. 64.

45 George Lamming, *The Emigrants* (London: Joseph, 1954); Samuel Selvon, *The Lonely Londoners* (Gateshead: Longman Caribbean, 1972).

46 Donald Hinds, *Journey to An Illusion: The West Indian in Britain* (London: Heinemann, 1966).

47 Ibid., p. 1.

48 Ibid., p. 12.

49 Ibid.

50 Ibid.

51 Ibid., p. 18.

52 Ibid., p. 32.

53 Edward Pilkington, *Beyond the Mother Country: West Indians and the Notting Hill Riots* (London: I.B. Tauris & Co. Ltd, 1988), p. 53.
54 Harris, 'Images of Blacks in Britain', p. 48.
55 Wendy Webster, ' "There'll Always Be an England"; Representations of Colonial Wars and Immigration, 1948–1968', *Journal of British Studies* 40 (2001), pp. 557–584.
56 Pilkington, *Mother Country*, pp. 5–6.
57 Steve Silver, 'Who Killed My Brother?' *Searchlight*, May 2006. www.searchlightmagazine. com/index.php?link=template&story=164 (accessed 4 November 2009).
58 Pilkington, *Mother Country*, p. 151.
59 Ibid., p. 143.
60 Sherwood, *Life in Exile*, pp. 62, 70–72.
61 Ibid. See also Diane Langford interview, part of the Hall-Carpenter Oral History Project held at the British Library. (C456/107/01-03); Dorothy Kuya interview, part of the Communist Party of Great Britain Biographical Project held at the British Library C1049/83/01-04.
62 Davies, *Left of Karl Marx*, p. 86.
63 Ibid., p. 93.
64 Ibid., p. 86.
65 This postcolonial formulation of black Britishness resurfaced in the anti-racist struggles and feminism of the 1970s and 1980s in Britain.
66 Schwarz, 'Claudia Jones', pp. 270–271.
67 Ibid., p. 268.
68 'A People's Art is the Genesis of Their Freedom', Davies, *Beyond Containment*, pp. 166–67.
69 Sherwood, *Life in Exile*, p. 158; Schwarz, 'Claudia Jones', p. 275.
70 *West Indian Gazette*, April 1961.
71 C.f Davies, *Left of Karl Marx*, p. 167.
72 Ibid., pp. 170–171.
73 Jones, 'A People's Art', p. 166.
74 Ibid.
75 Quoted in Sherwood, *Life in Exile*, p. 204.
76 Ibid.
77 This is likely a reference to Amy Ashwood Garvey's involvement in protesting against Apartheid in South Africa.
78 Quoted in Sherwood, *Life in Exile*, p. 180.
79 Tyson, *Woman of Our Times*, p. 10.
80 *Gazette*, May 1961, p. 10.
81 *Gazette*, December 1961, p. 10.
82 Interview with Donald Hinds, May 2012.
83 Quoted in Sherwood, *Life in Exile*, p. 53.
84 *Gazette*, December 1960, p. 6.
85 *Gazette*, December 1960, p. 6.
86 Quoted in Sherwood, *Life in Exile*, p. 190.
87 Schwarz, 'Claudia Jones', p. 268.
88 *Gazette*, November 1959, p. 7.
89 Sherwood, *Life in Exile*, p. 152; *Gazette*, December 1959, p. 3; *Gazette*, April 1961, p. 6.

90 Sherwood, *Life in Exile*, p. 209.
91 *Gazette*, November 1960.
92 Ibid.
93 *Gazette*, January 1960, p. 1.
94 *Gazette*, December 1961, p. 12.
95 Quoted in Sherwood, *Life in Exile*, p. 158.
96 *Gazette*, January 1962, p. 3.
97 Interview with Donald Hinds.
98 *Gazette*, December 1959, p. 3.
99 *Gazette*, April 1961, p. 4.
100 Ibid.
101 *Gazette*, September 1961, p. 8.
102 Ibid.
103 *Gazette*, November 1959, p. 7; Interview with Donald Hinds.
104 *Gazette*, September 1960, p. 7.
105 *Gazette*, September 1961, p. 9; *Gazette*, November 1961, p. 6.
106 *Gazette*, November 1960, p. 8.
107 *Gazette*, 1962, p. 3.
108 Quoted in Stephen Bourne, *Black in the British Frame: Black People in British Film and Television, 1896–1996* (London: Cassell, 1996), p. 171.
109 Ibid., p. 169.
110 For instance in 1971 it featured Jamaican-born London resident Dorothy Simpson who had trained at the London Academy of Modelling and was due to appear in *Vogue* magazine. *Jamaican Weekly Gleaner*, 11 April 1971, p. 11.
111 Theo Campbell had loaned office space to the *Gazette* above his Brixton record shop, and became editor of the *JOFFA* in 1968.

Afterword: a Grenadian 'Miss World', 1970

Beauty competitions in the Caribbean performed racialising and gendering work. They broadly reiterated the social lines between whiteness, brownness and blackness, yet this framework actually provided the opportunity to renegotiate such categories on the beauty stage, through the performance of modern, cultured, feminine beauty. Competitions began as a white space, but ultimately provided a register of exemplary brown femininity and helped to make brownness iconic of the region. Beauty contests established a distinctive brown glamour through the saturation of imagery of brown desirability affirmed by a social and political rationale. Though the exact composition of ideal brown womanhood could not in actual fact be settled upon (audiences continued to dispute beauty all the while), the process of the beauty competition reified racial categories and encouraged women to assess each other sideways as racially authentic or false beauties. By the end of the period hybridity was illustrated by the apparent universality of the representative capacity of brown femininity, which seemed to embody all races and harmonise competing interests whilst actually removing diversity from view as the beauty contest upheld enduring and conservative formulations of hybrid beauty all the while.

However, not only was brown iconicity well-established in beauty competitions by the 1960s, but dark-skinned, black-identified women were not invisible in the beauty parade and put themselves forward as beauty queens. As this study has revealed, there were significant episodes when the absence of black women in beauty competitions was decried and significant others when they were called upon to play a role, typically as symbols of Afro-Creole pride, but also of dramatic transformation and the potential for black modernity. In the harmonising beauty spectrum of 'Ten Types', 'Miss Ebony' proved to be crucial as the marker of 'fair play', assimilation and aspiration, and one that was so popular it was revived in Barbados, albeit unsuccessfully. The 'Miss Civil Service Association' and 'Miss Industry' titles in Barbados proved that beauty competitions, if identified with work, could be properly the domain of respectable dark women. In the hugely popular 'Miss Jamaica Nation' black women assumed the role of de facto cultural emissaries to Africa. In Claudia Jones's London 'Carnival Queen' competition dark-skinned black women used the opportunity as a launch pad for the glamorous careers they hoped for.

The real purpose of the discursive and visual construction of idealised femininity in the Caribbean beauty competition was to challenge notions of the Caribbean as a languid, tropical backwater, inhabited by subject peoples. To counter these images, nationalists promoted idealised coloured femininity that conflated ideals of cultural hybridity and racial blending, both of which ought to be accommodated in modern racial democracies. Idealised brown femininity allowed nationalists to construct an image of the Caribbean that had apparently 'overcome' racism *and* vanquished the primitivism associated with blackness and the 'lack' associated with Afro-Creole culture. However, in truth this competed with and suppressed other potential formulations of nation, citizen and subject, such as those more inclusive identities Jones experimented with in the London Carnival and 'Carnival Queen' contest.

However, while Jones's intervention in Caribbean beauty had important legacies for affirming inclusive African Diaspora identities and black womanhood, her radical experiment with the format of the beauty contest itself had little impact on the mainstream of competitive staged beauty. The mythology set in motion by the institutionalisation of brown middle-class beauty as national motif in the Caribbean created an enduring and serviceable formula. In 1970 the second ever Caribbean woman to win the 'Miss World' competition, 22-year-old BWIA air stewardess, Grenadian Jennifer Hosten, was crowned. Hosten became hugely popular in the Caribbean. So significant was her win that there was even a skirmish between officials of Trinidad and Grenada over who could properly claim her win, because she had also spent long periods in Trinidad.[1] The Barbadian press revealed in its coverage of Hosten's win that the notion of idealised ladylike behaviour favoured by the beauty contest had changed little in forty years. Hosten, it was revealed 'hate[d] bad manners, indiscretion, and insincerity' and admired 'honesty'. She was repeatedly praised for her poise and graciousness.[2] These were solidly middle-class and respectable values of an accomplished young lady, or in other words of cultured, modern beauty. However, Hosten's win took place in a memorable year. 1970 was the year that British feminists famously protested the 'Miss World' competition, disrupting the live presentation by compère Bob Hope with flour-bombs and rotten fruit.[3] It was also the first year in which South Africa sent two candidates, white Miss 'South Africa' and coloured 'Miss Africa South', Pearl Jansen. Jansen was placed as first runner-up and reportedly the sight of two 'non-white' finalists, in first and second place, prompted many complaints to the British press from TV audiences.[4] The reverberations of a peak of black-nationalist activism in New York and the anti-Apartheid struggle in South Africa were being felt throughout the African Diaspora. Thus Hosten was questioned on both black nationalism and feminism, two movements that had always been interdependent in the New World. Unsurprisingly, Hosten deftly batted away such queries, and it is unlikely the bourgeois journals that interviewed her, *Jet* (an African American magazine from the publishers of *Ebony*) and *The Bajan*, would have sought to dwell on such matters. Still it is noteworthy that in *Jet* Hosten, light-skinned and upper-middle-class, did not identify with the Black Power movement, but did chose to assert her identity as a Grenadian black woman: 'As a black woman this crown means a lot to me and to my people in Grenada', she remarked. However, Hosten said little more on the subject and talked only in terms of national pride in her island home.[5] The Johnson publications had long shown an interest in Caribbean beauty queens and consistently constructed all such women as being of 'black origin' and therefore black. Hosten's response to feminism was similarly evasive; while she was sympathetic to 'women's liberation', women in the Caribbean, in her view, were already emancipated.[6] Thus, on both subjects, race and gender, Hosten was able to claim a sort of regional exceptionalism that furthered the established image of Caribbean racial democracy. Hosten's ascent, then, helped to reiterate the vibrant mythologies that were now deeply ingrained in notions of Caribbeanness. Almost a decade after Trinidadian and Jamaican independence the Caribbean beauty contest continued as a reliable agent to broadcast notions of colour-blind democracy, alive and well in the Caribbean: social equality that emanated from principles of liberal meritocracy, the gift of British colonial rule, but now divorced from these origins and fabricated as a local, creolised standard. Thus, after the intensity of the 'crisis of decolonisation', the transition to self-rule, the Caribbean beauty contest born out of this era would continue to raise questions of national and regional identity, and of the racialisation and gendering of power.

Notes

1 Interview by the author with Jennifer Hosten, September 2010.
2 'The Reign of a Queen', *The Bajan* 218 (1971), p. 4.
3 Feminists had also protested in the previous year, though less memorably.
4 'New "Miss World" Talks About Fuss Over Her Title', *Jet* 7 (January 1971), pp. 28–29.
5 Ibid., p. 27.
6 'Reign of a Queen', *Bajan*, p. 4.

Bibliography

Personal testimony

Interviews conducted by the author:
Anna Adimira, Ngozi Aleme, Irico Aleme, Trevor Carter, Betty Hill, Donald Hinds, Jennifer Hosten, Frank Hunte, Sylvia John, Marcus Jordan, Olga Lope-Seale, Marvo Manning, Claudette Pickering

Recorded testimony archived at the British Library:
Dorothy Kuya interview, part of the Communist Party of Great Britain Biographical Project C1049/83/01–04
Diane Langford interview, part of the Hall-Carpenter Oral History Project (C456/107/01–03).

Printed primary sources

MANUSCRIPT SOURCES

Claudia Jones Memorial Collection 1935–38 (Schomberg Centre for Black Research, New York)
Norman Manley (National library of Jamaica)
Una Marson papers (National Library of Jamaica, Kingston, Jamaica)

PHOTOGRAPHIC COLLECTIONS

Beauty Contests (National Library of Jamaica)
Carnival Miscellaneous (National Archives of Trinidad and Tobago)
West Indies Committee (Institute for Commonwealth Studies, University of London)

SPECIAL COLLECTION

H/N Beauties and Beauty Contestants. Jamaica and West Indies (National Library of Jamaica)

GOVERNMENT PUBLICATIONS

Barbados

Barbados Independence Celebrations (Jaycees-Government publication)

Jamaica

Jamaica Hansard: 1954–55 Session
Cabinet Submission: Government Assistance to Beauty Contest Sponsored by the
Council on Afro-Jamaican Affairs. 18 June 1964, 1B/31/523–1964 (Jamaica Archives,
Spanish Town, Jamaica)
Pamphlet of Rules Governing Jamaica Festival 1965 (Jamaican Government
Stationers)

Trinidad

Legislative Council Paper No. 14, 4 February 1953
Trinidad Hansard: 1954–55, 1956–57, 1958–59, 1960–61 Sessions
Trinidad Carnival and Calypso 1960, 1961, 1962

PAMPHLETS

Barbados

The Nation's Second Anniversary Celebrations, 1968 (Jaycees)
The Nation's Third Anniversary Celebrations, 1969
Barbados Jaycees '70 Independence Queen Show
Queen of the Teens 1972

Jamaica

'Miss Jamaica' 1958 Beauty Contest Souvenir Programme (Jamaica Tourist Board)

Trinidad

Trinidad's Sensational Calypso Dance (Trinidad Tourist Board)
Carnival Souvenir Programme 1951, 1952, 1953, 1954, 1955. (Savannah Carnival
Committee)
Dimanche Gras 1960, 1961, 1962, 1965 (Trinidad Carnival Development Committee)
Carnival Queen Show 1964 (Trinidad Jaycees)
Souvenir Independence Day Celebration 1968, 1969
Trinidad Carnival: The World's Most Colourful Festival (1970)
Trinidad Carnival: The World's Most Colourful Festival (1971)

NEWSPAPERS AND PERIODICALS

Bajan, The
Barbados Advocate
Barbados Civil Service Association Monthly Newsletter
Barbados Jaycees Newsletter
Caribbean Post

Cosmopolitan
Daily Gleaner (Jamaica)
Ebony (USA)
Jamaican Housewife
Jamaica Journal
Jamaica Weekly Gleaner (London)
JOFFA (London)
Life (USA)
New Cosmopolitan
Newday
New York Age
Planter's Punch
Port of Spain Gazette
Spotlight
Star, The (Jamaica)
Tan (USA)
Time (USA)
Trinidad Guardian
Vanity
West Indian Gazette (London)

UNPUBLISHED RESEARCH PAPERS

De Freitas, Patricia, *Playing Mas; The Construction and Deconstruction of National Identity in the Trinidad Carnival*. PhD Thesis, McMaster University, 1994
Pasley, Victoria, *Gender, Race and Class in Urban Trinidad: Representations in the Construction and Maintenance of the Gender Order 1960–1980*. PhD Thesis, University of Houston, 1999
Vassell, Linette, *Voluntary Women's Associations in Jamaica: The Jamaican Federation of Women*. MPhil Thesis, University of the West Indies, 1993

Published sources

Abrahams, Peter, *Jamaica: An Island Mosaic* (London: HM Stationery Office, 1956)
Abreu, M., Boa, S., Newton, M., Paton, D., Scully, P. and Sheller, M., in Diana Paton and Pamela Scully (eds), *Gender and Slave Emancipation in the Atlantic World* (Durham: Duke University Press, 2005)
Altink, Henrice, 'Respectability on Trial: Notions of Womanhood in Two Jamaican Trials in the Interwar Years', *The Society for Caribbean Studies Annual Conference Papers* Sandra Courtman (ed.) 4 (2003) www.scsonline. freeserve.co.uk/olvol4.html (accessed 10 November 2006)
—— 'More Than Producers and Reproducers: Jamaican Slave Women's Dance and Song' in Sandra Courtman (ed.), *Beyond the Blood, the Beach and the Banana: New Perspectives in Caribbean Studies* (Kingston: Ian Randle Publishers, 2004)

—— 'The Misfortune of Being Black and Female: Black Feminist thought in Interwar Jamaica', *Thirdspace* 5(2) (2006)

—— 'An American Race Laboratory: Jamaica, 1865–1940', *Wadabagei* 10(3) (2007)

Anthony, Michael, *Parade of the Carnivals of Trinidad 1839–1989* (Port of Spain: Circle, 1989)

Bakhtin, M.M., *Rabelais and His World* trans. Helene Iswolksy (Bloomington: Indiana University Press, 1984)

Banet-Weiser, Sarah, *The Most Beautiful Girl in the World: Beauty Pageants and National Identity* (Berkeley: University of California Press, 1999)

Barnard, R. and Erasmus, Z., in Sarah Nuttall and Cheryl-Ann Michael (eds), *Senses of Culture: South African Culture Studies* (Oxford: Oxford University Press, 2000)

Barnes, Natasha, 'Face of a Nation; Race, Nationalisms and Identities in Jamaican Beauty Pageants', in Consuelo Lopez Springfield (ed.), *Daughters of Caliban, Caribbean Women in the Twentieth Century* (Bloomington: Indiana University Press, 1997)

—— 'Body Talk: Notes on Women and Spectacle in Contemporary Trinidad Carnival', *Small Axe* 4(7) (2000)

—— *Cultural Conundrums: Gender, Race, Nation, and the Making of Caribbean Cultural Politics* (Ann Arbor: University of Michigan Press, 2006)

Barriteau, Eudine, 'Theorising Gender Systems and the Project of Modernity in the Twentieth-Century Caribbean', *Feminist Review* 59(1) (1998)

Barry, Kathleen, M., *Femininity in Flight: A History of Flight Attendants* (Durham: Duke University Press, 2007)

Batson, D., Brereton, B., Elder, J.D., Martin, C., Schener, R. and Riggio, M.C., in Riggio, M.C. (ed.), *Carnival: Culture in Action: the Trinidad Experience* (New York and London: Routledge, 2004)

Beckles, Hilary, *Black Rebellion in Barbados: The Struggle Against Slavery* (Bridgetown: Carib Research, 1987)

—— *A History of Barbados: from Amerindian Settlement to Nation State* (Cambridge: Cambridge University Press, 1990), p. 41

Beckles, H., Brereton, B., Johnson, H. and Watson K., in Howard Johnson and Karl Watson (eds), *The White Minority in the Caribbean* (Oxford: J Currey, 1998)

Bennett, Louise, 'Colonisation in Reverse' in James Proctor (ed.), *Writing Black Britain: An Interdisciplinary Anthology* (Manchester: Manchester University Press, 2000)

Besson J. and Momsen J. in Momsen J. (ed.), *Women and Change in the Caribbean* (Kingston: Ian Randle, 1993)

Bhattacharyya, G., Mirza, H.S. and Weeks, D., in Mirza, H.S. (ed.), *Black British Feminism: A Reader* (London: Routledge, 1997)

Blackwelder, Julia Kirk, *Styling Jim Crow; African-American Beauty Training During Segregation* (College Station: Texas A&M University Press, 2003)

Blake, Evon, *Beautiful Jamaica* (Port Antonio: Jamaica, Vista Publications, 1978)

Bogues, Anthony, 'Nationalism and Jamaican Political Thought', in Kathleen Montieth and Glen Richards (eds), *Jamaica in Slavery and Freedom: History, Heritage and Culture* (Mona: University of West Indies Press, 2002)

Bogues A., Satchell V., and Vassell, L., in Brian Moore and Swithin Wilmot (eds), *Before and After 1865: Papers on Education, Politics and Regionalism in the Caribbean* (Kingston: Ian Randle, 1988)

Bolland, Nigel O., *The Politics of Labour in the British Caribbean* (Kingston: Ian Randle, 2001)

Bourne, Stephen, *Black in the British Frame: Black People in British Film and Television, 1896–1996* (London: Cassell, 1996)

Braithwaite, Lloyd, 'Social Stratification in Trinidad: A Preliminary Analysis', *Social and Economic Studies* 2(2–3) (1953)

Breiner, Laurence A., *An Introduction to West Indian Poetry* (Cambridge: Cambridge University Press, 1998)

Brereton, Bridget, *Race Relations in Colonial Trinidad 1870–1900* (Cambridge: Cambridge University Press, 1979)

——— *A History of Modern Trinidad, 1783–1962* (Exeter: New Hampshire, Heinmann, 1981)

Broder, Erna, *Perceptions of Caribbean Women: Towards a Documentation of Stereotypes* (Cave Hill: University of the West Indies, 1982)

Brown, Aggrey, *Colour, Class and Politics in Jamaica* (New Brunswick: Transaction Books, 1979)

Brown, Wenzell, *Angry Men-Laughing Men: The Caribbean Cauldron* (New York: Greenberg, 1947)

Bryan, Patrick, *The Jamaican People 1880–1902: Race, Class and Social Control* (London: Macmillan, 1991)

Burton, Antoinette, 'Introduction', in Antoinette Burton (ed.), *Gender, Sexuality and Colonial Modernities* (New York and London: Routledge, 1999)

Butler, Judith, *Gender Trouble: Feminism and the Subversion of Identity* (New York and London: Routledge, 1999)

Cameron, Linda (ed.), *The Story of the Gleaner: Memoires and Reminiscences* (Kingston: The Gleaner Company Ltd, 2000)

Campbell, Carl, *The Young Colonials: A Social History of Education in Trinidad and Tobago, 1834–1939* (Mona: The University of the West Indies Press, 1996)

Campbell, Susan, 'Carnival, Calypso, and Class Struggle in Nineteenth Century Trinidad', *History Workshop Journal* 26(1) (1988)

Carby H.V., Gilroy, B. and Tulloch, C. in Kwesi Owusu (ed.), *Black British Culture and Society, A Text Reader* (New York and London: Routledge, 2000)

Carter, B., Harris, C., Joshi S. and James W. in James W. and Harris, C. (eds), *Inside Babylon: The Caribbean Diaspora in Britain* (London: Verso, 1993)

Chamberlain, M., *Empire and Nation Building in the Caribbean: Barbados 1937–1966* (Manchester: Manchester University Press, 2010)

Cohen, Lizbeth, 'Citizens and Consumers in the United States in the Century of Mass Consumption', in Martin Daunton and Matthew Hilton, *The Politics of Consumption: On Material Culture and Citizenship in Europe and America* (Oxford: Berg, 2001)

Collins, Patricia Hill, *Knowledge, Consciousness and the Politics of Empowerment* (New York and London: Routledge, 2000)

Cooper, Carolyn, *Noises in the Blood: Orality, Gender and the 'Vulgar' Body of Jamaican Popular Culture.* (Warwick: Macmillan Caribbean, 1993)

—— 'Editorial: Jamaican Popular Culture', *Interventions* 6 (2004)

—— 'Caribbean Fashion Week: Remodelling Beauty in "Out of Many One" Jamaica', *Fashion Theory* 14(3) (2010), pp. 387–404

Cowley, John, *Carnival, Canboulay and Calypso: Traditions in the Making* (Cambridge: University of Cambridge Press, 1996)

Craig, Maxine Leeds, *Ain't I a Beauty Queen? Black Women, Beauty, and the Politics of Race* (Oxford: Oxford University Press, 2002)

Crenshaw K. and Morrison T., in Morrison T. (ed.), *Raceing Justice and En-Gendering Power: Essays on Anita Hill, Clarence Thomas and the Construction of Social Reality* (New York: Pantheon, 1992)

Dabydeen, David, Gilmore John and Jones, Cecily (eds), *The Oxford Companion to Black British History* (Oxford: Oxford University Press, 2008)

Davidson, Julia O'Connell and Taylor Jacqueline Sanchez, 'Exploring the Demand for Sex Tourism' in Kamala Kempadoo (ed.), *Sun, Sex, and Gold: Tourism and Sex Work in the Caribbean* (Lanham: Rowman and Littlefield, 1999)

Davies, Carol Boyce, *Left of Karl Marx: The Political Life of Black Communist Claudia Jones* (Durham: Duke University Press, 2008)

—— (ed.) *Claudia Jones: Beyond Containment* (Banbury, Oxfordshire: Ayebia Publishing, 2011)

Davis, Angela, *Women Race and Class* (London: The Women's Press, 1982)

De Boissiere R., *Rum and Coca-Cola* (Melbourne: Australasian Book Society, 1956)

—— *Crown Jewel* (London: Picador, 1981)

De Freitas, Patricia, Playing Mas; The Construction and Deconstruction of National Identity in the Trinidad Carnival, Unpublished doctoral thesis, McMaster University, 1994

De Grazia, Victoria, *Irresistible Empire: America's Advance Through Twentieth Centure Europe* (Cambridge, Mass: Harvard University Press, 2005)

De Lima, Arthur, *The De Limas of Frederick Street* (Trinidad: Imprint Caribbean Ltd, 1981)

De Lisser, Herbert, *Jane's Career* (London: Heinemann, 1972)

Donnell, Alison, 'Una Marson; Feminism, Anti-Colonialism and a Forgotten Fight for Freedom', in Bill Schwarz (ed.), *West Indian Intellectuals in Britain* (Manchester: Manchester University Press, 2003)

Donnell, Alison and Welsh, Sarah Lawson (eds), *The Routledge Reader in Caribbean Literature* (London: Routledge, 1996)

Downes, Aviston, 'Boys of Empire: Elite Education and the Construction of Hegemonic Masculinity in Barbados, 1875–1920', in Rhoda E. Reddock (ed.), *Interrogating Caribbean Masculinities* (Kingston: University of the West Indies Press, 2004)

DuBois, Laurent, *A Colony of Citizens: Revolution and Slave Emancipation in the French Caribbean, 1781–1804* (Chapel Hill: University of North Carolina Press, 2004)

Duncan, Neville, C. and O'Brien, Kenneth, *Women and Politics in Barbados, 1948–1981* (Cave Hill: University of the West Indies, 1983)

Edmondson, Belinda, 'Public Spectacles: Caribbean Women and the Politics of Public Performance', *Small Axe* 7(1) (2005)

—— *Caribbean Middlebrow: Leisure, Culture and the Middle-Class* (Ithaca, New York: Cornell University Press, 2009)

Edmondson B. and Smith F.L., in Belinda Edmondson (ed.), *Caribbean Romances: The Politics of Regional Representation* (Charlottesville: University Press of Virginia, 1999)

Espinet, C. and Pitts, H., *Land of Calypso: The Origin and Development of Trinidad's Folk Song* (Port of Spain: Guardian Commercial Printery, 1944)

Ezra, Elizabeth, *The Colonial Unconscious: Race and Culture in Interwar France* (Ithaca, New York: Cornell University Press, 2000)

Fanon, Frantz, *Black Skin, White Masks* (London: Pluto Press, 1986)

Fermor, Patrick Leigh, *The Traveller's Tree: A Journey Through the Caribbean Islands* (London: John Murray, 1950)

Flynn, Elizabeth Gurley, *The Alderson Story: My Life as a Political Prisoner* (New York: International Publishers, 1963)

Ford-Smith, Honor, 'Una Marson: Black Nationalist and Feminist Writer', *Caribbean Quarterly* 34(3,4) (1988)

—— 'Unruly Virtues of the Spectacular: Performing Engendered Nationalisms in the UNIA in Jamaica', *Interventions* 6(1) (2004)

—— 'Making White Ladies: Race, Gender and the Production of Identities in Late Colonial Jamaica', *Resources for Feminist Research* 23(4) (2005)

Franco, Jennifer, *When the Ti-Marie Closes* (Port of Spain: Franco, 2000)

Franco, Pamela, 'Dressing Up and Looking Good: Afro-Creole Female Maskers in Trinidad Carnival', *African Arts* 3(2) (1998)

—— 'The "Unruly Woman" in Nineteenth Century Trinidad Carnival', *Small Axe* 7(1) (2000)

French, Joan, 'Colonial Policy Towards Women after the 1938 Uprising: The Case of Jamaica,' *Caribbean Quarterly* 34(1,2) (1988)

Gilroy, Paul *The Black Atlantic: Modernity and Double Consciousness* (London: Verso, 1993)

—— (ed.) *Black Britain: A Photographic History* (London: Saqi, 2007)

Goldstein, Donna ' "Interracial" Sex and Racial Democracy in Brazil: Twin Concepts?' *American Anthropologist* 101 (1999)

Green, Garth, 'Marketing the Nation: Carnival and Tourism in Trinidad and Tobago', *Critique of Anthropology* 22 (2002)

Gregg, Veronica Mae, 'How With this Rage shall Beauty Hold a Plea: The Writings of Miss Amy Beckford Bailey as Moral Education in the Era of Jamaican Nation Building', *Small Axe* 11(23) (2007)

Gundle, Stephen, *Glamour: A History* (Oxford: Oxford University Press, 2008)

Haidarali, Laila, 'Polishing Brown Diamonds: African American Women, Popular Magazines, and the Advent of Modelling in Early Postwar America,' *Journal of Women's History* 17(2) (2005)

Hall, Catherine, 'White Visions, Black Lives: The Free Villages of Jamaica,' *History Workshop* 6 (1993), pp. 100–132

—— *Civilising Subjects: Metropole and Colony in the English Imagination 1830–1867* (Cambridge: Polity, 2002)

—— *White Male Middle-Class: Explorations in Feminism and History* (Cambridge: Polity Press, 2007)

Hall, Stuart 'Cultural Identity and Cinematic Representation', *Black British Cultural Studies: A Reader*, Houston A. Baker, Manthia Diawara, Ruth H, Lindeborg (eds) (Chicago: University of Chicago Press, 1996)

Hall, S. and Young, L., in Read, A. (eds), *Fact of Blackness* (London: Institute of Contemporary Arts, 1996)

Harris, Clive, 'Images of Blacks in Britain, 1930–1960', *Race and Social Policy* (London: Economic and Social Research Council, 1998)

Heuman, Gad, *Between Black and White: Race, Politics and the Free Coloured Population in Jamaica 1792 to 1865* (Westport: Greenwood, 1981)

Higginbotham, Evelyn Brooks, 'African-American Women's History and the Metalanguage of Race', in Ruth-Ellen B. Jones and Barbara Laslett (eds), *The Second Signs Reader: Feminist Scholarship, 1983–1996* (Chicago: The University of Chicago Press, 1996)

Hill, Donald, *Calypso Callaloo: Early Carnival Music in Trinidad* (Gainsville: University of Florida Press, 1993)

Hill, Errol, *The Trinidad Carnival: Mandate for National Theatre* (London: New Beacon, 1997)

Hinds, Donald, *Journey to an Illusion: The West Indian in Britain* (London: Heinemann, 1966)

—— 'The *West Indian Gazette*: Claudia Jones and the Black Press in Britain,' *Race and Class* 50 (2008)

Hooks, Bell, *Ain't I a Woman: Black Women and Feminism* (Boston: South End Press, 1981)

—— *Black Looks: Race and Representation* (London: Turnaround, 1992)

Iremonger, Lucille, *Yes My Darling Daughter* (London: Secker and Warburg, 1964)

James, C.L.R., *Beyond a Boundary* (London: Stanley Paul, 1963)

—— 'Triumph' and 'The Case for West Indian Self-Government', in Anna Grimshaw (ed.), *The C.L.R James Reader 1901–1989*, (Oxford: Blackwell, 1992)

James, Winston, *Holding Aloft the Banner of Ethiopia: Caribbean Radicalism in Early-Twentieth Century America* (London: Verso, 1998)

Jarrett-Macauley, Delia, *The Life of Una Marson. 1905–65* (Manchester: Manchester University Press, 1998)

Johnson, Buzz, 'Biographical Notes', in Johnson B (ed.), *I Think of My Mother: Notes on the Life and Times of Claudia Jones* (London: Karia Press, 1985)

Johnson, Howard, 'The "Jamaica 300" Celebrations of 1955: Commemoration in a Colonial Polity', *Journal of Imperial and Commonwealth History* 26(2) (1998)

Johnson, Michele A. and Moore, Brian L, *Neither Led Nor Driven: Contesting British Cultural Imperialism in Jamaica 1865–1920* (Kingston: University of the West Indies Press, 2004)

—— 'Married but not Parsoned: Attitudes to Conjugality in Jamaica, 1865–1920', in Gad Heuman and David Trotman (eds), *Contesting Freedom: Control and Resistance in the Post-Emancipation Caribbean* (London: Macmillan, 2005)

Jones, Claudia, 'The Caribbean Community in Britain', *Freedomways* 4(2) (1964)

—— 'An End to the Neglect of the Problems of the Negro Woman', in Johnson B (ed.), *I Think of My Mother: Notes on the Life and Times of Claudia Jones* (London: Karia Press, 1985)

Khan, A. and Segal, D., in Yelvington K.A. (ed.), *Trinidad Ethnicity* (Knoxville: University of Tennessee Press, 1993)

Kitch, Carolyn L., *The Girl on the Magazine Cover: The Origins of Visual Stereotypes in American Mass Media* (Chapel Hill: University of North Carolina Press, 2001)

Knight, F.W. and Palmer, C.A. (eds), *The Modern Caribbean* (Chapel Hill: University of North Carolina Press, 1989)

Kutzinski, Vera, *Sugar's Secrets: Race and the Erotics of Cuban Nationalism* (Charlottesville: University of Virginia Press, 1993)

Lai, Walton Look, *The Chinese in the West Indies: A Documentary History* (Kingston: University of the West Indies Press, 1998)

Lamming, George, *The Emigrants* (London: Joseph, 1954)

—— *In the Castle of My Skin* (New York: Schocken Books, 1983)

—— *The Pleasures of Exile* (London: Allison and Busby, 1984)

Larsen, Nella, *Passing* (New York: The Modern Library, 2002)

Lewis, Gordon, *The Growth of the Modern West Indies* (London: MacGibbon and Kee, 1968)

Lewis, L., 'The Contestation of Race in Barbadian Society and the Camouflage of Conservatism', in Brian Meeks and Folke Lindahl (eds), *New Caribbean Thought: A Reader* (Mona: University of the West Indies Press, 2001)

Lynch, Roslyn, *Gender Segregation in the Barbadian Labour Market, 1946–1980* (Mona: University of the West Indies, 1995)

McKay, Claude, *Banana Bottom* (Chatham: Chatham Bookseller, 1970)

McNay, Lois, *Feminism and Foucault: Power, Gender and the Self* (Cambridge: Polity Press, 1992)

Madsen, Deborah, 'Performing Community through the Feminine Body: The Beauty Pageant in Transnational Contexts; http://home.adm.unige.ch/%7Emadsen/Zurich_pageants.htm (accessed 25 July 2006)

Mama, Amina, *Beyond the Masks: Race, Gender and Subjectivity* (New York and London: Routledge, 1995)

Marson, Una, *The Moth and the Star* (Kingston: published by the author, 1937)

Massiah, Jocelyn, *Employed Women in Barbados: A Demographic Profile, 1946–1970* (Cave Hill: University of the West Indies, 1984)

Meighoo, Kirk, *Politics in a Half Made Society: Trinidad and Tobago 1925–2001* (Kingston: Ian Randle, 2003)

Mittelholzer, Edgar, *A Morning at the Office* (London: Heinemann, 1974)

Modleski, Tania, *Studies in Entertainment: Critical Approaches to Mass Culture* (Bloomington: Indiana Press, 1986)

Mohammed, Patricia, ' "But Most of All Mi Love Mi Browning": The Emergence in Eighteenth and Nineteenth Century Jamaica of the Mulatto Woman as Desired', *Feminist Review* 65(1) (2000)

—— 'A Blueprint for Gender in Creole Trinidad: Exploring Gender Mythology through Calypsos of the 1920s and 1930s', in Linden Lewis (ed.), *The Culture of Gender and Sexuality in the Caribbean* (Gainsville: University of Florida Press, 2003)

Moreno Figueroa, M.G. 'Displaced Looks: On Being Beautiful, Ordinary, Ugly or Insignificant: The Lived Experience of Beauty and Racism in Mexico,' *Feminist Theory* (forthcoming), 14(2)

Morgan, Jennifer, *Labouring Women: Reproduction and Gender in New World Slavery* (Philadelphia: University of Pennsylvania Press, 2004)

Munroe, Trevor, *The Politics of Constitutional Decolonisation: Jamaica 1944–1962* (Mona: University of West Indies Press, 1983)

Neptune, Harvey, 'White Lies: Race and Sexuality in Occupied Trinidad', *Journal of Colonialism and Colonial History* 2 (2001) //E:\2.1neptune.html (accessed 24 June 2006)

—— *Caliban and the Yankees: Trinidad and the United States Occupation* (Chapel Hill: University of North Carolina Press, 2007)

Nettleford, Rex (ed.) *Norman Washington Manley and the New Jamaica: Selected Speeches and Writings, 1938–68* (New York: Africana, 1971)

O'Rain, Rebecca Chiyoko King, *Pure Beauty: Judging Race in Japanese American Beauty Pageants* (Minneapolis: University of Minnesota Press, 2006)

Oxaal, Ivar, *Black Intellectuals Come to Power: The Rise of Creole Nationalism in Trinidad and Tobago* (Cambridge, Mass.: Schenkman Publishing Company, 1968)

Paton, Diana, *No Bond But the Law: Punishment Race and Gender in Jamaican State Formation 1780–1870* (Durham: Duke University Press, 2004)

Paul, Kathleen, *Whitewashing Britain: Race and Citizenship in the Postwar Era* (Ithaca, New York: Cornell University Press, 1997)

Pearce, Richard 'Toni Morrison's *Jazz*: Negotiations of the African-American Beauty Culture', *Narrative* 6(3) (1998)

Pearse, Andrew, 'Carnival in Nineteenth Century Trinidad', *Caribbean Quarterly* 4(3,4) (1956)

Peiss, Kathy, *Hope in the Jar: The Making of America's Beauty Culture* (New York: Metropolitan Book, 1998)

Phillips, Edsil, 'The Development of the Tourist Industry in Barbados 1956–1980', in DeLisle Worrell (ed.), *The Economy of Barbados, 1946–1980* (Bridgetown: Central Bank of Barbados, 1982)

Pilkington, Edward, *Beyond the Mother Country: West Indians and the Notting Hill Riots* (London: I.B Tauris & Co. Ltd, 1988)

Pinha, Patricia, 'Afro-Aesthetics in Brazil', in Sarah Nuttall (ed.), *Beautiful/Ugly: African and Diaspora Aesthetics* (Durham: Duke University Press, 2006)

Powrie, Barbara, 'The Changing Attitude of the Coloured Middle Class Towards Carnival', *Caribbean Quarterly* 4(3,4) (1956)

Proudfoot, Mary McDonald, *Britain and the United States in the Caribbean: A Comparative Study in Methods of Development* (London: Faber and Faber, 1954)

Quevedo, Raymond (Atilla the Hun) *Atilla's Kaiso: A Short Story of Trinidad Calypso* (St Augustine: University of the West Indies, 1983)

Reddock, Rhoda, *Women, Labour and Politics in Trinidad and Tobago: A History* (London: Zed Books, 1994)

Richardson, Bonham C., *Panama Money in Barbados 1900–1920* (Knoxville: University Tennessee Press, 1985)

Roach, Joseph, *Cities of the Dead: Circum-Atlantic performance* (New York: Columbia University Press, 1996)

Rohlehr, Gordon, *Calypso and Society in Pre-Independence Trinidad* (Port of Spain: Gordon Rohlehr, 1990)

Rooks, Noliwe, *Hair Raising: Beauty, Culture and African American Women* (New Brunswick NJ: Rutgers University Press, 1996)

—— *Ladies Pages: African American Women's Magazines and the Culture That Made Them* (New Brunswick, NJ: Rutgers University Press, 2004)

Rosenberg, Leah, *Nationalism and the Formation of Caribbean Literature* (Basingstoke: Palgrave Macmillan, 2007)

Rowe, R., 'Glorifying the Jamaican Girl: The "Ten Types" – One People' Beauty Contest, Racialized Femininities, and Jamaican Nationalism. *Radical History Review* 103 (2009), pp. 36–58

Ryan, Selwyn, *Race and Nationalism in Trinidad and Tobago: A Study of Decolonisation in a Multicultural Society* (Toronto: University of Toronto Press, 1972)

Salih, Sarah and Butler, Judith, 'Bodily Inscriptions, Performative Subversions', in Sara Salih and Judith Butler (eds), *The Judith Butler Reader* (Malden: Blackwell, 2004)

Sander, Richard, *From Trinidad: An Anthology of early West Indian Writing* (London: Hodder and Stoughton, 1978)

Schwarz, Bill, 'Claudia Jones and the *West Indian Gazette*: Reflections on the Emergence of Postcolonial Britain', *Twentieth Century British History* 14(3) (2003)

Segal, Daniel, A., 'Race and Colour in Pre-Independence Trinidad and Tobago', in Kevin Yelvington (ed.), *Trinidad Ethnicity* (Knoxville: University of Tennessee Press, 1993)

Sheller, Mimi, 'Quasheba. Mother, Queen: Black Women's Public Leadership and Political Protest in Post-emancipation Jamaica, 1834–65', *Slavery and Abolition* 19(3) (1998)

—— *Consuming the Caribbean: From Arawaks to Zombies* (New York and London: Routledge, 2003)

Shepherd, Verene, 'Introduction', in Verene Shepherd and Glen Richards (eds), *Questioning Creole: Creolisation Discourses in Caribbean Culture* (Kingston: Ian Randle, 2002)

Sherwood, Marika, *Claudia Jones: A Life in Exile* (London: Lawrence and Wishart, 1999)

Silver, Steve, 'Who Killed My Brother?', *Searchlight*, May 2006. ww.searchlight magazine.com/index.php?link=template&story=164 (accessed 4 November 2009)

Simey, TS, *Welfare and Planning in the West Indies* (Oxford: Clarendon Press, 1946)

Smith, Hope Munro, 'Performing Gender in the Trinidad Calypso', *Latin American Music Review* 25(1) (2004)

Stallybrass, Peter and White, Allon, *The Politics and Poetics of Transgression* (Ithaca, New York: Cornell University Press, 1986)

Stephens, Michelle, *Black Empire: The Masculine Global Imaginary of Caribbean Intellectual in the United States, 1914–1962* (Durham: Duke University Press, 2005)

Tate, Shirley Ann, 'Black Beauty: Shade, Hair and Anti-racist Aesthetics', *Ethnic and Racial Studies* 30 (2007)

—— *Black Beauty: Aesthetics, Stylization, Politics* (Farnham: Ashgate, 2009)

Thomas, Deborah, *Modern Blackness: Nationalism, Globalization and the Politics of Culture in Jamaica* (Durham: Duke University Press, 2004)

Thompson, Krista, 'Black Skin, Blue Eyes: Visualising Blackness in Jamaican Art, 1922–1944,' *Small Axe* 8(2) (2004)

Tyson, Jennifer, *Claudia Jones Woman of Our Times 1915–1964* (London: Camden Black Sisters, 1988)

Vassell, Linette (ed.), *Voices of Women in Jamaica, 1898–1939* (Mona: University of the West Indies, 1993)

—— 'Women of the Masses: Daphne Campbell and "Left" Politics in Jamaica in the 1950s,' in Verene Shepherd, Bridget Brereton and Barbara Bailey (eds), *Engendering History, Caribbean Women in Historical Perspective* (Kingston: Ian Randle, 1995)

Walker, Susannah, 'Black is Profitable: The Commodification of the Afro 1960–1975', *Enterprise and Society* 1(3) (2000)

—— *Style and Status; Selling Beauty to African American Women* (Lexington: University Press Kentucky, 2007)

Wallace, Elisabeth, *The British Caribbean: From the Decline of Colonialism to the End of Federation* (Toronto: University of Toronto Press, 1977)

Webster, Wendy, ' "There'll Always Be an England"; Representations of Colonial Wars and Immigration, 1948–1968', *Journal of British Studies* 40(4) (2001)

Western, John, *A Passage to England: Barbadian Londoners Speak of Home* (Minneapolis: University of Minnesota Press, 1992)

Weinbaum, Alys Eve *et al.* (eds), *The Modern Girl Around the World: Consumption, Modernity and Globalisation* (Durham: Duke University Press, 2008)

Williams, Megan E., 'The *Crisis* Cover Girl: Lena Horne, the NAACP, and Representations of African American Femininity, 1941–1945,' *American Periodicals* 16(2) (2006)

Willis, Susan, 'I Shop Therefore I Am: Is There a Place for Afro-American Culture in Commodity Culture?', in Robyn R. Warhol and Diane Price Herndl (eds), *Feminisms: An Anthology of Literary Theory and Criticism* (Basingstoke: Macmillan, 1997)

Wright, Michelle, *Becoming Black: Creating Identity in the African Diaspora* (Durham: Duke University Press, 2004)

Wrightman Fox R and Jackson Lears, TJ, 'Introduction' in Fox R and Lears TJ (eds), *The Culture of Consumption: Critical Essays in American History* (New York: Pantheon, 1983), pp. vii–xvii

Young, Lola, 'What is Black British Feminism?', *Women: A Cultural Review* 11 (2000), pp. 45–60

Young, Robert, *Colonial Desire: Hybridity in Theory, Culture and Race* (New York and London: Routledge, 1995)

Zobel, Joseph, *Black Shack Alley* trans. Keith Warner (Washington DC: Three Continents Press, 1980)

Index

advertising 134, 157
  and beauty queens 57–59, 133–134,
    141–146
  and Carnival in Trinidad, 50, 55,
    57–59
air hostess work
  and beauty queens 56, 72, 102–103,
    139–140

Bailey, Amy
  on beauty 24–32
  colour-consciousness in Jamaica
    24–27
  feminist activism 24
Barbados Progressive League 88
Barnes, Natasha 2–3, 43, 56, 118
Beauty culture
  in Harlem 156–157
  in Jamaica 25, 30–31, 129, 153
  in London 167–170
  see also hair
Beckles, Hilary 90, 106
black nationalism 16–18, 22
  and beauty competitions 128–130
  see also United Negro Improvement
    Association
Blake, Evon 32, 37, 72–73, 125–127
British Overseas Airways Corporation
  59, 72, 137–139
British West Indies Airways 56, 72, 74,
  103, 138–140, 182
Bustamante, Alexander 17

calypso 48–51, 66, 69–70, 74–75, 165
Carnival
  in Barbados 85, 92–93
  in London 163–167
  in Trinidad 43–84
Carnival Bands Union 51, 68, 74
Carnival Development Committee 74–79
Carnival Improvement Committee
  51–53, 61, 68–71
civilising mission 8, 16, 100
clubs
  social 51, 53–54, 56–57, 88, 169
  women's 24, 33, 91, 97, 102
  see also Jamaica Federation of Women;
    Women's Liberal Club
colour-consciousness
  in Barbados 95
  in Britain 155, 162
  in Jamaica 21–31
  in Trinidad 62–65
  see also Star, The, 'Ten Types'
    competition; pigmentocracy
Cooper, Carolyn 2–3, 5
crown colony rule 52, 87

Davies, Carole Boyce 152–155, 164, 166
De Lisser, Herbert 18–22
  see also Planter's Punch

Edmondson, Belinda 2–4, 6
education 22, 26, 30, 36, 62–63, 90,
  98–99, 102

EU authorised representative for GPSR:
Easy Access System Europe, Mustamäe tee 50,
10621 Tallinn, Estonia
gpsr.requests@easproject.com